OCCULT SCIENCE
AN OUTLINE

RULDOLF STEINER

translated by
George and Mary Adams

RUDOLF STEINER PRESS
LONDON

AN OUTLINE OF OCCULT SCIENCE, Theosophical Publishing Society, London, and Rand McNally and Co., New York & Chicago, 1914.

OCCULT SCIENCE — AN OUTLINE, Anthroposophic Press, New York, and Rudolf Steiner Publishing Co., London, 1939.

OCCULT SCIENCE — AN OUTLINE, Rudolf Steiner Publishing Co., London, and Anthroposophic Press, New York, 1949.

OCCULT SCIENCE — AN OUTLINE, (new translation) Rudolf Steiner Press, London, 1962/1963.

Reprinted 1969

Reprinted 1979 (taking into account the corrections made in the 27th, 28th and 29th German editions)

Reprinted 1984

Translation of the German text entitled
Die Geheimwissenschaft im Umriss
published in agreement with the
Rudolf Steiner Nachlassverwaltung
Dornach, Switzerland

ISBN 0 85440 207 1 cloth
0 85440 440 6 paper

Printed in Great Britain by
Whitstable Litho Ltd., Whitstable, Kent

CONTENTS

PREFACE TO THE 1925 EDITION

FIFTEEN YEARS having now elapsed since the first publication of this book, it may be suitable for me to say something more about the spiritual circumstances and my own state of mind when it originated. It had been my intention that its main content should form part of a new and enlarged version of my *Theosophy*, published several years before. But this did not prove possible. At the time when *Theosophy* was written the subject-matter of the present volume could not be brought into an equally finished form. In my Imaginative perceptions I beheld the spiritual life and being of individual Man and was able to describe this clearly. The facts of cosmic evolution were not present to me to the same extent. I was indeed aware of them in many details, but the picture as a whole was lacking.

I therefore resolved to make no appreciable change in the main content of the earlier volume. In the new edition as in the first, the book *Theosophy* should describe the essential features of the life of individual Man, as I had seen it in the spirit. Meanwhile I would quietly be working at a new and independent publication, *Occult Science — an Outline*.

My feeling at that time was that the contents of this book must be presented in scientific thought-forms — that is, in forms of thought akin to those of Natural Science, duly developed and adapted to the description of what is spiritual. How strongly I felt this 'scientific' obligation in all that I wrote at that time in the field of spiritual knowledge, will be evident from the Preface to the First Edition (1909), here reproduced on pages 20–24. But the world of the spirit as revealed to spiritual sight can only partly be described in

7

thought-forms of this kind. What is revealed cannot be fully contained in mere forms of thought. This will be known to anyone who has had experience of such revelation. Adapted as they are to the exposition of what is seen by the outer senses, the thoughts of our every-day consciousness are inadequate, fully to expound what is seen and experienced in the spirit. The latter can only be conveyed in picture-form, that is, in Imaginations, through which Inspirations speak, which in their turn proceed from spiritual reality of Being, experienced in Intuition. (Concerning 'Imagination, Inspiration and Intuition', the necessary explanations will be found both in the present volume and in my book *Knowledge of the Higher Worlds and its Attainment.*)

To-day however, one who sets out to tell of the spiritual world in Imaginations cannot rest content with such pictorial descriptions. He would be foisting on to the civilization of our time the outcome of a state of consciousness quite unrelated to existing forms of knowledge. It is to the normal consciousness of the present age that he must bring home the truths which can indeed only be discovered by a higher consciousness — one that sees into the spiritual world. The subject-matter of his exposition, namely the realities of the world of spirit, will then be cast into forms of thought which the prevailing consciousness of our time — scientifically thoughtful and wide-awake, though unable yet to see into the spiritual world — can understand.

An inability to understand will at most be due to hindrances that are self-imposed. The reader may have fixed in his mind some definition of the inherent limitations of human knowledge, due to a mistaken generalization of the limits of Natural Science. Spiritual cognition is a delicate and tender process in the human soul, and this is true not only of the actual 'seeing' in the spirit, but of the active understanding with which the normal, 'non-seeing' consciousness of our time can come to meet the results of seership. People with half-formed notions who allege auto-suggestion in this regard have little idea of the real depth and intimacy of such understanding. For the scientific understanding of the physical world there may be truth or error in our theories and concepts. For the spiritual world, it is no longer a merely theoretic issue; it is a matter of living experience. When a man's judgment is tinged however slightly by the dogmatic assertion that the ordinary (not yet clairvoyant) consciousness — through its inherent limitations — cannot really understand what is experienced by the seer, this mistaken judgment becomes a cloud of darkness in his feeling-life and does in fact obscure his understanding.

To an open mind however, though not yet 'seeing' in the spirit, what is experienced by the seer is comprehensible to a very full extent, if once the seer has cast it into forms of thought. It is no less intelligible than is a finished work of art to the non-artist. Nor is this understanding confined to the realm of aesthetic feeling as in the latter instance; it lives in full clarity of thought, even as in the scientific understanding of Nature.

To make such understanding possible however, the seer must have contrived to express what he has seen, in genuine forms of thought, without thereby depriving it of its 'Imaginative' character.

Such were my reflections while working at the subject-matter of my *Occult Science*, and, with these premises in mind, by 1909 I felt able to achieve a book, bringing the outcome of my spiritual researches, up to a point, into adequate forms of thought — a book moreover which should be intelligible to any thoughtful reader who did not himself impose unnecessary hindrances to understanding.

While saying this retrospectively today I must however admit that in the year 1909 the publication of this book appeared to me a venture of some temerity. For I was only too well aware that the professional scientists above all, and the vast number of others who in their judgment follow the 'scientific' authority, would be incapable of the necessary openness of mind. Yet I was equally aware that at the very time when the prevailing consciousness of mankind was farthest remote from the world of spirit, communications from that world would be answering to an urgent need. I counted on there also being many people feeling so weighed down by the prevailing estrangement from the living spirit that with sincere

9

longing they would welcome true communications from the spiritual world. This expectation was amply confirmed during the years that followed. The books *Theosophy* and *Occult Science* have been widely read, though they count not a little on the reader's good will. For it must be admitted, they are not written in an easy style. I purposely refrained from writing a 'popular' account, so-called. I wrote in such a way as to make it necessary to exert one's thinking while entering into the content of these books. In so doing, I gave them a specific character. The very reading of them is an initial step in spiritual training, inasmuch as the necessary effort of quiet thought and contemplation strengthens the powers of the soul, making them capable of drawing nearer to the spiritual world.

Misunderstandings were soon evoked by the chosen title, 'Occult Science'. A would-be science, people said, cannot in the nature of the case be 'occult' or 'secret'. Surely a rather thoughtless objection, for no man will deliberately publish what he desires to be secretive about or to keep obscure. The entire book is evidence that far from being claimed as a special 'secret', what is here presented is to be made accessible to human understanding like any other science. Speaking of 'Natural Science' we mean the science of Nature. 'Occult Science' is the science of what takes its course in realms which are 'occult' inasmuch as they are discerned, not in external Nature — Nature as seen by the outer senses — but in directions to which the soul of man becomes attentive when he turns his inner life towards the spirit. It is 'Occult Science' as against 'Natural Science'.

Of my clairvoyant researches into the world of spirit it has often been alleged that they are a re-hash, howsoever modified, of ideas about the spiritual world which have prevailed from time to time, above all in earlier epochs of human history. In the course of my reading I was said to have absorbed these things into the sub-conscious mind and then reproduced them in the fond belief that they were the outcome of my own independent seership. Gnostic doctrines, oriental fables and wisdom-teachings were alleged to be the real source of my descriptions. But these surmises too were the outcome of no

very deeply penetrating thought. My knowledge of the spiritual
— of this i am fully conscious — springs from my own spiritual
vision. At every stage — both in the details and in synthesis
and broad review — I have subjected myself to stringent tests,
making sure that wide-awake control accompanies each further
step in spiritual vision and research. Just as a mathematician
proceeds from thought to thought — where the unconscious
mind, auto-suggestion and the like can play no part at all —
so must the consciousness of the seer move on from one objective Imagination to another. Nothing affects the soul in this
process save the objective spiritual content, experienced in full
awareness.

It is by healthy inner experience that one knows a spiritual
'Imagination' to be no mere subjective picture but the expression of a spiritual reality in picture-form. Just as in sensory
perception anyone sound in mind and body can discriminate
between mere fancies and the perception of real facts, so a
like power of discernment can be attained by spiritual means.

So then I had before me the results of conscious spiritual
vision. They were things 'seen', living in my consciousness, to
begin with, without any names. To communicate them, some
terminology was needed, and it was only then—so as to put into
words what had been wordless to begin with — that I looked
for suitable expressions in the traditional literature. These too
I used quite freely. In the way I apply them, scarcely one of
them coincides exactly with its connotation in the source from
which I took it. Only after the spiritual content was known
to me from my own researches did I thus look for the way to
express it. As to whatever I might formerly have read — with
the clear consciousness and control above referred-to, I was
able to eliminate such things completely while engaged on
supersensible research.

But the critics then found echoes of traditional ideas in the
terms I used. Paying little heed to the real trend and content
of my descriptions, they focussed their attention on the words.
If I spoke of 'lotus flowers' in the human astral body, they
took it as proof that I was reproducing Indian doctrines in
which this term occurs. Nay, the term 'astral body' itself only

showed that I had been dipping into medieval writings. And if I used the terms Angeloi, Archangeloi and so on, I was merely reviving the ideas of Christian Gnosticism. Time and again I found myself confronted with comments of this kind.

I take the present opportunity of mentioning this too. *Occult Science — an Outline*, now to be published in a new edition, is after all an epitome of anthroposophical Spiritual Science as a whole, and is pre-eminently exposed to the same kinds of misunderstanding.

Since the Imaginations described in this book first grew into a total picture in my mind and spirit, I have unceasingly developed the researches of conscious seership into the being of individual Man, the history of Mankind, the nature and evolution of the Cosmos. The outline as presented fifteen years ago has in no way been shaken. Inserted in its proper place and context, everything that I have since been able to adduce becomes a further elaboration of the original picture.

RUDOLF STEINER

Goetheanum, Dornach,
Switzerland.
10th January 1925.

PREFACE TO THE 1920 EDITION

For this edition I have almost entirely rewritten the opening chapter on the character of Occult Science. I think there will now be less cause for misunderstanding. How often have I heard it said: While other branches of learning offer scientific proofs, this pretended science merely declares that such and such are the findings of Occult Science. It is a natural objection. The proof of supersensible knowledge can never be as tangible and compelling as with things seen and experienced by the outer senses. It is a misconception none the less, and in the altered version I have tried to bring this out more clearly than I appear to have succeeded in doing in the earlier editions.

For the rest, I have introduced changes and additions, trying to make the explanations clearer and more cogent. In many parts of the book, the oft-repeated experience of the spiritual realities described convinced me of the need to modify the forms of expression in which I try to clothe them, and I have done my best to make the necessary changes.

RUDOLF STEINER

Berlin, May 1920.

13

PREFACE TO THE 1913 EDITION

ONE WHO sets out to present results of spiritual science such as this book contains must reckon with the certain fact that in wide circles they will be held to be impossible. For in these pages many things are put forward which in our time — supposedly on good philosophic and scientific grounds — are pronounced inaccessible to man's intelligence.

The author can appreciate the weighty reasons leading so many serious thinkers to this conclusion. Therefore again and again he would renew the attempt to show up the misunderstandings underlying the all-too categorical belief that human cognition can never reach into the supersensible worlds.

Two things come into question here. The first is this: On deeper reflection no human soul can lastingly ignore the fact that the most vital questions about the purpose and meaning of life must be for ever unanswered if there is really no way of access to supersensible worlds. Theoretically we may deceive ourselves about it, but in our heart of hearts we do not share the deception. Those who refuse to listen to the voice of their inmost soul will naturally reject teachings about the supersensible worlds. But there are people — and not a few — who can no longer turn a deaf ear in this direction. They will forever be knocking at the doors which — as the others say — must remain barred and bolted, denying access to things 'beyond human comprehension'.

But there is also the second aspect. The 'good philosophic and scientific grounds' above-mentioned are in no way to be underrated, and those who hold to them in earnest deserve to be taken seriously. The writer would not like to be counted among those who lightly disregard the stupendous mental efforts that have been made to define the boundaries to which the human intellect is subject. These efforts cannot be dismissed with a few derogatory phrases. Seen at their best, they have their source in a real striving for knowledge and are worked out with genuine discernment. Nay, more than this. The reasons which have been adduced to show that the kind of knowledge, accepted nowadays as scientific, cannot reach into the supersensible are genuine and *in a sense irrefutable*.

People may think it strange that the author should admit all this and yet venture to put forward statements concerning supersensible worlds. It seems almost absurd that one should make however qualified an admission that there are valid reasons for asserting that supersensible worlds are beyond our ken, and yet go on to speak and write about these worlds.

Yet it is possible to do this, while understanding full well how contradictory it may appear. Not everyone can realize the experiences one undergoes when drawing near the realm of the supersensible with intellectual reflection. For it emerges then that intellectual proofs however cogent, however irrefutable, are not necessarily decisive as to what is real and what is not. In place of theoretical explanations we may here use a comparison. Comparisons, admittedly, have not the force of proof, but they are helpful in explaining.

In the form in which it works in everyday life, also in ordinary science, human cognition cannot penetrate into the supersensible worlds. This can be cogently proved, and yet there is a level of experience for which the proof has no more real value than if one set out to prove that the unaided eye cannot see the microscopic cells of living organisms or the detailed appearance of far-off heavenly bodies. That our unaided vision cannot reach to the living cells is true and demonstrable, and so it is that our ordinary faculties of cognition cannot reach into the supersensible worlds. Yet the proof that man's unaided sight falls short of the microscopic cells does not preclude their scientific investigation. Must then the proof that his ordinary faculties of cognition cannot reach into the supersensible worlds of necessity preclude the investigation of these worlds?

We can imagine the feelings this comparison will arouse in many people. Nay, we can sympathize if doubt is felt, whether the one who has recourse to it has any inkling of all the painstaking and searching thought that has gone into these questions. And yet the present author not only realizes it to the full but counts it among the noblest achievements of mankind. To demonstrate that human vision, unaided by optical instruments, cannot see the microscopic cells would be superfluous; to become aware of the nature and scope of human thought by dint of thought itself is an essential task. It is only too understandable if men who have given their lives to this task fail to perceive that the real facts may yet be contrary to their findings. Whereas this preface is certainly not the place to deal with would-be 'refutations' of the first edition by people void of sympathy or understanding — people who even direct their unfounded attacks against the author personally — it must be emphasized all the more strongly that serious philosophic thought, whatever its conclusions, is nowhere belittled in these pages. Any such tendency can only be imputed by those deliberately blind to the spirit in which the book is written.

Human cognition can be strengthened and enhanced, just as the range of vision of the eye can be. But the ways and means of strengthening the power of cognition are purely spiritual. Inner activities, entirely within the soul — they are described in this book as Meditation and Concentration, or Contemplation. Man's ordinary life of mind and soul is tied to the bodily organs; when duly strengthened and enhanced it becomes free of them. There are prevailing schools of thought to which this very claim will seem nonsensical — a mere outcome of delusion. From their own point of view, they will prove without difficulty that all our mental and psychological life is bound up with the nervous system. The author from his standpoint can appreciate these proofs. He knows how plausible it is to maintain that it is utterly superficial to speak of any life of soul being independent of the body. Those who maintain this will no doubt be convinced that in the inner experiences, alleged to be free of the body, there is still a connection with the nervous system — a hidden connection which the would-be occultist with his 'amateurish' science only fails to discern.

Such are the prevalent habits of thought for which due allowance must be made. They are so diametrically opposed to the main contents of this book that there is generally little prospect of any mutual understanding. In this respect one cannot help wishing for a change of heart in the intellectual and spiritual life of our time. People are far too ready to stigmatize a scientific quest or school of thought as visionary and fantastic merely because they find it radically different from their own. On the other hand there are undoubtedly many who in our time appreciate the kind of supersensible research presented in this book. They realize that the deeper meaning of life will be revealed not by vague references to the soul, to the 'true self' or the like, but by a study of the genuine results of supersensible research. With due humility, the author is profoundly glad to find a new edition called for after a relatively short interval of time. He realizes only too clearly how far this edition too will fall short of the essential aim — to be the outline of a world-conception founded on supersensible knowledge. For this edition the entire contents have been worked through again; further elucidations have been attempted and supplementary passages inserted at important points. Often however the author has been painfully aware of the inadequacy, the excessive rigidity of the only available means of presenting the revelations of supersensible research. Thus it was hardly possible to do more than suggest a way of reaching some idea, some mental picture of what this book has to relate concerning Saturn, Sun and Moon evolutions. One aspect of this chapter has been briefly re-cast in the new edition. The real experience of cosmic evolution differs so widely from all our experiences in the realm of sense-perceptible Nature that the description involves a constant struggle to find passably adequate forms of expression. A sympathetic study of this chapter may reveal that the effort has been made to convey by the quality and style of the description what is impossible to express in mere prosaic words. A different style has been used for Saturn evolution, a different style for Sun evolution, and so on.

Amplifications and additions to which the author attaches some importance will be found in the second part, dealing with 'Knowledge of Higher Worlds' — the way to its attainment. As clear as possible an account has been attempted of what the human soul must do and undergo so as to liberate the powers of cognition from the confines of the sense-world and fit them for the experience of supersensible worlds.

Acquired though it is and must be by inner ways and means — by the inner activity of each one who gains it — the experience has a more than subjective significance. In our descriptions we have tried to make this clear. He who eliminates in his own soul the personal peculiarities which separate him from the World reaches a common realm of experience — a realm which other men are reaching when they too transform their subjective inner life in the true pathway of spiritual development. Only if thus conceived is the real knowledge of supersensible worlds distinguishable from subjective mysticism and the like. The latter might to some extent be said to be the mystic's merely personal concern. The inner spiritual-scientific training here intended aims at objective experiences, the truth of which has to be recognized, no doubt, in an intimate and inner way by every one who has them; yet in this very process they are seen to be universally valid. Here once again, it is admittedly difficult to come to terms with habits of thought widely prevalent in our time.

In conclusion, the author ventures to express the wish that friendly readers too should take what is here set forth on its own merits. There is a frequent tendency to give a school of thought some venerable name, failing which, its value is somehow depreciated. But it may surely be asked: As to the real contents of this book, what do they gain by being called 'Rosicrucian' or given any other label? The essential thing is that with the means that are possible and proper to the human soul in the present epoch, insight be gained into the spiritual worlds, and that the riddles of man's destiny and of his life beyond the frontiers of birth and death be thereby penetrated.

What matters is the quest of truth, rather than a quest that claims some ancient title.

On the other hand, the world-conception presented in this book has been given names and labels by opponents, and with unfriendly intention. Apart from the fact that some of these descriptions — meant to discredit the author — are manifestly absurd and untrue, surely an independent quest of truth deserves to be judged on its merits. It is unworthy to insinuate that it be set aside for its alleged dependence on whatsoever cult or school of thought. Nor does it matter much whether this dependence is the critic's own surmise or he is carelessly repeating an unfounded rumour. Necessary as these few words were, the author has no wish — in the present context — to answer sundry charges and attacks in detail.

RUDOLF STEINER

Written in June, 1913.

PREFACE TO THE FIRST EDITION*

In publishing a work of this kind at the present time one must be resigned from the outset to every kind of criticism. A reader, for example, versed in the accepted theories, can be heard commenting on the way scientific themes have here been treated: 'It is amazing that such absurdities can be put forward in our time. The author betrays utter ignorance of the most elementary notions. He writes of 'heat' or 'warmth' as though untouched by the whole trend of modern Physics. Such vagaries do not even deserve to be called amateurish.' More in this vein can be imagined: 'One need only read a few pages to discard the book — according to one's temperament, with a smile or with indignation — shelving it with other literary curiosities such as turn up from time to time.'

What then will the author say to these damning criticisms? Will he not, from his own standpoint, have to regard his critics as without discernment or even lacking the good will for an intelligent judgment? The answer is, No — not necessarily. He is well aware that those who condemn his work will often be men of high intelligence, competent scientists and anxious to judge fairly. Knowing well the reasons for these adverse judgments, he can put himself in the critic's place. He must here be permitted a few personal observations which would be out of place save in so far as they relate to his resolve to write the book at all. For it would have no *raison d'être* if merely personal and subjective. The contents of this book must be accessible to *every* human mind; also the manner of presentation should as far as possible be free of personal colouring. The following remarks on the author's life and

* Slightly condensed in translation.

work are therefore only meant to show how he could come to write this book while understanding only too well the apparent grounds of adverse judgment. Even these remarks would be superfluous if it were possible to show in detail that the contents are after all in harmony with the known facts of science. But this would need several volumes, far more than can be done under present circumstances.

The author would certainly never have ventured to publish what is here said about 'heat' or 'warmth', for example, if he were not conversant with the commonly accepted view. In his student days, some thirty years ago, he made a thorough study of Physics. Concerning the phenomena of heat, the so-called 'Mechanical Theory of Heat' was in the forefront at that time, and this engaged his keen attention. He studied the historical development of all the explanations and lines of thought associated with such names as J. R. Mayer, Helmholtz, Clausius and Joule. This has enabled him also to keep abreast of subsequent developments. If he were not in this position, he would not have felt justified in writing about warmth or heat as in this book. For he has made it his principle only to speak or write of any subject from the aspect of spiritual science where he would also be qualified to give an adequate account of the accepted scientific knowledge. He does not mean that every writer should be subject to the same restriction. A man may naturally feel impelled to communicate what he arrives at by his own judgment and feeling for the truth, even if ignorant of what contemporary science has to say. But for his own part the author is resolved to adhere to the principle above-mentioned. Thus he would never have written the few sentences this book contains about the human glandular and nervous systems were he not also in a position to describe them in contemporary scientific terms.

Therefore however plausible the verdict that to speak of heat or warmth as in this book argues an utter ignorance of Physics, the fact is that the author feels justified in writing as he has done precisely because he has kept abreast of present-day research and would refrain from writing if he had not. No doubt this too may be mistaken for lack of scientific modesty. Yet it must be avowed, if only to forestall even worse misunderstandings.

Equally devastating criticisms might easily be voiced from a philosophic standpoint. One can imagine such a reader's question: 'Has the author been asleep to all the work that has been and is still being done in fundamental theory of knowledge? Has he never even heard of Kant, who proved how inadmissible it is to make such statements as are here contained? . . . To a trained mind this uncritical and amateurish stuff is quite intolerable — a sheer waste of time.'

Here once again and at the risk of fresh misunderstanding, the author has to introduce a more personal note. He began studying Kant at the age of sixteen, and believes himself to be up-to-date also in this respect — qualified to judge from a Kantian standpoint what is put forward in this volume. Here too, he would have had good reason to leave the book unwritten were he not fully aware how easily, how plausibly it can be judged to be naive by the accepted standards of criticism. One can feel justified in putting forward what this book contains precisely because one is well aware that the Kantian boundaries of knowledge are here overstepped. One can be equally well aware that Herbart would have found in it a 'naive realism' of which the concepts had not been properly worked-over; or that the pragmatic school of William James, Schiller and others would judge it to be trespassing beyond the bounds of those genuine conceptions which man is really able to assimilate, to make effective and to verify in action.*

In spite of all this — nay even because of it — one could feel justified in writing the book. The author himself has written critically and historically of these and other trends of thought in his philosophic works: *The Theory of Knowledge implicit in Goethe's World-Conception, Truth and Science, The Philosophy of Spiritual Activity, Goethe's Conception of the World, Nineteenth-century Philosophic Views of Life and of the World, Riddles of Philosophy.*

* Even the more recent schools — Bergson, the 'As if' philosophy, and the 'Critique of Language' — have been studied and appraised in this connection.

Other criticisms are imaginable. A reader of the author's earlier writings — for example his work on nineteenth century philosophies or his short essay on *Haeckel and his Opponents* — might well be saying: 'How can one and the same man be the author of these works and of the book *Theosophy* (published in 1904) or of the present volume? How can he take up the cudgels for Haeckel and then offend so grossly against the straightforward monism, the philosophic outcome of Haeckel's researches? One could well understand the writer of this *Occult Science* attacking all that Haeckel stood for; that he defended him and even dedicated to him one of his main works,* appears preposterously inconsistent. Haeckel would have declined the dedication in no uncertain terms, had he known that the same author would one day produce the unwieldy dualism of the present work.'

Yet in the author's view one can appreciate Haeckel without having to stigmatize as nonsense whatever is not the direct outcome of his range of thought and his assumptions. We do justice to Haeckel by entering into the spirit of his scientific work, not by attacking him — as has been done — with every weapon that comes to hand. Least of all does the author hold any brief for those of Haeckel's adversaries against whom he defended the great naturalist in his essay on *Haeckel and his Opponents*. If then he goes beyond Haeckel's assumptions and places the spiritual view side by side with Haeckel's purely naturalistic view of the Universe, this surely does not rank him with Haeckel's opponents. Anyone who takes sufficient trouble will perceive that there is no insuperable contradiction between the author's present work and his former writings.

The author can also put himself in the place of the kind of critic who without more ado will discard the whole book as an outpouring of wild fancy. This attitude is answered in the book itself, where it is pointed out that reasoned thinking can and must be the touchstone of all that is here presented. Only those who will apply to the contents of this book the test of

* *Nineteenth-century Philosophic Views of Life and of the World* (published in 1900).

reason — even as they would to a description of natural-scientific facts — will be in a position to decide.

A word may also be addressed to those already predisposed to give the book a sympathetic hearing. (They will find most of what is relevant in the introductory chapter.) Although the book concerns researches beyond the reach of the sense-bound intellect, nothing is here presented which cannot be grasped with open-minded thought and with the healthy feeling for the truth possessed by everyone who will apply these gifts of human nature. The author frankly confesses: he would like readers who will not accept what is here presented on blind faith, but rather put it to the test of their own insight and experience of life.* He desires careful readers — readers who will allow only what is sound and reasonable. This book would not be valid if relying on blind faith; it is of value only inasmuch as it can pass the test of open-minded thinking. Credulity too easily mistakes folly and superstition for the truth. People who are content with vague belief in the supersensible may criticize this book for its excessive appeal to the life of thought. But in these matters the scrupulous and conscientious *form of presentation* is no less essential than the substance. In the field of Occult Science irresponsible charlatanism and the highest truths, genuine knowledge and mere superstition are often separated by a thin dividing line, and it is all too easy to mistake the one for the other.

Readers already conversant with supersensible realities will no doubt recognize the author's care to keep within the bounds of what can and should be communicated at the present time. They will be well aware that there are aspects of supersensible knowledge for which a different form of communication is required, if not a later period of time should be awaited.

RUDOLF STEINER

December 1909.

* This does not only refer to the spiritual test of supersensible research, but to the test — unquestionably valid — of open-minded thought, the test of healthy human intelligence and reflection.

CHAPTER I

THE CHARACTER OF OCCULT SCIENCE

An ancient term — 'Occult Science' — is applied to the contents of this book. The term is likely to evoke the most contrary feelings among the people of our time. To many it will be downright repugnant, calling forth derision, a super cilious smile, even contempt. A way of thought — they will opine — which thus describes itself, must surely rest on idle dreams and the mere arbitrary play of fancy. Its claim to be a science can only be a blind, behind which is the wish to revive all manner of superstitions, justly eschewed by those who are familiar with the scientific spirit, the quest of genuine knowledge. Others are differently affected. They feel that what is signified by this term will bring them something unattainable in any other way, something to which they are drawn — according to their disposition — by a deep inner longing for knowledge or a refined curiosity of soul. Between these two sharply divergent opinions there are a multitude of intermediate views, implying conditional rejection or acceptance of the diverse things which people think of when they hear the term 'Occult Science'.

For some people, undeniably, it has a magic ring because it bids fair to satisfy their craving for information, inaccessible by straightforward methods, about something 'beyond our ken' — something mysterious, nay perhaps vague and confused. For there are those who do not want to meet the deepest longings of the soul with anything that is capable of being clearly known. In their conviction, beyond what is knowable there must be something more in the world that eludes our knowledge. It is a strange contradiction, which they fail to notice. Precisely where the deepest yearning for knowledge is

25

concerned, they would set aside clear knowledge and want to cherish what is incapable of discovery by natural and sound research. Whoever speaks of 'Occult Science' will do well to bear in mind the likelihood of misunderstandings due to the efforts of such champions, who in reality desire, not a true science but the reverse.

The contents of this book are addressed to readers who will not let their openness of mind be impaired because, for a variety of reasons, a word tends to awaken prejudices. Of knowledge claiming to be 'occult' in the sense of secret — accessible only to a few, by special favour or good fortune — there will be no mention here. The reader will do justice to our use of the term 'Occult Science' if he considers what Goethe had in mind when he spoke of the 'manifest secrets' in the phenomena of Nature. Whatever remains 'secret', that is to say unmanifest in these phenomena when we apprehend them only with the outer senses and with the intellect that is bound to the outer senses, will here be treated as the subject-matter of a supersensible way of knowledge.*

Needless to say, for anyone who will admit as science only what is manifest to the senses and to the intellect that serves them, what is here named 'Occult Science' can be no science. Such a man however, if willing to understand his own position, should candidly admit that his categorical rejection of any kind of 'Occult Science' springs not from reasoned insight but from an *ipse dixit*, due to his own individual feeling. To see that it is so, he need only reflect how sciences arise and what is

* Critics of earlier editions of this book have objected that the expression *Occult Science* is a contradiction in terms, since in the nature of the case a science cannot be kept 'occult' or 'secret'. (The German for 'Occult Science' — *Geheimwissenschaft* — begins with the adjective *geheim*, the ordinary word for 'secret'.) The criticism would be just if this were the intention, but it is not so. When we say 'Natural Science' we do not mean a science that is 'natural' to everyone — as it were, a natural endowment. No more does the author think of Occult Science as a science that is 'occult' or 'secret'. It is the science of what — to the ordinary methods of cognition — is present but unmanifest in the phenomena of the world. Occult Science is a science *concerning* the occult — or, to use Goethe's words again, concerning the 'manifest secret'. It has no secret to conceal from anyone who is prepared to seek for occult knowledge by the appropriate methods.

their significance in human life. How a pursuit comes to be a science cannot in the nature of the case be ascertained from the subject-matter to which it is devoted, but only by recognizing the mode of action of the human soul while engaged in scientific endeavour. What is the attitude and activity of the soul in the elaboration of a science? — this is the thing we must observe. If one is used to apply this mode of activity only where sense-data are concerned, one easily slides into the idea that sense-data are the essential factor. One misses the real point, which is that a certain inner attitude of the human soul has been applied to the revelations of the senses. For we can go beyond the self-imposed limitation. Apart from the special case to which it is here applied, we can envisage the character of scientific activity as such. Such is the underlying idea when in this book the knowledge of non-sensible World-contents is spoken of as 'scientific'. The human mind here sets to work at these World-contents, as in the other case it does at the World-contents given to Natural Science. Occult Science seeks to free the scientific method and spirit of research, which in its own domain holds fast to the sequence and relationship of sense-perceptible events, from this restricted application, while maintaining the same essential attitude and mode of thought. Thus it would speak of the non-sensible in the same spirit in which Natural Science speaks of the sensible. While Natural Science, in the employment of scientific thought and method of research, stops short within the sense-perceptible, Occult Science would like to regard the work of the human soul on Nature as a form of self-education, and apply the faculties, thus educated in the soul, to the realms of the non-sensible. Such is its method and procedure. It does not speak of sense-phenomena as such, but of the non-sensible World-contents in the same mood as does the natural scientist of those accessible to sense-perception. It preserves the essential bearing which the soul maintains in scientific procedure — i.e. the very element whereby alone our knowledge of Nature becomes a science. Hence it may justly call itself a science.

Whoever ponders on the significance of Natural Science in human life will find that its significance is by no means exhausted in the acquisition of so much detailed knowledge about Nature. The detailed items of knowledge can, in effect, only lead to an experience of what the human soul is *not*. The soul is living, not in the finished propositions about Nature, but in the *process* of scientific knowledge concerning Nature. In working upon Nature, the soul experiences her own conscious life and being, and what is livingly acquired in this activity is something more than so much information about Nature. It is an evolution of the Self that is experienced in building up our scientific knowledge of Nature. It is this gain in self-development which Occult Science seeks to activate in realms that lie beyond mere Nature. Far from misjudging Natural Science, the occultist thus values it even more than does the scientist himself. He knows that he can found no science without the integrity of thought with which Natural Science is imbued. And what is more, he knows that this integrity, once gained by really penetrating into the spirit of natural-scientific thinking, can by the requisite inner strength be maintained for other realms of being.

One thing, admittedly, can make one hesitate at this point. In contemplating Nature the soul is guided by the object of her study in a far higher degree than in the contemplation of non-sensible World-contents. The purely inner incentive whereby the essence of the scientific way of thought is maintained, must be far stronger in the latter case. Many people — unconsciously — imagine that it can only be maintained by holding to the leading-strings of natural phenomena. Hence they incline to decide *ex cathedra* that as soon as these leading-strings are left behind, the scientific endeavour of the mind and soul will needs be groping in the dark. Such people have never consciously faced the question: What is the essence of scientific procedure? They usually base their judgment on the inevitable aberrations which occur when scientific thinking has not been adequately strengthened by working at the phenomena of Nature, and the soul nevertheless sets out to contemplate the non-sensible or super-sensible domains of the World. Needless to say, much unscientific talk concerning these World-contents arises in this way. The reason is, however, not that the subject must in the nature of the case be outside the pale of science; it is only that in the given instance there has not been adequate self-discipline through the scientific study of Nature.

With due regard to what has just been said, those who would speak of Occult Science must indeed have a watchful eye for all the vagaries that arise when the 'manifest secrets' of the World are treated in an unscientific spirit. It would however be unfruitful if we were to deal with all these aberrations at the very outset of our exposition. In prejudiced minds, no doubt these aberrations bring discredit on any form of research into Occult Science. Their very existence — and they are only too numerous — is taken to justify the conclusion that the whole effort is fallacious. Yet as a rule the rejection of Occult Science by scientists or scientifically minded critics is only due, in the last resort, to the aforesaid *ex cathedra* decision. The reference to aberrations is but a pretext, howsoever unconscious. Lengthy initial argument with such opponents will therefore not be very fruitful. After all, they can observe with perfect justice that on the face of it there is no telling whether in seeing how others are caught up in error we ourselves are standing on the requisite firm ground. Therefore the claimant to Occult Science can do no other than simply bring forward what he has to say. Others alone can judge if he is right — though it must be added, only those others who will refrain from *ex cathedra* pronouncements and enter with open mind into the tenor of his communications about the 'manifest secrets' of the World. It will then be for him to show how what he brings forward is related to the existing achievements of life and knowledge. He must meet possible objections, and point out where the external, sense-perceptible realities of life confirm his statements. Nor should he ever speak or write in such terms as to rely on eloquence or on the arts of persuasion rather than on the pure content of his descriptions.

One often hears it objected that works on Occult Science do not prove what they adduce; they merely make their statements and declare: 'This is what Occult Science teaches.' It would be a misunderstanding to think that anything put forward in these pages was intended in this spirit. Our purpose is different; it is to encourage what is developed in the human soul through the knowledge of Nature to go on evolving, as indeed it can do by its own inherent power. We then point out that through this evolution the soul will encounter supersensible realities. The premise is that every reader, able to adopt this course, is bound to meet with these realities. There is however an important difference, the moment we enter the spiritual-scientific realm, as compared with natural-scientific study. In Natural Science the facts lie spread out before us within the sense-perceptible world. The scientist who describes them regards his own activity of mind and soul as something that recedes into the background over against the given sequence and relationship of the pure facts of the sense world. The spiritual scientist, on the other hand, puts the activity of the soul into the foreground and cannot but do so, for the reader will only reach the facts when by appropriate methods he makes this activity of soul his own. In Natural Science, the facts — however little understood — are there for man's perception even without the soul's activity. Not so the facts of Spiritual Science. They only enter the realm of man's perception by dint of the soul's activity. Thus the exponent of Spiritual Science has to presume that the reader is looking for the facts together with him. This will determine the character of his descriptions. He will narrate the discovery of the facts; and yet the style of his narration will be dominated not by any idiosyncracies of his own but by the purely scientific spirit, trained and developed through Natural Science. Hence he will also be obliged to speak of the means and methods whereby man rises to a contemplation of the non-sensible — that is to say, the super-sensible.

Anyone who really enters into the descriptions of Occult Science will presently perceive that in the process he acquires ideas and concepts he did not have before. He begins to have quite unexpected thoughts concerning what he formerly imagined to be the essence of a 'proof'. In natural-scientific thinking it is different. Here, the activity which is applied to the proof in natural-scientific thinking, already lies inherent in the seeking for the facts. One cannot even find the facts without the path towards them carrying its own inherent proof. Anyone who really goes along this path will in so doing have experienced the proof, and nothing more can be achieved by any added proof from outside. Failure to recognize this essential feature of Occult Science gives rise to numerous misunderstandings.

All Occult Science must spring from two thoughts — thoughts which can take root in every human being. For the occult scientist in our sense of the word, they express facts which every man can experience if he makes use of the proper means. Admittedly, for many people, even these thoughts will appear as statements highly questionable, or even liable to direct refutation.

The two thoughts are as follows. First, that there is behind the visible an invisible world, hidden *to begin with* from the senses and from the kind of thinking that is fettered to the senses. And secondly, that by the due development of forces slumbering within him it is possible for man to penetrate into this hidden world.

There is no such world, says one. The world man perceives with his senses is the one and only world, and the riddles it presents are soluble within its own domain. However far mankind may be as yet from the ability to answer all the problems, sensory observation and the science founded on it will in due time provide the answers.

No, says another, it cannot be said that there is no hidden world behind the visible; our human faculties of knowledge, however, cannot reach it. They are beset with insurmountable limitations. Let the longing for religious faith have recourse to such a world; genuine science, based on the ascertainable facts, can have no dealings with it.

There is still a third party, who deem it presumption for man to want to penetrate with his own active cognition into a region with regard to which he should resign the claim to knowledge and modestly content himself with faith. Those who adhere to this idea feel it wrong for weak humanity to want to press forward into a world which should belong to the religious life alone.

And then again it is argued that a universally accepted knowledge of the facts of the sense-world is possible; here there is common ground for all men. As to the super-sensible, on the other hand, it can only be a question of the individual's personal opinion; it is fallacious to allege any universally valid certainty upon these matters.

Others put forward many other viewpoints.

Yet it is possible to realize quite clearly that the contemplation of the visible world places riddles before man which can never be solved out of the facts of this world alone, even when scientific knowledge has advanced to the very utmost. The visible facts, by their very nature, distinctly indicate a hidden world. The man who does not see this, closes his eyes to the riddles which spring to view on every hand out of the facts of the sense-world. He does not *want* to see certain facts and problems; therefore he believes that all questions can be answered by the sense-perceptible facts alone. The questions he is willing to admit are indeed answerable by these facts, concerning which he is persuaded that they will all be discovered in course of time. We may concede this without controversy. But how should anyone who asks no further questions, expect answers to them? He who aspires to a science of the occult says no more than that for him these further questions are spontaneously there. Why should they not be recognized as a perfectly legitimate expression of the human soul? Science can not be forced into a strait-jacket by forbidding man to put questions freely.

To those who opine that there are limits to human knowledge which man cannot transcend and which compel him to stop short of an invisible world, the answer is: No doubt, with the mode of knowledge they have in mind, man will never penetrate into an unseen world. If one considers this to be the only mode of knowledge, one cannot but come to the conclusion that the human being is denied access to a higher world — if such a world exists. And yet, supposing it to be possible to evolve another mode of cognition, the latter may after all lead into a supersensible world. If such a mode of knowledge is ruled out, then indeed one arrives at a point of view from which any discussion of a supersensible world must appear meaningless. Yet for an open mind the only possible reason for this opinion is that the one who holds it is unacquainted with the other form of knowledge. No man can judge of a thing which from the very outset he declares to be unknown to him. Unbiased thinking must admit that a man should speak of what he knows, and refrain from making pronouncements on what he does not know. Sound thinking can only admit a man's right to communicate what he has really experienced; no man can claim the right to declare impossible what he does not know or does not want to know. We cannot deny a man's right *not* to concern himself with the supersensible; but he can never have the right to declare himself competent to judge, not only of what is known or knowable to himself, but of what he alleges to be unknowable to 'Man' in general!

As to those who think it presumption for man to penetrate into the supersensible, the occult scientist will ask them to reflect, what if man *can?* Is it not then a betrayal of faculties granted to man if he lets them lie waste instead of evolving and making good use of them?

Lastly, the one who thinks that any views about the super-sensible can only be a matter of personal feeling and opinion, denies the common and uniting element in all human beings. It is quite true that each of us can only gain insight into these things through his own efforts, but it is equally true that all those who do, provided they go far enough, reach no divergent views but come to the identical insight. Divergencies exist only so long as men try to approach the highest truths by arbitrary ways, instead of by a pathway that is scientifically sure. Once again it must be unreservedly admitted that he alone who is prepared to enter open-mindedly into the essence of the occult-scientific method will come to recognize its rightness.

The path to Occult Science can be found in due time by every man who perceives — or even only divines or surmises — in the manifest the presence of a hidden aspect. Aware that his powers of knowledge are capable of evolution, he will begin to feel that the hidden *can* become manifest to him. Once he is led to it by such experiences of the soul, Occult Science will open out to him the prospect not only of discovering the answer to many questions prompted by his thirst for knowledge, but the further prospect that he himself will be able to outgrow whatever may be hindering or weakening his life. For in a higher sense it does denote enfeeblement of life — even a kind of death to the soul — when a man feels himself compelled to turn away from the supersensible or to deny it. It may even lead him to despair when he loses hope that the hidden will ever be made manifest. This death and this despair — manifold in the forms they can assume — are at the same time inner opponents of man's striving towards Spiritual Science. They make themselves felt when his inner strength begins to wane. If he is then to have any strength for life, it has to be brought to him from outside. He perceives the objects and events which confront his outer senses; he analyses and dissects them with his intellect. They give him joy or pain; they impel him to such actions as lie within his scope. For a while he may go on in this way; sooner or later however, he will inevitably reach a point where he begins to die an inner death. Sooner or later, what the outer world can give him in this way becomes exhausted. This is no mere assertion of any one man's personal experience; it derives from an open-minded contemplation of all human life. It is the hidden world, latent in the depths of things, which preserves us from this exhaustion. And when the power of fathoming the depths, so as to draw forth from thence ever new strength for life, is waning in man, the outer aspect too will in the end cease to sustain him.

Nor does this only concern the individual's personal weal or woe. More than any other thing, the study of true Occult Science gives us the ever-growing certainty that from a higher point of view the weal and woe of the individual is bound up with that of all the world. Here is a path whereby man reaches the insight that he does harm to the whole world and to all other beings if he fails in the right development of his own powers. When a man renders his life waste and void by losing his connection with the supersensible, he not only destroys within himself something of which the death may ultimately lead him to despair; by his own weakness he becomes a hindrance to the evolution of the entire world in which he lives.

Now it is quite possible for man to deceive himself. He can give himself up to the belief that there is no hidden side to things; that that which meets his outer senses and his intellect is all-inclusive. This delusion however is only possible on the surface of consciousness, not in the depths. Our feeling-life, our aspirations and desires, do not partake in the illusory belief. In one way or another they will always crave for the hidden side; when it is taken from them, they drive the human being into doubt and bewilderment, even into despair, as we have seen. A way of knowledge which brings the hidden to revelation is apt to overcome all hopelessness, perplexity and despair — in short, all that weakens human life on Earth and incapacitates it from contributing its service to the cosmic whole.

One of the fairest fruits of the pursuit of Spiritual Science is that it lends strength and firmness to life, instead of merely satisfying a man's craving for knowledge. Inexhaustible is the fountain head from which it draws, giving man strength for work and confidence in life. No man who has once truly found his way to this source will ever go away unstrengthened, however often he may have recourse to it.

There are those who will have nothing to do with Spiritual Science because they think there is something unhealthy even in what has just been said. As to the surface, the outward aspect of life, they are not altogether wrong. They do not want any neglect of the 'realities' of life, as they see them. They see it as a weakness when man turns away from these realities and seeks salvation in a hidden world, which for them is equivalent to a world of mere dreams and fancies. If in the quest of Spiritual Science we are not to succumb to morbidity and weakness, we must admit the partial justice of such objections. They rest on a sound enough judgment, but one which only leads to a half-truth instead of to the whole truth, inasmuch as it stops short at the surface and fails to penetrate into the depths. If the striving for supersensible knowledge were such as to weaken life and turn man away from reality, objections of this kind would assuredly be strong enough to undermine it.

Here too, however, Occult Science would not be taking the right path by seeking to defend itself, in the everyday sense of the word, as against such opinions. Here too it can only try to express — recognizably to any open mind — its own inherent value, making it felt how it can enhance the strength and energy of life for those who devote themselves to it. For the true quest of Spiritual Science will never make a man a dreamer or an escapist from the world; rather will it fortify him from those deeper founts of life from which as a being of soul and spirit he himself proceeds.

There are yet other hindrances to understanding which for some people bar the way to the pursuit of Occult Science. To mention one: it is true in principle that the reader will find in the expositions of Occult Science a description of experiences of soul which, if he follows them, can lead him towards the supersensible realities. In practice however, this is an ultimate ideal. The reader must first receive as simple communication a wealth of supersensible discoveries which he cannot yet experience for himself. It cannot be otherwise, and will be so in this book. The author will be describing what he believes himself to know about the being of man, including what man undergoes in birth and death and in the body-free condition in the spiritual world; also about the evolution of the Earth and of mankind. It might then seem as though he were putting forward all these alleged items of knowledge as dogmas, which the reader was being asked to accept on the writer's authority. But it is not so. For in reality, whatever can be known of the supersensible world, lives — as a living content of soul — in the spiritual investigator who expounds it, and as the reader finds his way into this living content it kindles in his soul the impulses leading towards the supersensible realities in question. The way we live in reading the descriptions of Spiritual Science is quite different from what it is when reading communications about sense-perceptible events. We simply read *about* the latter; but when we read communications of supersensible realities in the right way, we ourselves are entering into a stream of spiritual life and being. In receiving the results of research, we are receiving at the same time our own inner path towards these results. True, to begin with, the reader will often fail to notice that this is so. For he is far too apt to conceive the entry into the spiritual world on the analogy of sensory experience. Therefore what he experiences of this world in reading of it will seem to him like 'mere thoughts' and nothing more. Yet in the true receiving of it even in the form of thoughts, man is already *within* the spiritual world; it only remains for him to become aware that he has been experiencing in all reality what he imagined himself to be receiving as the mere communication of thoughts.

The true character of the experience will be made fully clear to him when he proceeds to carry out in practice what is described in the later portions of this book, namely the 'path' leading to supersensible knowledge. It might easily be imagined that the reverse was the right order — the pathway should first be described. But it is not so. One who, without first turning his attention to some of the essential facts of the supersensible world, merely does 'exercises' with the idea of gaining entrance there, will find in it a vague and confusing chaos. Man finds his way into that world — to begin with, as it were, naively — by learning to understand its essential features. Then he can gain a clear idea of how — leaving this 'naive' stage behind him — he will himself attain, in full consciousness, to the experiences which have been related to him. Anyone who really enters into Occult Science will become convinced that this and this alone is the reliable way to supersensible knowledge. As to the opinion that information about the supersensible world might influence the reader by way of 'suggestion' or mere dogma, he will perceive that this is quite unfounded. The contents of supersensible knowledge are experienced in a form of inner life which excludes anything in the nature of suggestion and leaves no other possibility than to impart the knowledge to one's fellow-man in the same way as any other kind of truth would be imparted, appealing only to his wide-awake and thoughtful judgment. And if, to begin with, the one who hears or reads the description does not notice how he himself is living in the spiritual world, the reason lies not in any passive or thoughtless receiving of the information, but in the delicate and unwonted nature of the experience.

Therefore by studying the communications given in the first part of this book, one is enabled in the first place to share in the knowledge of the supersensible world; thereafter, by the practical application of the procedures indicated in the second part, one can gain independent knowledge in that world.

A scientific man, entering into the spirit of this book, will find no essential contradiction between his form of science, built as it is upon the facts of the sense-perceptible world, and the way the supersensible world is here investigated. Every scientist makes use of instruments and methods. He prepares his instruments by working upon the things which 'Nature' gives him. The supersensible form of knowledge also makes use of an instrument, only that here the instrument is Man himself. This instrument too must first be prepared — prepared for the purposes of a higher kind of research. The faculties and forces with which the human instrument has been endowed by 'Nature' without man's active cooperation must be transformed into higher ones. Thus can man make of himself the instrument of research — research into the supersensible world.

CHAPTER II

THE NATURE OF HUMANITY

WHAT WE have seen to be true of the supersensible way of cognition in general, becomes immediately evident when we set out to study Man from this standpoint. For the essential thing will be to recognize the 'manifest secret' of our own human nature. What is accessible to the senses, and to the intellect that rests on sense-perception, is but a part of human nature as known to supersensible cognition. It is the *physical body* of man.

To reach a clear and accurate idea of the 'physical body', our attention must first be directed to the phenomenon of death — the great riddle that confronts us wherever we turn to observe life. And in connection with death, we have to think of lifeless Nature so-called — the kingdom of the mineral, which carries death perpetually within it. All these are facts of which the full explanation is only possible with the help of supersensible knowledge, and an important section of this work must be devoted to them. We will begin by suggesting certain ideas and lines of thought with a view to clearer understanding.

Within the manifest world it is the physical body in which man is of like nature with the mineral creation. Anything that distinguishes man from the mineral cannot properly be regarded as 'physical body'. To clear and open-minded reflection the important fact will be that death lays bare the part of the human being which — after death — is of like nature with the mineral world. We can point to the corpse as to that part of man, which, after death, is subject to processes such as are also found in the mineral kindgom. We can emphasize that in this member of man's nature, which we now call the corpse, the same substances and forces are at work as in the mineral

39

world. Equal stress must however be laid upon the fact that for the physical body of man, disintegration sets in the moment death occurs. Moreover we shall be justified in saying: while the same substances and forces are indeed at work in the physical body of man and in the mineral, during man's life their activity is made to serve a higher function. It is only when death has taken place that they work identically with the mineral world. Then they appear, as indeed they must in accordance with their own nature, as the destroyer of the form and structure of man's physical body.

Thus we are able clearly to distinguish what is manifest from what is hidden in the human being. Throughout the life of man something that is hidden must perpetually be battling with the mineral substances and forces in the physical body. The moment the battle ceases, the mineral form of activity makes its appearance. This is the point where the science of the supersensible must enter in; it has to discover what it is that maintains the battle. For this is hidden from the outer senses; it is accessible only to supersensible observation. The way man can attain such observation, so that the 'hidden reality' becomes as manifest to him as are the phenomena of the sense-world to his ordinary vision, will be dealt with in a later chapter. Here, the results of supersensible observation must first be described. As has already been pointed out, information about the path to the attainment of higher faculties of cognition can only be of value to a man when he has first made himself acquainted, through simple narrative, with that which supersensible research reveals. In this domain it is indeed possible to *comprehend* what one cannot yet *observe*. Nay more, the right path to seership is one that takes its start from such comprehension.

Although the hidden something which battles against the disintegration of the physical body can be observed by seership alone, in its effects it is plainly evident even to the kind of judgment which is restricted to the outwardly manifest. For its effects are expressed in the form and shape into which the substances and forces of the physical body are combined during life. When death has taken place, this form gradually disappears and the physical body becomes part of the mineral kingdom pure and simple. Supersensible perception can observe, as an independent member of the human being, what it is that prevents the physical substances and forces during life from going their own way, which would, as we have seen, lead to the disintegration of the physical body. We will call this independent member of man's being the Etheric Body or Life-Body.

If misunderstandings are not to creep in at the outset, two things must be borne in mind when these terms are used. In the first place, the word 'ether' is here applied in a different sense from that of modern Physics, which denotes as ether, for example, the supposed carrier of light — the 'luminiferous ether'.* Here the word 'ether' will be strictly limited to the meaning above indicated. It will be applied to the reality, accessible to higher perception, which makes itself known to sense-observation only by its effects, namely by its power to give definite form and configuration to the mineral substances and forces present in the physical body. Nor, in the second place, must the word 'body' be misunderstood. To designate these more spiritual entities there is no avoiding the use of words taken from ordinary language, which to begin with apply to material, sense-perceptible things. The etheric body is of course nothing 'bodily' in the sensual meaning of the term, in however refined a way we might conceive it.†

With the mention of the etheric body or life-body, our description of supersensible realities is already bound to come into conflict with contemporary opinions. As an outcome of the development of human thought hitherto, the mention of a 'life-body' as an essential principle of human nature can at the present time scarcely fail to be regarded as unscientific. Materialistic thought has reached a point where it sees no

---

* *Note by Translators.* At the time when these words were written, the hypothetical 'luminiferous ether' was still part of the accepted teachings of Physics; hence it was necessary to guard against a possible misunderstanding.

† That the terms 'etheric body' and 'life-body' are not intended as a mere revival of the long since discarded idea of a 'vital force' was pointed out by the author in his earlier work, *Theosophy.*

more in the living organism than a combination of physical substances and forces such as are also found in the so-called lifeless body, or in the mineral. The combination is only supposed to be far more complex.

Yet it is not so very long since other views were held, even by official science. If we study the writings of many serious thinkers of the first half of the nineteenth century, we realize how at that time even 'genuine scientists' were aware that something more is present in the living body than in the mineral. They spoke of a vital force or life-force. True, they did not conceive it as a 'life-body' in the sense above described, but there was in their minds a dim underlying feeling that something of the sort exists. To their way of thinking, it was as though the life-force were present in the living body over and above the physical substances and forces, in much the same way as in the magnet the magnetic force is present over and above the mere iron. Then the time came when the idea of a life-force was eliminated from the accepted scientific teachings. It was claimed that physical and chemical causes alone are a sufficient explanation. Latterly, there has again been a reaction. Some scientific thinkers are disposed to admit that something like a vital force is, after all, not entirely out of the question. But even scientists who admit this much will hardly be disposed to make common cause with the conception here put forward of the life-body.

Generally speaking, to enter into a discussion of these scientific theories from the standpoint of supersensible knowledge will be of little value. Rather should it be recognized that the materialistic conception is an inevitable concomitant of the great progress of Natural Science in our time. This progress has been due to an extreme refinement in the methods of observation by the external senses. And it is characteristic of human nature: again and again in the course of his evolution man brings certain faculties to a high degree of perfection at the expense of others. The faculty of precise sensory observation, which has evolved so significantly with the rise of Natural Science, was bound to eclipse the cultivation of those human faculties which lead into the hidden worlds. But the time has come round again when their cultivation is urgently needed. The recognition of the hidden world will not be furthered by combating judgments which are only the logical outcome of its denial; rather, by putting forward the hidden reality itself in a true light. Then those for whom the time has come will recognize it.

Yet it was necessary to say this much, lest mere ignorance of scientific viewpoints should be presumed when mention is made of an etheric body, which, we are well aware, will widely be regarded as a mere figment of the imagination.

The etheric body, then, constitutes a second member of the human being. For supersensible perception it has indeed a higher degree of reality than the physical. A description of how supersensible perception sees it can only be given in the later sections of this book, when the way of understanding such descriptions will have been made clear. For the present it will suffice to say that the etheric body completely permeates the physical, of which it may be regarded as a kind of architect. All the organs of the physical body are maintained in their form and structure by the currents and movements of the etheric body. Underlying the physical heart there is an etheric heart, underlying the physical brain an etheric brain, and so on. The etheric body is in effect a differentiated body like the physical, only far more complicated. And whereas in the physical body there are relatively separated parts, in the etheric all is in living interflow and movement.

Man has the etheric body in common with the plant world, just as he has the physical body in common with the mineral. Everything that is alive has an etheric body.

From the etheric body, the science of the supersensible advances to a further member of human nature. And as in leading up to the etheric body attention had to be drawn to death, so, to form a conception of this further member of man's nature, supersensible science points to the phenomenon of sleep. All the creative work of man depends — so far as the manifest world is concerned — on his activity in waking life. But this activity is only possible if he again and again derives from sleep a strengthening of his exhausted forces. In sleep, action and thought disappear; pain and joy vanish from conscious life. On awakening, man's conscious powers well up from the unconsciousness of sleep as if from mysterious and hidden springs. It is the *same* consciousness which sinks into dark depths when man falls asleep, and then arises again when he awakens. To the science of the supersensible, what rouses life again and again from the unconscious state is the third member of the human being. It may be called the Astral Body.

As the physical body cannot maintain its form through the mineral substances and forces it contains, but needs to be permeated by the etheric body, so too the forces of the etheric body cannot of themselves become illumined with the light of consciousness. Left to itself, an etheric body would of necessity be in a perpetual state of sleep — or, we may also say, could only maintain in the physical body a vegetable form of life. An etheric body that is awake is illumined by an astral body. For outer observation the effect of the astral body disappears when man falls asleep. For supersensible observation however, the astral body still remains, but it is now seen to be separated from the etheric body, or lifted out of it. Sensory observation is in fact concerned, not with the astral body itself, but only with its effects within the manifest world, and these are not immediately present during sleep.

Man has his physical body in common with the minerals and his etheric body with the plants. In the same sense he is of like nature with the animals in respect of the astral body. The plant is in a perpetual state of sleep. Anyone who does not judge accurately in these matters may easily fall into the error of attributing to plants too a kind of consciousness such as the animals and man have in their waking state. But this mistake is only possible when one's idea of consciousness is inexact. One may then aver that a plant too, when subjected to an outer stimulus, will perform movements, just as an animal will do. One will refer to the 'sensitiveness' of many plants, which for example contract their leaves when certain outer things affect them. But the criterion of consciousness does not lie in the fact that to a given action a being shows a definite reaction. It lies in this, that the being has an inner experience, and this

44

is a new factor, over and above the mere reaction. Otherwise we might as well speak of consciousness when a piece of iron expands under the influence of heat. Consciousness is only there when for example, through the effect of heat, the being inwardly experiences pain.

The fourth member* which supersensible science attributes to the human being, is one he no longer has in common with any of the manifest world around him. Indeed it is this fourth member which distinguishes him from all his fellow-creatures and marks him as the crown of the creation — or of that realm of the creation to which man belongs. Supersensible science arrives at an idea of this fourth member of the human being by pointing to an essential differentiation between the kinds of experience we have even within waking life. This difference becomes directly evident when man observes that in the waking state he is on the one hand in the midst of experiences which *must* come and go, while on the other hand he also has experiences of which this cannot be said. It comes out most distinctly when we compare the conscious experiences of man with those of the animal. The animal experiences the influences of the outer world with great regularity. Under the influence of heat and cold it becomes conscious of pain or pleasure, and its experience of thirst and hunger is subject to bodily processes which take a regular and periodic course. Man's life is not exhausted by experiences such as these. He can develop wishes and cravings transcending all these things. For the animal, could we but pursue the matter far enough, we should always be able to indicate — within the body or outside it — the precise cause for any given action or sensation. With man it is not so. He can give birth to wishes and desires for whose origin no external cause — whether in the body or outside it — is sufficient. Everything that belongs to this domain must be attributed to a special source, which the science of the

* In rendering Rudolf Steiner's chosen term *das Ich* for the fourth and central member of the sevenfold being of Man, it is desirable also to use the direct English equivalent 'the I' and not be restricted to the Latin alternative ,'the Ego'. In this and other translated works, we have adopted the convention of leaving a little extra space on either side of the word I when used as a noun in this hitherto unfamiliar way. (*Note by Translators.*)

super-sensible recognizes to be the I or Ego of man. The I may therefore be described as the fourth member of the human being.

If the astral body were left to itself, pleasure and pain, feelings of hunger or of thirst would come and go in it, but one thing would never come about — namely, the sense of something permanent in all these things. Not the permanent itself, but that which has conscious experience of the permanent, is here called the I. (We must form our concepts with great precision if misunderstandings are not to arise in this domain.) With the awareness of something permanent and lasting in the changing flow of inner experiences, the feeling of 'I', of inner selfhood begins to dawn. The mere fact that a creature experiences hunger, for example, cannot give it the feeling of 'I'. On every new occasion when the causes of hunger make themselves felt, hunger arises. The creature falls upon its food simply because the causes of hunger are there anew. The feeling of 'I' comes in when the creature is not merely impelled to take food by the renewed causes of hunger, but when a previous satisfaction gave rise to a sense of pleasure and the consciousness of the pleasure has remained. Here it is not only the *present* experience of hunger but the *past* experience of satisfaction which provides the impulse.

The physical body disintegrates when it is not held together by the etheric; the etheric body falls into unconsciousness when it is not irradiated by the astral body. In like manner the astral body would ever and again have to let the past sink into oblivion, if the I did not preserve the past and carry it over into the present. Forgetting is for the astral body what death is for the physical body and sleep for the etheric. Or, as we may also express it: *life* is proper to the etheric body, *consciousness* to the astral body, and *memory* to the Ego.

To attribute memory to animals is an error still easier to fall into than the mistake of ascribing consciousness to plants. It is natural enough to think of memory when a dog recognizes its master, whom it may not have seen for some time past. Yet in reality the recognition depends not on memory, but on something else. The attraction proceeds from the master's nature, which gives pleasure to the dog when in his presence. Every time the master's presence is renewed this causes a renewal of the pleasure. Now memory is only there when a being not only feels the experiences of the present moment but preserves those of the past. Even when this is granted, it is however still possible to make the mistake of attributing memory to the dog. Surely, one might rejoin, since the dog grieves when its master goes away, it must retain some memory of him. This too, however, is a wrong conclusion. By living with him, the master's presence has become a need to the dog; it feels his absence just as it experiences hunger. If we are not ready to make clear distinctions of this kind, insight into the true relationships of life remains impaired.

Prevalent misconceptions may even now lead to the retort that we surely cannot know whether anything like human memory is present in the animal or not. This difficulty is due to untrained observation. Anyone who can observe in a really sensible way how the animal behaves in the whole nexus of its experiences, will notice an essential difference between the behaviour of the animal and that of man. He will realize that the animal's behaviour implies the absence of all memory. To supersensible perception this is directly evident; but in these matters, what the supersensible observer is aware of directly, can also be recognized *in its effects* by sense-perception and the penetration of sense-perception with clear thinking.

If we say that man is aware of his memory by looking into his own inner life — a method he obviously cannot apply to the animal — we make a fatal mistake. Man is of course aware of his own faculty of memory, but he can not derive this knowledge from mere introspection. He derives it from what he experiences with himself *in relation to* the things and events of the external world. This kind of experience he has with himself, with his fellow-man, and with the animals too, in precisely the same way. It is an illusion to imagine that we judge of the presence of memory simply on the strength of introspection. The power underlying memory may indeed be called an inner one; the judgment about it is acquired, even for one's own person, by the tests of the external world, — by observing the whole sequence and continuity of life. Of this we can form a judgment in the case of the animal no less than in our own. In such matters the psychology of our time suffers greatly from crude and inexact conceptions — conceptions based on faulty observation and therefore highly misleading.

The significance for the Ego of remembering and forgetting is like that of waking and sleeping for the astral body. As sleep lets the cares and troubles of the day vanish into nothingness, so does forgetting spread a veil over the unhappy experiences of life, thus extinguishing a portion of the past. And as sleep is necessary to refresh the exhausted powers of life, so must the human being blot out from memory certain portions of his past if he is to meet new experiences openly and freely. From the very forgetting he gains strength for the perception of the new. Think for instance of how we learn to write. The many details which a child must live through as he learns to write are afterwards forgotten. It is only the faculty of writing that remains. How would a man ever manage to write, if every time he put pen to paper there rose up in his soul the memory of all the experiences he had to undergo as a child during his writing lessons!

Now memory appears in different stages and degrees. We have it in its simplest form when a man perceives an object and, having turned away, is able still to recall an image of it to his mind. It was while he was perceiving the object that he formed the mental image. A process was then taking place between his astral body and his Ego. The astral body brought the external impression of the object to his consciousness. But his awareness of the object would have lasted no longer than it was actually there before him, if it were not for the Ego receiving this awareness into itself and making it its own.

It is at this point that the science of the supersensible distinguishes 'body' from 'soul'. We speak of the 'astral body' so long as we have in mind how the knowledge or awareness of an actually present object comes about, while we designate as 'soul' what gives the knowledge permanence, duration. From this it will also be evident how close is the connection of the astral body with the part of the soul which gives permanence to knowledge. In a sense, they may even be said to be united — to constitute a single member of the human being. Hence it is also possible to refer to them jointly as the astral body. Or, if we desire a more exact description, we may call the astral body of man the 'Soul-Body' and the soul, in so far as it is united with the astral body, the 'Sentient Soul'.

The Ego rises to a higher stage of being when it directs its activity to what it has received and has made its own by taking cognizance of external objects. In this activity it liberates itself increasingly from the external objects of perception, to work within its own sphere and property. The part of the soul to which this faculty belongs may be described as the Intellectual or Mind-Soul.

It is characteristic both of the sentient and of the intellectual soul that they work with what is received through the impressions of sense-perceived objects and with what memory retains of these impressions. The soul is here entirely given up to things external to it. For even what it has made its own through memory, — even this was received originally from outside. But it is able to transcend all this; the soul is not only sentient and intelligent. Supersensible perception can most readily form an idea of this transcendent faculty by pointing to a simple fact, the far-reaching significance of which needs only to be rightly valued, — the fact that in the whole domain of language there is one name which differs in its essence from all other names. It is the name 'I'. Every other name can be given by every man to the thing or being to which it belongs. 'I', on the other hand, as the designation of a being, only has meaning when the being gives itself this name. The name 'I' can never reach a man from without as a designation of himself. It is only to himself that any being can apply this name. 'I am an I only to myself; to every other being I am a you, and every other being is a you to me.'

This is the outer expression of a deeply significant truth. The real being of the I is independent of all external things and for this very reason no external thing or person can call it by its name. Hence those religious faiths which have consciously maintained their connection with the supersensible wisdom speak of the I as the Unutterable Name of God. For this is what they mean to indicate. Nothing external has access to the part of the human soul which is here envisaged. Here is the 'hidden Holy of Holies' of the soul, to which no entry is possible save for a Being with whom the soul is of like kind and essence. 'The God who dwells in man, — He it is who speaks when the soul perceives and knows itself as 'I'.' As the sentient soul and intellectual soul live in the outer world, so does a third member of the soul immerse itself in the Divine when the soul comes to a perception of its own essence and nature.

One may all too easily be misunderstood at this point — as though one were asserting that the human I and God were one and the same. Yet it is not said that the I is God, but only that it is of like kind and essence with the Divine. When we say that a drop of water taken from the ocean is of the same essence or substance as the ocean, are we thereby stating that the drop *is* the ocean? If we must use a comparison, we may put it thus: as the drop is to the ocean, so is the I to the Divine. Man can find a Divine within himself, because his own and most essential being springs from the Divine.

In this way man reaches up to a third member of his soul — to an inner knowledge and awareness of himself, even as through the astral body he gains knowledge and awareness of the outer world. Hence too, Occult Science calls this third member of the soul, the Consciousness-Soul or Spiritual Soul.* Thus Occult Science sees the soul as consisting of three members: Sentient Soul, Intellectual Soul and Spiritual Soul; just as the bodily nature consists of the three members: Physical Body, Etheric Body and Astral Body.

Errors in psychological observation, not unlike those already discussed with reference to memory, give rise to difficulties

---

* *Note by Translators.* 'Consciousness-Soul' is the literal translation of the original German word *Bewusstseins-Seele*, and will be found in the earlier English editions of this and other works. In later years Rudolf Steiner — who often did not favour a merely literal translation — suggested 'Spiritual Soul' as the best English equivalent. 'Spiritual Soul' will therefore be used throughout this book, the alternative 'Consciousness-Soul' being occasionally added where it would seem to throw light on a particular context.

once again when seeking insight into the nature of the I. Much that people think they see may easily be taken by them for a refutation of what has here been said, whereas in truth it serves only to confirm it. Such is the case, for instance, with Eduard von Hartmann's remarks on page 55 of his *Outline of Psychology*. *'To begin with', says von Hartmann, 'self-consciousness is older than the word 'I'. The personal pronouns are a comparatively late product in the evolution of language, and have for language merely the value of abbreviations. The word 'I' is a short substitute for the proper name of the speaker — with this peculiarity, that every speaker applies it to himself, no matter by what proper name the others call him. In animals and in the untrained deaf and dumb, self-consciousness may evolve to a high degree, even without the initial connection with a proper name. Also the consciousness of the proper name may completely replace the use of the word 'I' when this is absent. The recognition of this fact will suffice to remove the magic halo with which the little word 'I' is invested for so many people. The word contributes nothing to the concept of self-consciousness; it receives its own content purely from this concept.'

We need not quarrel with such a point of view. We may well agree that the little word 'I' should not be invested with a magic halo — such as could, after all, only blur the thoughtful perception of the truth. But the essence of a matter is not decided by the way in which the word, the designation for it, has evolved. That the real essence and nature of the I in self-consciousness is 'older than the word 'I' ' — this is precisely the point. The point is, moreover, that the human being needs this word, with its unique properties, to express what he experiences in relation to the outer world in a different way from an animal. Nothing is ascertained about the nature of the triangle by showing how the word 'triangle' evolved. No more can the nature of the I or Ego be determined by anything that we may know as to how the use of the word 'I' arose from other usages of words in the evolution of language.

* E. von Hartmann: *System der Philosophie im Grundriss*. Vol. III: *Grundriss der Psychologie*.

In the spiritual soul the real nature of the I first becomes revealed. For while in sentient and intellectual activity the soul is given up to other things, *qua* spiritual soul it seizes hold of its own being. Hence too, the spiritual soul can only perceive the I by dint of a certain *inner* activity. The mental images and representations of external objects are formed as these objects come and go; in the intellect they go on working by their own impetus. But if the I is to perceive itself, it can no longer passively devote itself to other things. To become conscious of its own essence and being, it must first call it forth — by dint of inner activity — out of the depths of its own nature. With the perception of 'I' — with self-contemplation — an inner activity of the I itself begins. By virtue of this activity, the perception of the I in the spiritual soul has a fundamentally different significance for man from the observation of what comes to him through the three bodily members and the other two members of the soul.

The power which brings the I to manifestation in the spiritual soul is indeed the selfsame power which reveals itself throughout the world. In the body however, and in the lower members of the soul, it does not come forth directly but is revealed stage by stage in its effects. The lowest revelation of it is through the physical body; thence it arises, step by step, up to the content of the intellectual soul. We might say that with each step in the ascent one of the veils by which the Unmanifest is shrouded falls away. In the experience and content of the spiritual soul, the Unmanifest in its own essence enters unveiled into the inmost temple of the soul. Admittedly it shows itself as a mere drop out of the ocean of the all-pervading spiritual essence. Yet it is here that man must first seize the spiritual essence. He must know it by discovering it within himself; then he can also find it in all other revelations.

What penetrates in this way like a drop into the spiritual soul is what Occult Science calls the Spirit. Thus the spiritual soul is connected with the universal Spirit which is the hidden reality within all things manifest. If man would apprehend the hidden Spirit in all the other manifestations of the World, he must needs do so in the same way in which he apprehends the

Ego in the 'Consciousness-Soul' — the spiritual soul. He must apply to the manifest world the same activity which has led him to a perception of the I within himself. By this means he evolves to higher stages of his being. To the bodily members and the members of the soul he now adds something new.

The first step along this path consists in his conquering and making his own all that lies hidden in the lower members of his soul. He does this by working upon his soul — working upon it out of the inmost resources of the Ego. We have a vivid picture of the way the human being is engaged upon this work when we compare a man still given up to lower cravings and so-called sensual pleasures with a high-minded idealist. The former evolves into the latter in that he withdraws from lower inclinations and turns to higher ones. In so doing, he works from the Ego upon his soul, ennobling and spiritualizing it. The Ego becomes master in the soul's life.

This process can go so far that no desires or enjoyments can gain access to the soul without the I itself being the power which makes possible their entry. And in this way the soul in its entirety becomes at length a revelation of the I , as was hitherto the spiritual soul alone. This is the meaning of all civilization, of all the spiritual strivings and aspirations of mankind. There is this constant endeavour for the mastery of the Ego. Every human being living at the present time is engaged in this great work — whether he will or no, whether he is conscious of the fact or not.

This work leads on to ever higher levels of human nature. Through it man evolves new members of his being, which lie — as yet unmanifest — behind what is manifest in him. Moreover, it is not only the soul over which a man can attain mastery by working upon it from the Ego, till from the manifest within the soul the unmanifest springs forth. He can extend this work still further, carrying it over to the astral body. As he does so, the Ego gains power over the astral body, entering into union with its hidden nature. The astral body thus mastered and transformed by the I may be called the 'Spirit-Self'. (This is identical with what is called, in connection with Oriental wisdom, 'Manas'). In the Spirit-Self we have therefore a higher member of man's nature, one which is already present in him — germinally, as it were — and comes forth ever more and more as he continues to work upon himself.

As man gains mastery over his astral body by penetrating to the hidden forces that underlie it, so in the course of evolution does he gain mastery over the etheric body too. The work upon the etheric body is however more intense and more exacting. For what lies hidden in the etheric body is shrouded beneath a double veil; the hidden in the astral body beneath a single veil only. We can get some idea of the difference in the work upon the two bodies by noticing the changes which take place in a human being in the course of his life. Think of the qualities that are developed when the Ego works upon the soul. How very different a man's pleasures and desires, his joys and sufferings become! A man need only look back to the time of his childhood. What was it that he then delighted in, or that caused him pain? And what has he not learned and added to the faculties he had in childhood? These changes are but an expression of the way the Ego has been gaining mastery over the astral body. For the astral body is the bearer of pleasure and pain, of joy and suffering. And now compare with this the small extent to which certain other qualities of man will change in course of time: his temperament, for instance, his deeper traits of character. One who as a child is given to sudden fits of anger will often show signs of violent temper right on into later life. This is indeed so evident a fact that some thinkers tend altogether to dismiss the possibility of change in the basic character of any man. They assume it to be something that persists throughout his life, though it may be revealed in varying directions. Such a judgment rests however on insufficient observation. One who has sensitive perception will realize that even the character and temperament of man can change under the influence of his Ego, although the change is comparatively slow. We might even say that the two types of change are to one another as the movement of the hour hand to that of the minute hand of a clock.

Now the forces that affect these changes in character or temperament belong to the hidden domain of the etheric body.

They are alike in kind with the forces that govern the kingdom of life — the forces of growth and nourishment and those that serve the reproductive process. All this will appear in the proper light in the further course of this book.

It is not when man is merely given up to pleasure or suffering, to joy or pain, that the Ego works upon the astral body; rather, when these proclivities are actually being changed. In like manner, the work of the Ego extends to the etheric body when it applies itself to changing the qualities of character, temperament and so forth. And at this transformation too, every man is working, whether or no he be aware of it. The impulses that work most strongly in this direction are those of religion. When the Ego lays itself open to these influences again and again, they work within it as a power which reaches down to the etheric body and transforms it, just as the lesser incentives of life will bring about the changing of the astral body. These lesser incentives, which come to man through learning, through thoughtful reflection, through the refinement of his feelings and so on, are subject to many variations; the religious emotions, on the other hand, impress a kind of unity on all his thinking, feeling and willing. They pour out as it were a common light, a light that is 'single', over the whole life of the soul. A man thinks and feels one thing to-day, another to-morrow. Many and varied circumstances provide occasion for his thoughts and feelings. But one who is aware through his religious life, of whatsoever kind it be, of something that outlasts all changes, will refer to the same underlying emotion his thoughts and feelings of to-day and his experiences of to-morrow. A man's religious faith thus has a penetrating influence in his soul's life — an influence which grows as time goes on through constant repetition. It thereby gains the power to work on the etheric body. So do the influences of true art affect the human being. When through the outer form, colour or sound of a work of art man penetrates with thought and feeling to the spiritual sources that underlie it, the impulses the Ego thus receives do in effect reach the etheric body. Thinking this through to its conclusion, we may gain some idea of the immense significance of art in human evolution.

We have thus indicated some of the incentives enabling the Ego to work at the etheric body. There are other such influences in human life, though outwardly less evident than the ones here mentioned. From these, however, it can already be seen that there lies hidden in man a further member of human nature, which, once again, the Ego is progressively elaborating. It is the second member of man's spiritual being, and may be called the 'Life-Spirit'. (It is identical with what is named 'Budhi' in connection with Oriental wisdom.) The term Life-Spirit is right and proper because the same forces are working in it as in the life-body. Where they reveal themselves as life-body the I of man is not yet active in them; when they come to expression as Life-Spirit they are penetrated through and through by its activity.

Man's intellectual development, the purification and refinement of his feelings and of the manifestations of his will, are the measure of his transmutation of the astral body into Spirit-Self. His religious experiences, and other experiences too which life affords, become engraved in his etheric body, changing it into Life-Spirit. In the ordinary course of life all this goes on more or less unconsciously. There is, on the other hand, what is called the Initiation of man. Initiation consists in his being shown, through supersensible knowledge, the means whereby he may take in hand with full consciousness this work upon the Spirit-Self and the Life-Spirit. This will be spoken of in subsequent chapters. For the moment, the point was to show that in addition to the Soul and Body the Spirit too is at work in man. In contrast to the transitory body, the Spirit belongs to the Eternal in man. This too will emerge more clearly in further course.

Now the activity of the Ego is not exhausted with the work upon the astral and etheric bodies. It extends also to the physical. We see a faint suggestion of the influence of the Ego on the physical body when, for example, a human being blushes or grows pale. For the I is here the underlying motive power of a process taking place in the physical body. If now, through the Ego's own activity and initiative, its influence upon the physical body undergoes essential changes, the Ego will then be working in unison with the hidden forces of the physical body. It will be united, in effect, with the same forces which bring about the physical processes in this body. The Ego itself may then be said to be working upon the physical body to transform it. But this expression must not be misunderstood. It must not be supposed that the work is of a crude material kind. For what appears crudely material in the physical body is merely what is manifest in it. Behind this manifest there lie the hidden forces of its being, and these are of a spiritual kind. Here we are speaking, not of a working upon the material appearance of the physical body, but of a spiritual working — a working upon the invisible forces to which the coming-into-being and also the decay of the physical body are due. In ordinary life man can at most become very dimly conscious of this work of the Ego upon the physical body. Full clarity is only reached when under the influence of spiritual knowledge he takes the work consciously in hand. It then becomes manifest that there is yet a third spiritual member in the human being. It may be called, in contrast to the physical man, the 'Spirit-Man'. (In Oriental wisdom it is called 'Atma'.)

With regard to Spirit-Man it is easy to be led astray by the fact that the physical appears to be the lowest member of the human being. One finds difficulty in conceiving that work upon the physical body should culminate in the highest member of man's nature. But for the very reason that the physical body conceals beneath a threefold veil the Spirit that is active in it, the highest form of human activity is needed to unite the Ego with this hidden Spirit.

Thus in the light of Occult Science man appears as a being composed of several members. Those of a bodily nature are: physical body, etheric body and astral body. Those of the soul are: sentient soul, intellectual soul and spiritual soul. In the soul the Ego sheds its light. Lastly we have the spiritual members: Spirit-Self, Life-Spirit and Spirit-Man.

From the above explanations it will be seen that the sentient soul and the astral body are intimately united, forming in one respect a single whole. The same is true of the spiritual

57

soul and the Spirit-Self. For in the spiritual soul the light of the Spirit arises, to radiate from thence throughout the other members of man's nature. Taking this into account, the constitution of the human being may also be described as follows: The astral body and the sentient soul can be taken together as a single member; likewise the spiritual soul and the Spirit-Self. Lastly the intellectual soul, since it partakes of the nature of the I — since in a certain respect it *is* the I, though not yet conscious of its spiritual being — may be designated simply as the I or Ego. We thus obtain the following seven members of the human being:

1. Physical body
2. Etheric body or life-body
3. Astral body
4. I, Ego
5. Spirit-Self
6. Life-Spirit
7. Spirit-Man

Even for those accustomed to materialistic notions, this organisation of the human being according to the number seven would not have the vaguely magical and superstitious quality often attributed to it, if they could simply follow the given explanations, and not themselves bring in the 'magical' significance which they presume. We speak of the seven colours of the rainbow, or of the seven notes of the scale (treating the octave as a repetition of the keynote). In no other sense — only from the standpoint of a higher kind of observation — do we refer to the seven members of man's being. As light appears in seven colours and the musical scale in seven notes, so does human nature — for all its singleness and unity — appear in the seven members here described. In sound and colour the number seven does not imply any kind of superstition; nor does it in the constitution of the human being. (On one occasion when this was mentioned in a lecture, it was objected that the number seven does not apply to colour, since there are other 'colours' beyond the red and violet, only the human eye cannot perceive them. But even taking this into account, the comparison is still valid; for the human being too reaches beyond the physical body on the one hand and beyond Spirit-Man on the other. Only these extensions of man's being are 'spiritually invisible' to the available methods of spiritual observation, just as the colours beyond red and violet are invisible to the physical eye. This remark was necessary because it is too easily concluded that supersensible vision and the ideas to which it leads are scientifically inexact. If one really enters into what is here intended, it will in no case be found inconsistent with genuine Science. There is no contradiction — neither when scientific facts are cited by way of illustration, nor when a direct relation to the discoveries of Natural Science is pointed out.)

CHAPTER III

SLEEP AND DEATH

THE ESSENCE of man's waking consciousness cannot be penetrated without observing the condition he lives through in sleep; so too, is the riddle of life insoluble without the study of death. People who have no feeling for the importance of supersensible knowledge will find grounds for scepticism in the very fact that it dwells so much on the facts of sleep and death. We can appreciate the motives of this kind of scepticism. For it is not unreasonable to insist that man is here to lead an active life, and that the more he is devoted to this life, the more efficient and creative he will be; to delve into such things as sleep and death can only spring from a tendency to idle dreaming and lead to nothing more than empty figments of the mind.

People may easily regard the refusal to indulge in such 'empty figments' as a sign of mental health, and see in the pursuit of these 'idle dreamings' something morbid, natural enough to those deficient in vitality and vigour, without ability to do creative work. We should do wrong merely to brush aside this opinion. There is in it a modicum of truth; it is a quarter-truth, and only needs to be complemented by the remaining three quarters. By arguing against it we only kindle the mistrust of those who see the one quarter well enough but are unaware of the other three.

A study of what lies hidden behind sleep and death is only morbid if it produces weakness and aversion from the realities of life. This may be granted without reservation. Admittedly moreover, much that has claimed the title of 'Occult Science' in the past or is pursued to-day under this name, bears an unhealthy stamp, inimical to life. But the true science of the supersensible does not give rise to anything unhealthy of this kind.

The fact is rather this. — As a man cannot always be awake, so for the full reality of life he cannot do without what the supersensible provides. Life goes on in sleep; the faculties with which we work and achieve results in waking consciousness derive strength and renewal from what sleep imparts. So too it is with what man is able to observe within the manifest world. The real world is wider than the field of this type of observation. Therefore the knowledge man can gain within the visible domain needs to be fertilized and complemented by all that he can come to know of the invisible. A man who did not ever and again derive from sleep the renewal of his exhausted powers would destroy his life; likewise, a way of thinking which is not made fruitful by the knowledge of hidden worlds must ultimately lead to emptiness and desolation.

So too with 'death'. All living things are subject to death, to the end that new life may arise. It is the knowledge of the supersensible which throws clear light on Goethe's well-known saying: 'Nature herself invented death, to have abundant life.' As without death there could be no life in the ordinary meaning of the term, so without insight into the supersensible there can be no true knowledge even of the visible world. Our knowledge of the visible must penetrate again and again to the invisible, that it may live and grow. Thus it becomes apparent that the science of the manifest world is awakened to essential life by the science of the supersensible. In its true form, the latter never has a weakening effect. Time and again it brings refreshment and healing into the outer existence which when abandoned to its own resources becomes weak and ill.

When a man falls asleep the connection between the members of his being undergoes a change. What we see lying there on the bed includes the physical and the etheric body of the sleeper, but not the astral body nor the I or Ego. Inasmuch as the etheric body remains connected with the physical, the vital functions continue during sleep; left to itself alone, the physical body would of necessity disintegrate. It is the thoughts, the mental images, it is pain and pleasure, joy and grief, the power of giving conscious direction to the will, and all other things of this kind, which are blotted out in sleep. Now of all this the astral body is the bearer.

For an unbiased mind there can of course be no question of supposing that the astral body with its pains and pleasures, with its whole world of ideation and volition, is annihilated during sleep. It is still there, only in a different state. If the human I and astral body are not merely to contain pain and pleasure and all the other things above named, but to have conscious perception of them, the astral body must be united with the physical and etheric bodies, as indeed it is in waking life. In sleep it is not so; it has then withdrawn from the physical and the etheric and entered into quite another mode of existence than pertains to it when united with them.

It is the task of supersensible science to investigate this other mode of existence. In sleep the astral body vanishes from external observation; supersensible perception must now trace it through the stages of its life, till on awakening it once more takes possession of the physical and the etheric body.

As with all other knowledge of the world's hidden realities, supersensible observation is necessary for the discovery of the spiritual facts concerning sleep; properly stated, however, what has thus been discovered is intelligible to unbiased thinking. For the realities of hidden worlds are manifest in their effects. If we perceive how the processes of the sense-world are made intelligible by the information derived from supersensible perception, such confirmation by the facts of life is the kind of proof we may expect. Anyone not wishing to apply the methods — later to be described — for the attainment of supersensible perception, can have the following experience. To begin with, he may simply take the statements of supersensible science and apply them to what is manifest within the compass of his experience. He will discover that life becomes clear and intelligible to him in the process. Indeed the more exact and searching his study of the ordinary life he knows, the more will he be led to this conviction.

Although the astral body during sleep experiences no ideas

or thoughts in consciousness, though it is unaware of pain or pleasure or the like, yet it does not remain inactive. On the contrary, it is precisely during sleep that a most vital activity devolves upon it — an activity into which it has to enter again and again in rhythmical succession, when for a time it has been working in unison with the physical and the etheric body. A pendulum, returning to the middle after swinging to the left, will swing to the right through the very momentum it has gathered on the left. So it is with the astral body and the I or Ego which it bears within it. Having been active in the physical and etheric body for a time, for a succeeding period of time — precisely as an outcome of this activity — they need to live and move and have their being in a body-free condition, in an environment of pure soul and spirit.

As man is constituted in ordinary life, unconsciousness ensues during this body-free condition of the astral body and Ego. Unconsciousness is in effect the antithesis of the state of consciousness evolved in waking life by union with the physical and the etheric bodies, just as the swing of a pendulum to the right is the antithesis of the swing to the left. The need to enter into this unconscious state is felt by the human soul and spirit as tiredness, fatigue. Fatigue itself is the expression of the fact that during sleep the astral body and Ego are making themselves ready for the next waking state, when they will once again be undoing and reversing in the physical and etheric body what has arisen in the latter — through a purely organic and unconscious formative activity — while free from the soul-and-spirit. This unconscious formative activity, and what takes place in man during his conscious life and by virtue of it, are contrasting states which have to alternate in rhythmical succession.*

The form and shape, proper to the physical body of man, can only be maintained by means of a human etheric body, which in its turn must be endowed with the appropriate forces by the astral body. The ether-body is the form-giving agent or architect of the physical. But it can only form the physical body aright if it receives from the astral body the necessary

* Concerning fatigue, see also the Note on page 327.

guidance and stimulation. In the astral body are the 'pattern-forms' or archetypes according to which the etheric body gives the physical its appointed shape.

Now in the waking life the astral body is not imbued with these archetypal patterns for the physical body, or only to a limited extent. For while awake the soul puts its own pictures, its own images, in their place. Turning his senses to the surrounding world, in the very act of perception man forms pictures, mental images of his surroundings. These images are, to begin with, 'disturbers of the peace' for those pattern-forms which stimulate the etheric body in its work of building and maintaining the physical. Only if a man were able by his own inner activity to supply his astral body with such pictures as could give to the etheric body the right kind of stimulus, only then would there be no such disturbance. Yet the fact is that this very disturbance plays an essential part in human life, and as an outcome, while a man is awake the archetypal pictures for his etheric body cannot work with their full power. The astral body fulfils its waking function *within* the physical body; in sleep it works upon the latter *from without*.

Just as the physical body — in the supply of nourishment for example — has need of the outer world to which it is akin, a similar thing is also true of the astral body. Imagine a human physical body taken right away from its appropriate surroundings; it would inevitably perish. The physical body's existence is impossible without the entire physical environment. The whole Earth must be as it is, if human physical bodies are   be present on it. In truth, this human body is but a portion of the Earth-planet, and in a wider sense of the whole physical Universe. In this respect it is as the finger is to the human body as a whole. Separate the finger from the hand — it cannot remain a finger; it will shrink and wither. Such too would be the fate of the human body if severed from the body of which it is a member — from the life-conditions with which the Earth provides it. Raise it a sufficient number of miles above the Earth and it will perish, as the finger does when cut off from the hand. As to his physical body, man may be less aware of this fact than with regard to the finger in relation to this body as a whole. But this is merely because the finger cannot walk about the body as man does about the Earth; hence the dependence is more obvious in the one case than in the other.

Even as the physical body is embedded in the physical world to which it belongs, so too the astral body belongs to a world of its own, from which however it is torn away by man's waking life. This may be illustrated by a comparison. Imagine a vessel full of water. Within the mass of water a single drop has no separate existence. But take a little sponge and draw a drop away, thus severing it from the total mass. Something of this kind happens to the human astral body on awaking. During sleep it is in a world of its own kind, a world to which it properly belongs. On awaking, the physical and the etheric body draw it in and fill themselves with it. These two bodies contain the organs whereby the astral body perceives the external world, to attain which perception it has to be detached from its own world. Yet from the latter alone can it derive the archetypal patterns which it needs for the etheric body.

As food and other necessities are received by the physical body from its environment, so do the *pictures* of the astral body's environment come to it during sleep. The fact is that the astral body is then living, outside the physical and the etheric, in the great Universe — the selfsame Universe out of which the entire man is born. For in that Universe is the source of the creative patterns, — the archetypal pictures to which man owes his form. In his true being he belongs to the great Universe and is in harmony with it. In waking life he detaches himself from the all-embracing harmony, in order to have outer perceptions. In sleep his astral body returns into the harmony of the Universe, whence on awakening he brings sufficient force into his bodies to enable him for a time once more to forgo the sojourn there.

The astral body thus returns to its pristine home during sleep, and on awakening brings with it into life newly strengthened forces. All this finds expression in the refreshment which a healthy sleep affords. As the further exposition of Occult Science will reveal, the home of the astral body is of far wider compass than the more obvious physical environment to which the physical body belongs. While as a physical being man is a member of the Earth, his astral body belongs to worlds wherein other heavenly bodies are contained besides our planet Earth. The astral body therefore, during sleep, enters a Universe to which other worlds than the Earth belong. But this can only be made fully clear in the further course of our explanations.

Though it should really be superfluous, prevalent habits of materialistic thought render it not unnecessary to set aside a possible misunderstanding in this connection. People adhering to these ways of thought will be inclined to say: 'Surely the scientific procedure is to investigate the physical conditions of such a thing as sleep. Though scientists may not yet be agreed as to its precise causation, this much at any rate is certain: physical processes of one kind or another can be assumed to underlie the phenomenon of sleep'. If only it were realized that supersensible science is not at all against such a contention! All that is said from this quarter is readily accepted, just as it will be admitted that for a house to come into physical existence one brick must be laid on the other, and that when the house is finished its form and its stability are explainable by purely mechanical laws. Yet for the house to come into being the thought of the architect was also necessary. This thought will not be discovered by mere investigation of the mechanical and physical laws. — Behind the physical laws in terms of which the structure of the house can be explained, there are the thoughts of its creator. So too, behind what physical science and physiology are perfectly right in bringing forward, there are the hidden realities of which the science of the supersensible is telling.

Admittedly, the same comparison is frequently adduced to justify belief in a spiritual background of the world, and one may find it trite. But in these matters the point is not whether a line of thought is familiar, but whether we have given it due weight. We may well be prevented from appreciating the true weight of an idea because ideas derived from a contrary way of thinking have too much influence upon our judgment.

A midway condition between waking and sleeping is dreaming. Reflecting on our dream-experiences, we are confronted by a world of pictures, iridescent and in manifold confusion, though not without some hint of underlying method. Pictures arise and fade away again, often bewildering in their sequence. Man in his dream-life is released from the laws which bind his waking consciousness to the perceptions of the senses and the logical rules of judgment. Yet in the world of dreams we seem to divine mysterious laws of its own, fascinating and alluring. This is the deeper reason why we are prone to compare with dreaming the play of fancy and creative imagination which our aesthetic and artistic sense delights in.

We need only call to mind a few characteristic dreams to find all this confirmed. A man will dream, for example, that he is chasing away a dog which has been rushing at him. He awakens and finds himself in the unconscious act of pushing away a portion of the bed-clothes which had been weighing on an unaccustomed part of his body and had become oppressive. In such an instance, what does the dream make of the real, sense-perceptible event? To begin with, the life of sleep leaves entirely in the unconscious what the senses would have perceived in waking life. But it holds fast to one essential — the fact that we are wanting to ward something off — and around this it weaves an imaginary sequence of events. In substance these imaginary pictures are like echoes from the waking life of the day-time, echoes selected at random. The dreamer will generally feel that with the same external cause his dream might just as well have conjured up quite other pictures. Only in one way or another they would relate, in this instance, to the sensation of having to ward something off. The dream, therefore, creates symbolic pictures; it is in fact a symbolist. Inner bodily conditions too can be translated into dream-symbols of this kind. A man will dream that a fire is crackling beside him; he sees the very flames. On awakening he finds that he put on too many bed-clothes and has grown too hot. The feeling of excessive heat comes out symbolically in the picture of the fire.

Experiences of the most dramatic kind can be enacted in a dream. For instance, a man dreams that he is standing near the edge of a cliff and sees a child running towards it. The dream lets him undergo all the tortures of the thought, 'What if the child should fail to notice and fall over!' Presently he sees the child fall and hears the dull thud of the body down below. He wakes up and finds that a familar object, hanging on the wall of the room, had worked loose and made a dull sound as it fell. A simple enough event — the dream-life turns it into a sequence of dramatic pictures, full of suspense and excitement.

For the present we need not stop to ponder, how and why — in the last example — the instantaneous thud of the falling object gets extended into a whole series of events, seeming to occupy a considerable time. The point is that the dream translates what waking sense-perception would have shown, into scenes and pictures.

We see from this that when the senses cease from their activity, immediately a creative faculty begins to stir in man. It is the same creative faculty which is at work in fully dreamless sleep, there giving rise to the state of soul we were describing as the antithesis of the waking state. For dreamless sleep, the astral body has to be withdrawn both from the etheric body and from the physical. In dreaming, while separated from the physical body — no longer joined to the physical sense-organs — it still remains connected to some extent with the etheric. The very fact that what is going on in the astral body is perceived in pictures, is due to its connection with the etheric body. The moment this connection too is severed, the pictures fade into complete unconsciousness; dreamless sleep ensues.

The arbitrary, often nonsensical character of dream-pictures is due to the fact that the astral body, disconnected as it is from the sense-organs of the physical, cannot relate its pictures to the proper objects and events of the external world. This becomes very evident when we contemplate the kind of dream in which the I, the Ego, is in a sense divided. For instance, one dreams of oneself as a pupil who cannot answer a question the schoolmaster is putting; yet in the very next moment the master himself gives the required answer. Unable to make use of the organs of perception of his physical body, the dreamer cannot relate the two events to himself as to one and the same person. Even to recognize himself as a continuous and coherent I, man therefore needs to be equipped with outer organs of perception. Only if he had attained the faculty to be aware of his own I without the help of such organs of perception, only then would the continuity and oneness of the I still be perceptible to him even outside the physical body. For super-sensible consciousness, faculties of this kind must indeed be acquired. The way to do so will be dealt with in a later chapter.

Not only sleep; death too is due to a change in the mutual connection between the members of man's being. And here once more, what is apparent to supersensible perception can also be seen in its effects within the manifest world. Here once again, unbiased thinking will find the statements of super-sensible science confirmed by the facts of external life, though in this instance the impress of the invisible in the visible domain is less in evidence, and it is therefore not so easy to realize the weight and bearing of those realities of outer life which answer to the statements of supersensible science. Here even more than for other things already dealt with in this volume, if the mind is not open to discern the way in which the sense-perceptible domain relates to the supersensible and indicates the latter's presence, it is only too easy to pronounce the findings of Occult Science mere figments of imagination.

When a man falls asleep, whereas his astral body is released from its connection with the etheric and physical bodies, the latter still remain united. Not so in death. In death the physical is severed from the etheric body. Left to its own unaided forces, the physical body will now inevitably disintegrate. For the etheric body, on the other hand, death brings about a condi-tion in which it never was throughout the whole time between birth and death, save in exceptional circumstances to be men-tioned later. For the etheric is now united with its astral body, and the physical body is no longer with them. The fact is that the etheric and astral bodies do not separate immediately after death. They hold together for a time, by virtue of a force which obviously must be there, for otherwise the etheric body could never have freed itself from the physical, to which it is tenaciously attached, as is shown by the fact that in sleep the astral body fails to part them. At death the force that holds the etheric and astral bodies together becomes at last effective, detaching the etheric from the physical. To begin with therefore, the etheric body after death is united with the astral body. Supersensible observation shows that this their union varies from one individual to another. All we need say at the moment is that it lasts for a short time — for a few days — after which the astral body frees itself from the etheric body also, and goes on its way without it. While the connection of the two persists, man is in a condition consciously to perceive the experiences of his astral body. So long as the physical body was there, the separation of the astral body from the physical in sleep involved the immediate commencement of its work upon the physical body from without, for the renewal of the outworn organs. With the severance of the physical body at death, this work is at an end. But the spiritual forces which were expended on it during sleep are still there and can now serve a different end, namely to make perceptible the processes within the astral body as such.

From a point of view which would restrict scientific observation to the outer aspects of life, it will be said: 'These are so many assertions, evident no doubt to those endowed with supersensible perception; men who are not thus endowed have no way of assessing their truth.' Yet this is not so. Even in this domain, remote though it may seem from ordinary sight and thought, what the science of the supersensible observes can be taken hold of, *once discovered*, by the normal faculties of thought and judgment. One need only ponder with due judgment the manifest and given relationships of human life. The thinking, feeling and willing of man are related to one another, and to his experiences in and with the outer world, in ways that are unintelligible unless the manifest activities and relationships are understood as the expression of an unmanifest. To thoughtful contemplation, what is here manifest remains opaque and untransparent till we are able to interpret the way it takes its course within the physical life of man, as an outcome of nonphysical realities disclosed by supersensible cognition. Un-illumined by the science of the supersensible, it is as though we were in a dark room without a light. Just as we cannot see the physical objects around us until we have a light, so too we cannot explain what goes on in and through the soul-life of man till we have knowledge of the supersensible.

While man is joined to his physical body, the outer world enters his consciousness in images. After the physical body has been laid aside, he becomes aware of the experiences the astral body undergoes when unconnected with the outer world by physical sense-organs. To begin with, the astral body has no essentially new experiences. Its still remaining connection with the etheric body stands in the way of any new experience. But it possesses in an enhanced degree the memory of the past earth-life, which memory the etheric body — being still united with it — makes to appear in a vivid, all-embracing tableau.

Such is the first experience of the human being after death. He sees his past life from birth till death in a vast series of pictures, simultaneously spread out before him. During this earthly life, memory is only present while — in the waking state — man is united with his physical body. Moreover, it is only present to the limited extent the physical body permits. Yet to the soul herself nothing is lost; everything that has ever made an impression on the soul during this life is preserved. If the physical body were but a perfect instrument for the purpose, it would be possible for us at every moment to conjure up before the soul the whole of our past earthly life. At death all hindrance is removed, and while man still retains the ether-body he has a relatively perfect memory. This vanishes, however, in proportion as the ether-body loses the form it had while it indwelt the physical — a form which bears a funda-mental likeness to the latter. This also is the reason why the astral body after a time separates from the etheric. For the astral body can only remain united with the etheric while the latter retains the imprint, the form that corresponds to the physical body.

During the life between birth and death a severance of the etheric body from the physical only takes place in exceptional cases, and then only for a short duration. When, for example, a man subjects an arm or leg to an unusual pressure, a portion of the etheric body may become separated from the physical. We say then that the limb has 'gone to sleep'. The peculiar sensation it gives is in fact due to the severance of the etheric body. (Here too, of course, materialistic thinking can deny the invisible within the visible, maintaining that the effect is *merely* due to the physical or physiological disturbances induced by the excessive pressure.) In such a case supersensible perception actually sees the corresponding part of the etheric body moving out and away from the physical. Now when a man undergoes an altogether unaccustomed shock or something of that nature, a like severance of the etheric may ensue for a brief space of time over a large proportion of the body. This happens if he is brought very near to death, as on the point of drowning, or when in imminent danger of a fall in mountaineering.

What is related by individuals who have had such experiences comes very near the truth. Supersensible observation confirms it. They tell how at such a moment the whole of their past life appeared before them in a vast tableau of memory. Among the many examples that might be cited, we select one, the author of which — by the whole tenor of his thought - - would have rejected as empty fancies what is here said about these matters. Incidentally, when one is taking the first steps in supersensible observation it is always useful to familiarize oneself with the findings of those who think the science of the supersensible fantastic. They are less easily attributed to favourable bias. (Let occult scientists learn as much as they can from those who deem their efforts futile. If the latter do not respond in kind we need not feel discouraged. Supersensible observation does not of course depend on these evidences for the verification of its results, and in adducing them the intention is not to prove, only to illustrate.)

The eminent anthropologist and criminologist Moritz Benedict, a scientist distinguished too in other branches of research, tells in his reminiscences of an experience of his own. Once he was very nearly drowned while bathing. He saw the whole of his past life in memory before him as though in a single picture.

It is no contradiction if others have described quite differently the pictures they experienced on such occasions, to the extent sometimes that there seemed little connection with the events of their past lives. For the pictures that arise during this altogether unaccustomed state of severance from the physical body are often not so easy to elucidate in their relation to the human being's life. None the less, if thoroughly gone into, some such relation will always be discerned. Nor is it valid to object that someone on the point of drowning did not have the experience at all. For the experience is only possible when the etheric body, while severed from the physical, remains united with the astral. It will not occur if the shock brings about a detachment of the etheric from the astral body too, since there will then be complete unconsciousness, just as there is in dreamless sleep.

Once more, then: gathered together in a great memory-tableau, the past life of man comes before him during the time immediately following his death. Thereafter, the astral body — severed now from the etheric — goes on its further way alone and by itself. It is not difficult to see that in this astral body there will now remain whatever it has made its own by dint of its own activity while living in the physical. The Ego has to some extent elaborated Spirit-Self, Life-Spirit and Spirit-Man. These, in so far as they are evolved, owe their existence to the Ego, to the I , — not to the organs of the bodies. Now by its very essence the I is the being which needs no outer organs for its perception. No more does it need outer organs to retain what it has once united with itself.

It may perhaps be objected: why, then, in sleep is there no perception of the evolved Spirit-Self, Life-Spirit and Spirit-Man? There is none because from birth until death the Ego is chained to the physical body. In sleep, it is true, it is with the astral body outside the physical. Yet even then it remains in close connection with the latter, for to the physical body the activity of the astral body, closely associated with the Ego, is directed. Bound as it is to the physical throughout earthly life, the Ego is dependent for its perceptions on the outer world of the senses; it cannot yet receive the manifestations of the spiritual in its original and proper form. Such manifestations can only come to the human Ego when released by death from its connection with the physical and etheric bodies. In life, the physical world holds the soul's activity chained to itself; another world can light up for the soul the moment it has been drawn forth, out of the physical body.

Yet there are reasons why even at this juncture man's connection with the external, sense-perceptible world does not altogether cease. Cravings, in effect, persist, maintaining the connection. These are the cravings man engenders for himself through the very fact that he is Ego-conscious — endowed with an Ego, the fourth member of his being. The cravings and desires which spring from the nature of the three lower bodies can only take effect in the outer world; when these bodies are laid aside, these cravings cease. Due as it is to the external body, hunger is naturally silenced when this body is no longer joined to the Ego. When death has taken place, the Ego, if it had now no other cravings than derive from its own spiritual nature, could draw full satisfaction from the spiritual world into which it is then transplanted. But life has given it other cravings besides these. Life has kindled in it a longing for enjoyments which, while only satisfiable by means of physical organs, are not in essence attributable to these organs. Not only the three bodies crave for satisfaction through the physical world; the Ego too finds enjoyments in this world — enjoyments such that in the spiritual world there are no objects to satisfy the longing for them.

Two kinds of wishes are proper to the Ego during earthly life. First are the wishes which, originating as they do in the three bodies, have to be satisfied in and through the bodies; these wishes naturally cease when the bodies disintegrate. Secondly there are the wishes which originate in the spiritual nature of the Ego. So long as the Ego is living in the bodies, these wishes too will find their satisfaction by means of bodily organs. For the unmanifest, the spirit, is at work here too — manifested through the organs of the body. In and with all that they perceive, the outer senses are at the same time receiving a spiritual portion. This spiritual portion is present also after death, though in a different form. Therefore the spiritual that the Ego craves for in the world of the senses is still available to it when these senses are no longer there.

If then a third kind of wish were not added to these two, death would merely signify the passing on from cravings satisfiable by means of bodily senses, to such as find fulfilment in the direct revelations of the spiritual world. But there are wishes of a third kind — wishes which the Ego engenders for itself while living in the sense-world inasmuch as it takes pleasure in this world even where the latter is not making manifest the spirit.

The lowest kinds of enjoyment can be true manifestations of the spirit. The satisfaction food affords to a hungry creature — this too is a manifestation of the spirit. For by the creature's nourishment something is accomplished, without which — in one essential direction — the spiritual itself could not evolve. But the I of man is able to go beyond this due enjoyment. The I can long for the tasty dish, quite apart from the function nourishment fulfils and in the fulfilling of it serves the spirit. The same applies to many other things belonging to the 'sensual' world — that is to say, the world of the senses. Desires are thus engendered which would never have occurred in the sense-perceptible world of Nature, had not the I of man entered this world. Nor is it from the spiritual being of the I as such that these desires spring. The natural enjoyments of the senses are needed by the Ego — even as a spiritual being — whilst living in the body. In and through sense-perceptible Nature the spiritual manifests itself; it is none other than the spirit which the Ego is enjoying when given up to sensual manifestations through which the spirit-light is shining. In the enjoyment of this light it will continue, even when the nature of the outer senses is no longer the medium through which the spiritual light is radiating.

For sensual desires on the other hand, from which the living spirit is absent, there can be no fulfilment in the spiritual world. Therefore when death ensues the possibility of their assuagement is utterly cut off. The enjoyment of tasty food can only be brought about by means of the bodily organs —

tongue, palate and the like — used in the taking of food. These organs man no longer has when the physical body has been laid aside. And if the Ego still feels need of such enjoyment, the need must remain unsatisfied. In so far as the enjoyment is in harmony with the spirit, it will be present only as long as the physical organs are there. But in so far as the human I has fostered it without thereby serving the spirit, the wish for the enjoyment will persist after death, vainly thirsting for satisfaction.

What now goes on in man can only be imagined if we think of one who has to suffer burning thirst in a desert country where no water is to be found. Such is the lot of the human I after death in so far as it harbours unextinguished cravings for the enjoyments of the outer world and has no organs for their satisfaction. Only, if thirst is here to serve as a comparison for the Ego's plight after death, we must imagine it boundlessly enhanced and extended to all the manifold cravings which may still persist, for the assuagement of which there is no possibility whatever.

The next stage through which the Ego passes is that it gradually frees itself from all these bonds of attachment to the outer world. In this respect it has to bring about within itself a purging and a liberation. All the desires the Ego has engendered while living in the body and that have not their rightful home within the spiritual world, must now be extirpated. As a combustible material is seized and burned by fire, so is the world of cravings dissolved and annihilated after death.

Herewith we peer into a world which supersensible wisdom has very properly described as 'the consuming fire of the spirit'. This 'fire' seizes hold of every craving which is not only sensual — related, that is, to the sense-perceptible world — but is so in such a way that in its sensual nature it does not express the spirit. Pictures like these, in terms of which supersensible insight cannot but describe what actually happens after death, may appear terrible and cheerless. Well may it seem appalling that a hope, for the satisfaction of which sensory organs are required, must after death give way to utter hopelessness, or that a wish which the physical world alone is able to fulfil, must change into the burning want of its fulfilment. Yet one can only think in this way while failing to perceive that all the wishes and cravings, seized upon after death by the 'consuming fire', represent forces which are not wholesome but in a higher sense destructive, inimical to life. These forces cause the Ego to form closer bonds of attachment to the sense-world than are needed in order to receive from this world that which will serve the Ego's progress. Nature — the 'world of the senses' — is a manifestation of the hidden spiritual. There is a form in which the spiritual can only become manifest by means of bodily senses, and in this form the Ego would never be able to receive it, were it not to use the senses for the enjoyment of what is spiritual in the garb of Nature. But the Ego becomes estranged from the world's real and true and spiritual content when craving for sensual enjoyments through which the spirit is no longer speaking. While sensual enjoyment as an expression of the spirit helps to uplift and evolve the Ego, that which does not express the spirit spells its impoverishment and desolation. And though a craving of this latter kind may lead to satisfaction and enjoyment within the sense-world, its emptying and de-vastating effect upon the I of man is still there. Only that this effect does not become perceptible to the I until after death. While life goes on, the enjoyment consequent on such a craving can beget new wishes of its kind, and man does not become aware that by his own doing he is enveloping himself in a consuming fire. The fire that enveloped him already during life is made perceptible to him after death, and in so doing becomes transmuted into its wholesome and beneficial con-sequences.

When one human being loves another, he is not only attracted by those of the other's features which are directly sensible by physical organs of perception. And yet of these alone can it be said that death will render him unable any longer to perceive them. On the other hand, after death there becomes visible in the beloved the very reality of being for the perception of which the physical organs were but the means. Moreover then the one thing that will mar this perfect visibility will be the persistence of cravings which can only be satisfied by means of physical organs. Nay, if these cravings were not purged, conscious perception of the beloved would not be possible at all after death. Looked at in this light, the terrible and hopeless picture which the after-death events described by supersensible science might at first sight be seeming to convey, gives place to one that is deeply comforting and satisfying.

In yet another respect our experiences after death are different from those we have in life. During the time of purification, man — in a sense — lives backwards. He goes again through all that he experienced in life, ever since his birth. Starting from the events immediately preceding death, he re-experiences it all in reverse order, back into childhood. And as he does so, there become visible to him all those things in his life which did not truly spring from the spiritual nature of the Ego. These too he now experiences in an inverted way. Say for example that a man dies in his sixtieth year, and that at the age of forty, in an outburst of anger, he caused another person pain in body or in soul. He will experience the event in consciousness again after death, when in his backward journeying through life he arrives at his fortieth year — the moment when it happened. But he will now experience, not the satisfaction he felt in giving vent to his anger, but instead the suffering the other person underwent through his unkindness. The example shows that what is painful in the after-death experience of an event of this kind is due to a craving to which the Ego gave way — a craving which had its origin in the outer material world and in this alone. In truth, by giving vent to such a craving the Ego was doing harm not only to the other human being but to itself; only the harm done to itself remained invisible during life. After death the whole world of harmful cravings becomes perceptible to the Ego. The man now feels drawn to every being and to every object by contact with which a craving of this kind was ever kindled in him, so that the craving may be destroyed even as it originated — destroyed in the consuming fire.

When in his backward journeying man has attained the moment of his birth, all such cravings having now undergone the cleansing fire, there is no longer anything to hinder his unimpaired devotion to the spiritual world. He enters on a new stage of existence. Just as in death the physical body, and soon after it the etheric body was laid aside, so now there falls away and disintegrates the part of the astral body which is unable to live save in the consciousness of the external, physical world. Therefore for supersensible science there are no less than three corpses — physical, etheric and astral. The point of time at which the astral corpse is shed is given by the fact that the period of purification lasts about a third as long as the past life between birth and death. Why this is so will only be made clear at a later stage, when the whole course of human life has been more thoroughly gone into in the light of Occult Science. For supersensible perception there are ever present in man's environment the astral corpses cast aside by those who are passing from the stage of purification on to higher levels of existence. It is analogous to what is obviously true for physical perception: physical corpses come into being where human communities are living.

After the time of purification an entirely new state of consciousness begins for the I of man. Before death, perceptions came to him from without, for the light of his consciousness to fall upon them. Now, as it were, a world is coming to him — into his consciousness — from within. It is a spiritual world, in which the I is also living between birth and death. Here however, it is veiled in the manifestations of the senses; and only when — turning aside from all outward perceptions — the I becomes aware of itself in the inmost 'holy of holies' of its being, what otherwise is shrouded in the veils of sense-perceptible Nature, makes itself known directly and in its pristine form. Like to this inner perception of the I before death, 'from within outward' is the manifestation of the spiritual world in its fulness, after death and when the time of purification has been absolved.

This kind of manifestation is indeed already there as soon as the etheric body has been laid aside, but like a darkening cloud the world of cravings obscures it, clinging still to the external world. It is as though a blissful world of purely spiritual consciousness were to be interspersed with black, demonic shadows, due to the cravings that are being purged in the consuming fire. Indeed these cravings are now revealed to be no mere shadows but very real beings; this becomes evident to man's Ego as soon as the physical organs are taken from him and he is thereby enabled to perceive what is spiritual. The beings look like distortions and caricatures of what was known to him hitherto by sense-perception. For of this realm of the purging fire, supersensible observation must relate that it is inhabited by beings whose appearance to the spiritual eye can only kindle pain and ghastly horror. Their very joy seems to consist in destruction; their passion is directed to an evil compared to which the evils known to us in the outer world seem insignificant. Whatever man takes with him thither by way of cravings of the kind above defined, appears as nourishment to these beings — nourishment by means of which they constantly renew and reinforce their powers.

The picture we have thus been painting of a world imperceptible to the outer senses may seem less incredible if one will look with open mind at well-known aspects of the animal creation. What, to the eye of the spirit, is a ruthlessly prowling wolf? What is revealing itself in the figure of the wolf as the outer senses see it? Surely it is none other than a soul that lives in cravings and acts out of its cravings. The very form of the wolf may be described as an embodiment of its cravings. Even if man had no organs to perceive this outer form, he would still have to recognize the wolf's existence if the cravings, though invisible, made themselves felt in their effects — if there were on the prowl a power invisible to human eye, yet by whose agency all that the visible wolf is doing were being done.

The beings of the purging fire are not present to the outer senses — only to supersensible consciousness. Their effects however are only too evident, in that they tend to destroy the Ego that gives them nourishment. When right enjoyment is carried to intemperance or to excess these effects are made visible enough.

Nature too, as perceived by the outer senses, would entice the Ego, but only in so far as the enjoyment were true to the Ego's own essential being. An animal is urged by instinct to desire that alone of the outer world for which its three bodies crave. Man has higher forms of enjoyment because he has not only the three bodily members but the fourth, the I — the Ego. If then the Ego craves for forms of satisfaction which serve, not the furtherance or maintenance but the destruction of its own being, such desires can neither be the outcome of the three bodies nor of the Ego's proper nature. They can only be the work of beings whose true shape and form remain hidden from the senses, but who gain access precisely to the higher nature of the Ego and entice it into cravings unfounded in the nature of the senses, yet only satisfiable by its means. In effect, there are beings whose food consists of cravings and passions more evil and pernicious than those of any animal, for they live not in the true nature of the senses but seize the spiritual and drag it down on to the sensual level. Their forms and features are to the spiritual eye more hideous and ghastly than those of the most savage animals. The latter, after all, do but incorporate natural passions, natural desires. The destructiveness of these beings boundlessly exceeds the wildest ravings known to us in the animal world as seen by the outer senses. Supersensible knowledge must in this way extend man's outlook to a world of beings who in a sense are on a lower level than any visible animal, even the most noxious and destructive.

When after death man has passed through this world, he finds himself face to face with a world of pure spiritual content — a world, moreover, which begets in him only such longings as will find satisfaction in the purely spiritual. But he still distinguishes what appertains to his own I or Ego from what constitutes his environment, which we might also call the 'spiritual outer world' for the Ego. Only, once more, his experiences of this environment come to him in the same way in which the inner perception of his own I came to him while living in the body. Whilst in the life between birth and death the environment of man speaks to him through the organs of his bodies, when he has laid all the bodies aside the language of his new environment speaks directly into the inmost 'holy of holies' of the *I am*. Now therefore the whole environment of man is replete with beings alike in kind to his own I , for in effect, only an I has access to an I . Even as minerals, plants and animals, surrounding him in the world of sense, constitute sense-perceptible Nature, so after death man is surrounded by a world composed of spiritual Beings.

Yet he brings with him thither something more — something which in yonder world is *not* his environment. In effect, he brings with him what his Ego has experienced while living in the sense-world. The sum-total of these his experiences first appeared to him in an all-embracing memory-tableau immediately after death, while the etheric body was still connected with his Ego. The ether-body was then laid aside, but something of the memory-tableau remained as an enduring possession of the Ego. It is as though an extract, a quintessence, were distilled of all the experiences that had come to the human being between birth and death. This is the thing that endures. It is the spiritual yield, the fruit of life. The yield, once more, is of a purely spiritual nature. It contains all the spiritual content, manifested during life through the outer senses. Spiritual though it is, without man's sojourn in the sense-world it could never have come into existence. After death, the I of man feels this spiritual fruit, culled in the world of the senses, to be his own — *his* inner world. With this possession he is entering the spiritual world — a world composed of beings who manifest themselves as an I alone can manifest itself in its own inmost depths. A seed, which is a kind of extract of the whole plant, can only develop when planted in another world — the earthly soil. What the Ego brings with it from the sense-world is like a seed — a seed received into the spiritual world, under whose influences it will now develop.

The science of the supersensible can at most give pictures in attempting to describe what happens in this 'Land of Spirits'. Yet the pictures can be true to the reality. Experiencing the facts invisible to the external eye, supersensible consciousness can feel these pictures of them to be true. The spiritual realities can thus be illustrated by comparisons from sense-perceptible Nature. Purely spiritual though they are, they none the less bear a certain likeness to this world of Nature. As in this world a colour will appear when the eye receives an influence from the appropriate object, so too in Spirit-land, under the influence of a spiritual Being, the Ego will experience a kind of colour. Only the colour-experience will come about in the way in which the Ego's own inner self-perception — and this alone — comes about during the life between birth and death. It is not as though light from outside were imping-ing on him; rather as though another Being directly influenced the Ego of man, impelling him to represent the influence to himself in a colour-picture. Thus do all Beings in the spiritual environment of the Ego find expression in a world radiant with colour.

Needless to say, since the manner of their origin is so very different, the colour-experiences of the spiritual world differ in character from those we enjoy in the world of Nature. The same applies to other kinds of sense-impression which man receives from this world. It is the sounds of the spiritual world which are most like the corresponding impressions of the sense-world. The more man lives his way into the spiritual world, the more does it become for him an inner life and movement, comparable to the sounds and harmonies of sense-perceptible reality. Only he feels the sound, not as approaching an organ of perception from outside, but as a power flowing outward into the world from his own Ego. He feels it as in the sense-world he would feel his own speech or song; yet in the spiritual world he is aware that the sounds, even while pro-ceeding from himself, are in reality the manifestation of other Beings, pouring themselves into the World through him.

There is a yet higher form of manifestation in the Spirit-land, when spiritual sound is enhanced to become the 'spiritual Word'. Not only does the surging life and movement of an-other spiritual Being then pour through the I of man; the Being himself communicates his inmost being to the I. With-out the remnant of separation which in the world of the senses even the most intimate companionship must have, two beings live in one-another when the Ego is thus poured through and through by the spiritual Word. In all reality, such is the Ego's companionship with other spiritual beings after death.

Three distinct regions of Spirit-land — the land of Spirits —

are apparent to supersensible consciousness. We may compare them with three domains of sense-perceptible Nature. The first is as it were the 'solid land' of the spiritual world; the second the 'region of oceans and rivers'; the third the 'air' or 'atmosphere'.

Whatever assumes physical form upon Earth and is thus made perceptible to physical organs, is seen in its spiritual essence in the first region of Spirit-land. For example, one may there perceive the power which builds the form of a crystal. Only what there reveals itself is like the antithesis of what appears to the senses in the outer world. The space which is here filled by the rocky material appears to the spiritual eye as a kind of hollow or vacuum; while all around the hollow space is seen the force building the form of the stone. The characteristic colour which the stone has in the sense-world is experienced in the spiritual world as its complementary. Seen therefore from Spirit-land, a red stone is experienced with a greenish and a green stone with a reddish hue. Other properties too appear as their antithesis. Even as stones, rocks and geological formations constitute the solid land — the continental region — of the world of Nature, so do the entities we have been describing constitute the 'solid land' of the spiritual world.

All that is life in the sense-world is the oceanic region of the spiritual world. To the eye of sense, life appears in its effects — in plants and animals and human beings. To the eye of the spirit, life is a flowing essence, like seas and rivers pervading the Spirit-land. Better still is the comparison with the circulation of the blood in the human body. For while the seas and rivers in external Nature appear as though distributed irregularly, there is a certain regularity in the distribution of the flowing life in Spirit-land, even as in the circulation of the blood. It is this flowing life above all which is experienced as living spiritual sound.

The third region of Spirit-land is the airy sphere or 'atmosphere'. All that is feeling and sensation in the outer world is present in the spirit-realm as an all-pervading element, comparable to the air on Earth. We must imagine an ocean of flowing sensation. Sorrow and pain, joy and delight, are wafted in that region as are wind and tempest in the atmosphere of the outer world. Think of a battle being fought on Earth. Not only are there facing one another the figures of the combatants which the outer eye can see. Feelings are pitted against feelings, passions against passions. Pain fills the battlefield no less than the forms of men. All that is there of passion, pain, victorious exultation, exists not only in its outer sense-perceptible effects; the spiritual sense becomes aware of it as a real event in the airy sphere of Spirit-land. Such an event is in the spiritual like a thunderstorm in the physical world. Moreover the perception of such events may be compared to the hearing of words in the physical world. Hence it is said: Even as the air enwraps and permeates the inhabitants of Earth, so does the wind of the Spirit — the 'wafting of the spiritual Words' — enwrap and permeate the beings and events of Spirit-land.

Further perceptions are possible in the spiritual world, comparable to the warmth and also to the light of the physical world. Warmth permeates all earthly things and creatures, and it is none other than the world of *thoughts* which in like manner permeates all things in Spirit-land. Only these thoughts must be conceived as independent living Beings. The thoughts man apprehends within the manifest world are but a shadow of the real thought-being, living in the land of Spirits. One should imagine the thought, such as it is in man, lifted out of him and as an active being endowed with an inner life of its own. Even this is but a feeble illustration of what pervades the fourth region of Spirit-land. Thoughts in the form in which man perceives them in the physical world between birth and death are but a manifestation of the real world of thoughts — the kind of manifestation that is possible by means of bodily organs. The thoughts man cultivates — those above all which signify an *enrichment* of the physical world — originate in this region of Spirit-land. This does not only apply to the ideas of great inventors or men of genius. Fruitful ideas 'occur' to every human being — ideas he does not merely borrow from the outer world, but which enable him to work upon this world and change it. While feelings and passions occasioned by the external world belong to the third region of Spirit-land, all that can come to life in the soul of man so that he becomes creative, acting on his environment in such a way as to transform and fertilize it, is manifested in its archetypal being in the fourth region of the spiritual world.

The prevailing element of the fifth region may be likened to the light of the physical world. It is none other than *Wisdom*, manifested in its pristine, archetypal form. Beings belong to that region who pour Wisdom into their environment, even as the Sun sheds light upon physical creatures. Whatsoever the Wisdom shines upon, is revealed in its true significance for the spiritual world, just as a physical creature reveals its colour when the light is shining on it. There are yet higher regions of Spirit-land; we shall refer to them again in later chapters.

Such is the world in which the I of man is steeped after death, with the yield he brings with him from his life in the outer world of sense. This yield, this harvest, is still united with the part of the astral body which was not cast off when the time of purification was over. For, as we saw, only part of the astral body then falls away — namely the part which with its wishes and cravings clung to the physical life even after death. The merging of the Ego into the spiritual world with all that it has gained from the sense-world may be likened to the embedding of a seed into the ripening earth. The seed draws to it the substances and forces of the surrounding soil, so that it may unfold into a new plant. In like manner, development and growth are of the essence of the I of man when planted in the spiritual world.

In what an organ perceives also lies hidden the creative force to which the organ is due. It is the eye that perceives the light, and yet without the light there would be no eye. Creatures that live perpetually in the dark fail to develop organs of sight. Thus the whole bodily man is created out of the hidden forces of what the several members of his bodies are able to perceive. The physical body is built by the forces of the physical world, the ether-body by those of the world of life; the astral body has been formed out of the astral world. Transplanted into Spirit-land, the Ego meets with these creative forces, which remain concealed from physical perception. Spiritual beings who, though unseen, surround man all the time, and who have built his physical body, become perceptible to him in the first region of Spirit-land. Whilst in the physical world he can perceive no more than the outer manifestation of the creative and formative spiritual powers to which his own physical body is due, after death he is in their very midst. They now reveal themselves to him in their original and proper form, previously hidden from him. In like manner, throughout the second region he is amid the creative forces of which his ether-body consists, and in the third there flow towards him the powers of which his astral body is formed and organized. The higher regions too of Spirit-land now pour in upon him the creative powers to which he owes the very form and substance of his life between birth and death.

These Beings of the spiritual world henceforth collaborate with the fruit of his former life which man himself has brought with him — the fruit which is now about to become the seed. And by this collaboration man is built up anew — built, to begin with, as a spiritual being. In sleep the physical and etheric bodies are still there; the astral body and the Ego, although outside, are in communication with them. The influences from the spiritual world received by the astral body and the Ego during sleep can only serve to repair the faculties and forces exhausted in the waking hours. But when the physical and the etheric body, and after purification the parts of the astral body which were still chained to the physical world by desire, have been cast off, what flows to the Ego from the spiritual world becomes not only the repairer; henceforth it is the re-creator. And after a lapse of time (as to the length of which we shall have more to say), the Ego is again invested with an astral body, able to live in an etheric and physical body such as are proper to the human being between birth and death. He can be born again and re-appear in a new earthly life, in which the fruits of his former life have been incorporated.

Till his investment with a new astral body, man is the conscious witness of his own re-creation. And as the Beings of

Spirit-land reveal themselves to him not through external organs but from within, like his own inmost I in the act of self-awareness, he can perceive the revelation so long as his attention does not yet incline towards a world of outer percepts. But from the moment when his astral body has been newly formed, he begins again to turn his attention outward. The astral once again demands an external body — physical and etheric — and in so doing turns away from what is manifested purely from within. Hence there now comes an intermediate condition during which man is plunged into unconsciousness. Consciousness will only be able to re-awaken when in the physical world the necessary organs — organs of physical perception — have been developed. During this intermediate time — the spiritual consciousness illumined by purely inner perception having faded — a new etheric body begins to be formed and organized about the astral body. This being done, man is prepared to re-enter into a physical body. Consciously to partake in the last two events — his re-equipment with an etheric and with a physical body — would only be possible for an Ego which by its own spiritual activity had developed the hidden creative forces of these bodies, in other words, Life-Spirit and Spirit-Man. So long as man has not yet reached this stage, Beings more advanced in evolution than himself have to direct the process. Such Beings guide the astral body towards a father and mother, so as to endow it with the appropriate etheric and physical bodies.

Now before the new etheric body has been formed and incorporated with the astral body, an event of great significance is undergone by the human being about to re-enter physical existence. In his preceding life, as we saw, he engendered hindering and disturbing forces, revealed to him during his backward journeying after death. Let us return to the above example. At the age of forty in his former life, in a sudden upsurge of anger, a man did harm to another. He was confronted after death by the other's suffering, as a force hindering the development of his own Ego. So too with all such occurrences of the preceding life. Now on re-entry into physical life these hindrances to his development confront the I of man.

As after death a kind of memory-tableau of the past, he now experiences a pre-vision of his coming life. He sees it in a kind of tableau once again, showing him all the obstacles he must remove if his development is to go forward. What he thus sees becomes the source of active forces which he must carry with him into the coming life. The picture of the suffering he caused his fellow-man becomes a force impelling his Ego, now about to enter earthly life once more, to make good the hurt which he inflicted. Thus does the former life wield a determining influence upon the new; the deeds of the new life are, in a way, caused by the deeds of the old. In this relationship of law and causation between an earlier and a later life we have to recognize the real Law of Destiny — often denoted by a word taken from Oriental Wisdom, the law of 'Karma'.

The building of a new bodily organization is however not the only activity incumbent upon man between death and a new birth. While this is going on he lives outside the physical world. But this world too is going forward in its evolution all the time. In comparatively short periods of time the face of the Earth is changed. What did it look like a few thousand years ago, say in the regions of Middle Europe? When man appears again in a new life, the Earth will as a rule be looking very different from what it did last time. Much will have altered during his absence, and in this changing of the face of the Earth, here once again hidden spiritual forces are at work. These forces issue from the very same spiritual world in which man sojourns after death, and he himself is working in and with them; he too has to cooperate in the necessary transformation of the Earth. So long as he has not yet developed Life-Spirit and Spirit-Man and thus attained clear consciousness of the connection between the spiritual and its physical expression, he can of course only do this under the guidance of higher Beings. None the less, he participates in the work of transforming the conditions upon Earth, and it is true to say: During the time between death and a new birth human beings are at work transforming the condition of the Earth so that it shall accord with what has been evolving in themselves. Picture a region or locality on Earth such as it was at a given time in the past, and then again — profoundly changed — a long time after; the forces which have wrought the change are in the realm of the dead. Thus are the souls of men still in communication with the Earth even between death and a new birth. Supersensible consciousness sees in all physical existence the outer manifestation of hidden spiritual realities. To physical observation, it is the rays of the Sun, changes of climate and the like which bring about the transformation of the Earth. To supersensible observation, in the light-ray falling from the Sun upon the plants the virtues of the dead are working. We become conscious of how the souls of men are hovering about the plants, changing the earthly soil, and other things of this kind. Man's activity after death is devoted not only to himself — not only to the preparation for his own new earthly life — but he is called to work upon the outer world in a spiritual way, even as in the life between birth and death it is his task to work upon it physically.

Not only does the life of man in Spirit-land influence and modify the prevailing conditions of the physical world, but conversely too, his life and action in physical existence have their effect in the spiritual. To take one example: there is a bond of love between a mother and her child. The love proceeds from a natural attraction, rooted in forces of sense-perceptible Nature. Yet in course of time it is transformed. The natural grows ever more into a spiritual bond, and this is welded not only for the physical world but for the spiritual.

So too it is with many other relationships of life. Threads that are spun in the physical world by spiritual beings persist in the spiritual world. Friends who were closely united in this life belong together in Spirit-land as well; nay, when their bodies have been laid aside, they are in still more intimate communion. For as pure spirits they are there for each other in the way that was described before; it is from within that spiritual beings manifest themselves to one-another. Moreover, bonds that have once been woven between one human being and another will lead them together again in a new life on Earth. Thus in the deepest sense it is true that we find one-another again after death.

The cycle of human life from birth till death and thence to a new birth repeats itself periodically. Again and again man returns to the Earth when the fruits gained in a preceding physical life have ripened in Spirit-land. But this is not a repetition without beginning or end. Time was when man advanced from other forms of existence to those here described, and in the future he will pass on to different ones again. We shall gain an idea of these transitions in due course, when in the light of supersensible consciousness we shall be describing the evolution of the World in its relation to Man.

For outer observation, what goes on between death and a new birth is of course still more hidden than the underlying spiritual reality of manifest existence between birth and death. As to this part of the hidden world, sensory observation will only see the corresponding effects when they enter into physical existence. The question is, therefore, whether on entering this life through birth man brings with him any evidence of the events since a preceding death, described by supersensible science. Finding a snail's shell in which no trace of any animal can be detected, we shall admit that the shell was produced by an animal's activity and vital functions. We cannot imagine this form to have been the product of mere inorganic forces. In like manner, if in our contemplation of man's earthly life we find what cannot possibly have had its origin in this present life, we can admit with reason that it may be the outcome of what the science of the supersensible describes, if in fact a light of explanation thereby falls on the otherwise inexplicable. Here therefore too, wide-awake observation with the senses and the thinking mind can find the visible effects intelligible in the light of invisible causes. A man who looks at life with fully open mind will come to see increasingly that this is right; it will impress itself on him with every new observation. The question only is to find the appropriate point of view in each instance. Where, for example, are the effects to be seen of what the human being underwent during the time of purification described by supersensible science? How do the effects appear of his experiences after purification in a purely spiritual realm — once more, according to the researches of spiritual science?

Riddles enough impress themselves upon our thought whenever we earnestly reflect on human life. We see one man born in misery and need, equipped with scanty talents. By the very circumstances of his birth he seems predestined to a life of hardship and limitation. Another is tended and looked after with every care and solicitude from the first moment of his existence. Brilliant faculties unfold in him; he seems predestined to a fruitful and fully satisfying life. In face of such questions two different ways of thought and feeling can make themselves felt. The one wants strictly to adhere to what is seen by the outer senses and understood by the intellect which takes its data from them. A man of this way of thinking will see no deeper question in the fact that one human being is born to happiness, another to ill fortune. And even if he does not have recourse to the word 'chance', he will not think of looking for a deeper law or causal nexus to which these things might be due. As to the presence or the lack of innate talents, he will insist that these are 'inherited' from parents, grandparents and other forebears. He will decline to seek the causes in spiritual experiences the individual himself went through before his birth, whereby he shaped his gifts and talents for himself quite apart from physical heredity.

A man imbued with the other way of thought and feeling will not be satisfied with this. Surely — he will aver — even in the manifest world nothing happens in a given locality and environment without some underlying causes. And though in many instances our science may not yet have found them, we can assume the causes to be there. An alpine flower does not grow in low-lying plains; there is something in its nature belonging to the alpine heights. So too there must be something in a human being, causing him to be born into a given environment. Nor is it adequate to look for causes within the physical world alone. To one who thinks more deeply, undue insistence on these causes is like attempting to explain the fact that one man hit another, not by the feelings of the one who dealt the blow but by the physical mechanism of his hand.

This other way of thinking will feel equally dissatisfied with the attributing of gifts and talents to 'heredity' alone. Of course it may be pointed out how talents have been and are sometimes inherited in families. For two and a half centuries musical talents were inherited by members of the Bach family. No less than eight mathematicians of distinction sprang from the Bernoulli family. Though some had very different careers mapped out for them in childhood, again and again the 'hereditary' talent drew them into the family profession. It might also be contended that by a detailed study of his ancestry a particular man's talents can be shown to have appeared in one way or another in his forebears, so that he is merely benefiting by the summation of inherited potentialities.

A man whose thinking leans towards the spiritual will certainly not disregard evidences of this kind, and yet for him they cannot be what they are to those who want to base all their explanations on facts accessible to the outer senses. He will point out that inherited potentialities cannot of their own accord add up into a complete and integrated personality, any more than the several metallic parts will of their own accord assemble into the watch. And if objection is made that the conjunction of the parents can surely have brought about the combination, thus as it were taking the watchmaker's place, he will answer: Look but with open vision, how altogether new a thing is the personality of every child we see! This cannot possibly come from the parents, for the simple reason that it is not there in them.

Unclear thinking may give rise to much confusion here. It is silliest of all when those of the former way of thinking represent those of the latter as disregarding and opposing well-established facts. For it need never occur to them to deny the truth or value of the facts alleged. They too can fully see that a mental or spiritual gift or even bent of mind will be 'inherited' in a particular family, or that inherited potentialities, added and combined in a descendant, have produced a man or woman of eminence. Readily will they acquiesce when told that the most eminent name is seldom to be found at the head but generally at the latter end of a line of descent. But it should not be taken amiss when they derive from all these things quite other thoughts than do those who will not go beyond sense-perceptible data. For to the latter the following answer can be made. Certainly a man bears the stamp of his forebears, for the soul-and-spirit, entering physical existence through birth, derives the bodily element from what heredity provides. But this is to say no more than that an entity naturally bears the features of the medium in which it is immersed! It is a quaint and no doubt a trite comparison, yet to an open mind it is surely apposite: A man who has fallen into the water will be wet, but his wetness is no evidence of his inner nature. No more is a human being's however obvious investment with some of the characteristics of his forebears evidence as to the origin of those which are uniquely his. Moreover this too may be said: If the most eminent name comes at the end of a line of descent, it shows that the bearer of the name required that very line of blood-relationship to form the body needed in this life for his own individual development and expression. It is no proof of the hereditary character of what he — individually — was. Indeed to healthy logic it proves, if anything, the reverse. For if individual gifts were inherited, they surely would appear at the beginning of a line of descent and be handed down from thence to the individual descendants. That they appear at the end, is evidence that they are not hereditary.

Now it cannot be denied that many of those who believe in spiritual causes also tend to make confusion worse confounded. They talk too much in vague and general terms. To maintain that a man is the mere sum-total of his inherited character-istics may indeed be like saying that the metallic parts have assembled of their own accord into the watch. Yet it must also be granted that many would-be arguments on behalf of a spiritual world are as though one were to say: 'The metallic parts of a watch cannot of themselves join up so as to drive the hands forward; therefore there must be some spiritual entity driving them forward.' As against such a contention, the man who answers: 'What do I care for 'mystical' beings of this kind? I want to know the mechanical construction by means of which the forward movement is in fact produced', is building on far better ground. The point is not to be vaguely aware that underlying the mechanical contrivance — the watch, in this instance — there is the spiritual entity, the watchmaker. The thing of practical significance is to get to know the thoughts in the mind of the watchmaker — thoughts which preceded the making of the watch. These thoughts are in the mechanism and can be found there.

Merely to dream and spin fancies about the supersensible can only lead to confusion and is least likely to satisfy opponents. They are quite right in contending that the vague reference to supersensible beings in no way helps one to understand the facts. Many opponents, it is true, will make the same objection to the precise and clear descriptions of spiritual science. But in this case it can be pointed out how the effects of hidden spiritual causes are manifested in external life. It can be said: Assume for once that what is claimed to have been found by spiritual observation is actually true. Assume that after death a man passed through a time of purification, when he experienced in soul how a thing done by him in a preceding life was going to be an evolutionary hindrance. While he had this experience, there grew in him the impulse to make good the consequences of his action. This impulse he brings with him into a new life; the presence of it is a trait in his nature, leading him to the place and situation where the needed opportunity is given. Think of all impulses of this kind, and you have a cause for the particular human environment into which the man was destined to be born.

Or take another assumption. Suppose once more: what spiritual science tells is true. The fruits of a past life on Earth are embodied in the spiritual seed of man. The Spirit-land wherein he sojourns between death and a new earthly life is the realm where these fruits ripen, to re-emerge in the new life transmuted into aptitudes and talents and making him the man he is, so that his present character and being appear as the effect of what was gained in a former life. Take this as a hypothesis and with it candidly look out into life. It is consistent, in the first place, with a healthy recognition of the outer facts — facts accessible to the senses — in their full truth and import. At the same time it makes intelligible ever so many things which, if one had to rely upon the outer facts alone, must remain unintelligible to anyone whose mind and feeling do not incline towards the spiritual world. Above all, it will put an end to that inverted logic, of which a typical instance was the proposition that because the most eminent name occurs at the end of a hereditary tree, therefore the man who bears it must have inherited his gifts. The supersensible facts ascertained by spiritual science make life intelligible to sound logic and straightforward thinking.

Still, the conscientious seeker after truth, without experience of his own in the supersensible world yet looking for a deeper understanding of the facts, may have another difficulty at this point, the force of which should be admitted. He may contend: Surely we cannot assume that a thing is true merely because it helps explain the otherwise inexplicable. Needless to say, this objection will not trouble those who know the thing in question by their own supersensible experience. Later on in this book a path will be indicated which one may go along, to learn to know by one's own experience not only the other spiritual facts here described but the law of spiritual causation too. But for those who do not want to take this path, the difficulty remains. Moreover even for those who do, what will now be said in answer to it may be of value. Rightly received and understood, it is indeed the very best way of taking the first step.

Certainly we ought not to assume things of the existence of which we have no other knowledge, merely because they give a satisfying explanation of the otherwise inexplicable. But with the spiritual facts here adduced the case is really different. To assume them has not the mere intellectual consequence of making life intelligible theoretically. When we receive them — even as hypotheses — into our thoughts, we experience far more than this, and different in kind. Think of a man to whom a great misfortune happens, from which he suffers deeply. He can meet the occurrence in either of two ways. He can experience the pain of it, give himself up to this emotion and maybe even succumb to his distress. But he can face it in a different way, saying to himself: 'In reality, it was I who in a past life planted in myself the forces which have now confronted me with this occurrence. I have inflicted it upon myself.' He can now kindle in himself all the feelings which this thought may carry in its train. Of course the thought must be entertained with great earnestness and intensity to have an adequate effect upon his life of feeling. But anyone who manages to do this will make a very significant discovery — best illustrated by a comparison. Each of two men, let us suppose, is given a stick of sealing-wax. The one indulges in intellectual reflections upon its 'inner nature'. His thoughts may be profound, but if this inner nature is in no way revealed he will very soon be told that they are vain speculation. The other rubs the sealing-wax with a silken cloth and demonstrates how it will attract small bodies. There is a vital difference between the thoughts that passed through the first man's head, giving rise to his philosophical reflections, and those of the second man. The former are without factual consequence, whereas the latter have led to a force of Nature — a real and potent fact — being conjured forth from its hidden state.

Such are the thoughts of one who thinks how in a former life he planted in himself the force that led him into a painful misfortune. The mere idea that this was so kindles in him a real power — a power to meet the event quite differently than he could do without it. It dawns upon him how inherently necessary, how essential was the event which he could otherwise only have looked upon as an unfortunate mischance. With direct insight he will realize: 'This thought was right, for it has had the power to reveal to me the real state of affairs.' Inner experiments of this kind, actively repeated, become an ever increasing source of inner strength, and by their fruitful outcome prove their truth. The demonstration grows impressive — ever more so. In spirit and in soul, and physically too, the experience is health-giving — in all respects a positive and beneficial influence upon one's life. A man becomes aware that with such thoughts he takes his proper stand amid the ups and downs of life, whereas if he were only thinking of the single life between birth and death he would be giving himself up to illusions. Knowledge of reincarnation fortifies his inner life.

Admittedly, this intimate and searching proof of the spiritual law of causation can only be gained by each man for himself, in his own inner life. And it is really possible for everyone. No-one who has not gained it for himself can judge of its demonstrative power, while those who have can hardly doubt it any more. We need not be surprised that this is so. For where a thing is so bound up with a man's individuality, his inmost being, it is but natural that it can only be adequately proved by his own inner experience.

This does not mean however that because it answers to an inner experience of the soul the question can only be settled by each man for himself and therefore cannot be the subject-matter of a valid spiritual science. True, every one must have the experience himself, just as every one has to perceive for himself the proof of a theorem in mathematics. But the pathway by which the experience is reached, no less than the method of proving the mathematical theorem, is universally valid.

Apart of course from actual observation in the supersensible, the proof above described is undeniably the only one which by the potency and fertile outcome of its thoughts stands firm in face of every fair and rational approach. Other considerations may be of great significance, and yet in all of them a sincere opponent may find loopholes. One other thought — evident enough to fair-minded insight — does however deserve mention. The very fact of education — that man is educable — goes a long way to prove that in the human child there is a spiritual being clad in a bodily garment and working his way through into life. Compare man with the animal. The characteristic properties and faculties of the animal are apparent from birth onward — a well-defined totality, of which the plan is manifestly given by heredity and then develops by contact with the outer world. See how the chick begins to fulfil the functions of its life as soon as ever it is hatched. How different with man! While he is being educated things which may well have no connection whatever with his heredity meet him and come into relation with his inner life. He proves able to assimilate and make his own the effects of these external influences. As every educator is aware, powers and faculties from the pupil's own inner life must come to meet these influences; if they do not, schooling and education are useless. An educator of sufficient insight will even mark the clear dividing line between the inherited tendencies and those inner faculties of his pupils which ray right through the latter, originating as they do in former lives.

True, in this field we cannot offer proofs as literally 'weighty' as are the scientific proofs for which a balance is used in a physical experiment. But we are dealing here with the more intimate realities of life. To a sensitive thinker the kind of evidence just indicated, intangible though it is, has a validity even more cogent than that of tangible and ponderable data.

Animals too can of course be trained to develop special qualities and aptitudes, as though by education. But if we once discern what is essential, this is no valid objection. Quite apart from the fact that transitions between one thing and another are everywhere to be found, the effects of training do not merge into the animal's individual being as in the case of man. We are even told how the skills and aptitudes domestic animals acquire by their association with man or by deliberate training can be inherited. In other words, the effect is not individual but generic. Darwin describes how dogs will 'fetch and carry' without previous training and without ever having seen it done. Who would say the same of human education?

Now there are thinkers who see beyond the mistaken notion that man is outwardly pieced together by mere hereditary forces. They rise to the idea that a spiritual being, an individuality, precedes and helps to form the bodily existence. But many of them are not yet able to realize the fact of repeated lives on Earth, the fruits of earlier lives playing a decisive part during an intermediate spiritual form of existence. We will cite one of these thinkers, Immanuel Hermann Fichte — son of the great philosopher — who in his *Anthropologie* (p. 528) sums up his observations as follows:—

'The parents are by no means the progenitors in the full sense of the word. What they contribute is the organic material, and not only this; also the intermediate qualities of heart and mind and sensibility, shown in the temperament, in shades of feeling, instinctive tendencies and the like, the common source of all which we found in the imaginative power — *Phantasie* — using this word in the wider sense already indicated. In all these elements of a man's personality, the mingling and conjunction of the souls of his parents is unmistakeable. These we may justly regard as a simple outcome of procreation, the more so since the act of procreation — as we were driven to admit — is an event in the soul-life too. Yet in all this the core and coping-stone of the individuality is not yet contained. For as a deeper penetration shows, even these subtler traits of heart and mind and feeling are but a sheath, an instrument, a vestment to contain the essentially spiritual, ideal potentialities of the man himself. True, they can further — or, it may be, hinder — these potentialities in their development, but they can never bring them forth out of themselves.'

A little later on (p. 532) Fichte adds:

'As to his archetypal spiritual form each human being pre-exists. Spiritually seen, two human *individuals* are no more like one another than are two animal *species*.'

These ideas only go so far as to allow that a spiritual being enters the physical, bodily nature of man to indwell it. But as they fail to attribute the form-giving powers of this being to causes originating in former lives, a fresh spiritual being would have to issue from the Divine Source of all, every time a human personality arose. On this assumption it would not be possible to explain the undoubted relationship between the innate tendencies which work their way outward from a man's inner being, and what comes to meet this inner being from his external, earthly and social environment during the course of his life. The inner being of man, springing for each single one — as it were, new-born — from the Divine Fount, would then confront what is to meet him in the earthly life as a complete stranger. This will only *not* be the case as indeed we know it is not — if the man's inner being has already been connected with this outer world and is not living in it for the first time. An open-minded teacher and educator can attain this perception: 'What I am bringing to my pupil out of the fruits of human life on Earth is to a great extent foreign to his mere hereditary endowment, and yet it somehow touches him as though he had already been a participant — partaking in the work to which these fruits are due.'

Only repeated lives on Earth — taken together with the events in the spiritual realm between, as shown by spiritual science — can give a satisfying explanation of the life of present-day mankind when looked at in an all-round way. We say expressly, 'present-day mankind'. Spiritual research reveals that there was a time when the cycle of man's earthly lives first began. Moreover the conditions then obtaining for the entry of his spiritual being into the bodily sheaths differed from those of to-day. In the next chapters we shall be going back to that primeval state of man, and in so doing it will emerge from the results of spiritual science how he evolved into his present form, in close connection with the evolution of the Earth as such. Then too it will be possible to indicate more fully how the spiritual core of man's being enters from supersensible worlds into the bodily vestments, and how the spiritual law of causation — how human destiny works itself out.

CHAPTER IV

MAN AND THE EVOLUTION OF THE WORLD

WE HAVE seen from the foregoing chapters that the being of man is built up of four members: physical body, life-body, astral body, and the bearer of the Ego. The I or Ego of man works in the three other members and transforms them. Through this transformation arise at a lower stage sentient soul, intellectual soul and spiritual soul, whilst at a higher stage of man's existence Spirit-Self, Life-Spirit and Spirit-Man are evolved. These several members of man's nature stand in the most varied relations to the whole Universe. Their evolution is connected with the evolution of the Universe, and by a study of the latter we can gain insight into the deeper secrets of the being of man.

It can easily be seen that the life of man is related in many different directions to the environment, to the dwelling-place wherein he evolves. External science has already by its own recognized facts and data been driven to the conclusion that the Earth — this dwelling-place of man in the widest sense of the word — has itself undergone evolution. It can tell us of conditions that once prevailed in the Earth, where man in his present form did not yet exist upon our planet, and can then go on to show how humanity has evolved, slowly and gradually, from quite simple conditions of civilization to those that obtain to-day. Thus has external science too been led to the idea that there is a connection between the evolution of man and that of the heavenly body on which he lives — the Earth.

Spiritual science* traces this connection by means of a cogni-

* The term 'spiritual science' is here used — as will be evident from the whole context — with the same meaning as 'Occult Science' — that is to say, the Science of the Supersensible.

tion that derives its facts from a perception that has been quickened by the spiritual organs. It follows man back on the path of his development, and perceives how the real, inner, spiritual being of man has passed through a succession of lives upon this Earth; and as it continues to pursue these researches, it arrives at length at a far distant point of time, when the inner being of man first entered upon an outward life (in the present-day meaning of the word). It was in that earliest earthly incarnation that the I or Ego first began its activity within the three bodies — astral body, life-body and physical body; and it took with it, on into the life that followed, the fruits of this activity.

When we go back in the way thus indicated, we become aware that at that distant point of time the Ego finds the Earth in a condition wherein the three bodies of man are already evolved and have a certain connection with one another. Now for the first time the Ego unites with the entity that consists of these three bodies, and from this point onwards partakes in their further evolution. Hitherto they have been evolving without a human Ego and have in this way reached the stage at which the Ego finds them.

Spiritual science must go still further back with its researches if it would find an answer to the question: How did the three bodies reach a stage of evolution such as enabled them to receive into themselves an I, and then too to the further question: How did the I itself come into being and how did it acquire the ability to work within the bodies?

An answer to these questions is possible only by tracing the rise and evolution of the Earth-planet itself in the light of spiritual science. By means of such research we arrive at a beginning of this Earth-planet. The mode of thought which builds on the facts of the physical senses alone, cannot pursue its inferences far enough to deal at all with this beginning of the Earth. There is a theory which, by inferences of this kind, arrives at the result that all the substance of the Earth has evolved from a primeval nebula. There is no occasion for us to enter here into a discussion of such ideas as this. For spiritual research has to consider not merely the material processes of

Earth evolution, but before all the spiritual causes which lie behind all matter and substance. If we see before us a man in the act of lifting up his hand, this can start us on two different lines of thought. We may investigate the mechanism of the arm and of the remainder of the body with the intention of describing how the action takes place as a purely physical process. But we can also direct our mind's eye to that which is going on in the man's soul and constitutes his motive for lifting up his hand. In a similar way the scientist trained in spiritual perception sees spiritual processes behind all the processes of the world of the physical senses. For him, all the changes in the material nature of the Earth-planet are manifestations of spiritual forces which are there behind the material. And as his spiritual observation reaches farther and farther back in the Earth's life, he comes at length to a point in evolution where the material first begins to be. The material evolves out of the spiritual; until then, the spiritual alone existed. By the exercise of spiritual observation we perceive the spiritual, and note how, as time goes on, it partially condenses, so to speak, to the material. We watch this taking place and, but that the process is on a higher level, it is very much as though we might be looking at a vessel filled with water, where by a finely regulated cooling process, lumps of ice were gradually taking shape. We see the ice condense out of what was water through and through. Similarly, by spiritual observation we can trace how the material things, events and entities condense, as it were, out of a previous existence which was spiritual through and through.

Thus the Earth-planet has evolved out of a cosmic spiritual entity. Everything material connected with the planet has condensed out of what was once united with it spiritually. But we must not imagine that a time ever came when *all* spiritual being had been transformed into material. That which confronts us in the latter is never more than part of the original and spiritual. Even throughout Earth's material evolution, the spiritual always remains the guiding and directing principle.

It stands to reason that the way of thought which would hold fast to the physical, sense-perceptible processes alone — and to what the intellect is able to infer from these — can say nothing whatever about the spiritual of which we are here speaking. If a being could exist, endowed with senses to perceive only the ice and not the finer state of water from which the ice on cooling separates itself, then for such a being the water would not be there; he could perceive nothing of it until some of it was changed into ice. So too for the man who will admit only what presents itself to the physical senses, the spiritual which underlies the earthly processes must ever remain hidden. And if from the physical facts that he perceives to-day he is able to form correct conclusions as to earlier conditions of the planet, he will still reach back only to that evolutionary point where the spiritual began its partial condensation to the material. His mode of thought will not perceive the spiritual that preceded that process, any more than it can perceive the spiritual substance which even now holds sway, invisibly, behind the world of matter.

Not until the later chapters of this book will it be possible to speak of the paths whereby man attains the faculty to look back, in spiritual perception, to the earlier conditions of the Earth with which we are now dealing. Suffice it for the moment to point out that for spiritual research the facts of the most distant early times are not obliterated. When a creature has come into bodily existence, its bodily death involves the passing away of what was material. But the spiritual forces which brought forth the bodily nature are not obliterated in the same way. They leave behind their traces, nay their exact images, in the spiritual foundation of the world. And if we are able to raise our faculty of perception and look through the visible world to the invisible, we arrive at length at a point where we have before us what may be compared to a mighty spiritual panorama wherein all the past events of the world are displayed. These abiding traces of all spiritual happenings may be called the 'Akashic Records', denoting as 'Akasha-essence' that which is spiritually permanent in the world process, in contrast with the transient forms. Here once again it must be emphasized that researches in the supersensible realms of existence can only be made with the help of spiritual perception — that is to say, as regards the region we are now considering, by actual reading of the Akashic Records. Nevertheless here too, what has been said already in similar connections holds good: to *investigate* and *discover* the supersensible facts is possible only by supersensible perception; once found however, and communicated in the science of the supersensible, these facts can be *understood* with man's ordinary faculty of thought. There must only be the readiness to approach the subject with an open mind. In the following pages the evolutionary conditions of the Earth according to the science of the supersensible will be communicated. The transformations of our planet will be followed down to the state of life in which it is to-day. Let anyone consider what he has before him to-day in pure sense-perception, and then give his attention to what supersensible knowledge tells of how this present has evolved from the primeval past. If he be truly open-minded, he will then be able to say to himself: In the first place, what this science tells is inherently logical; secondly, if I assume the truth of what is communicated from supersensible research, I find I can understand how it is that things have eventually come to be such as they appear before me now.

The use of the word 'logical' in this connection does not of course imply that errors in logic can never be contained in any particular statement from supersensible research. We are using the term here in no other way than it is used in ordinary life in the physical world, where logicality of statement is universally demanded — although some individual describing a particular set of facts may now and again be guilty of mistakes in logic. The situation is just the same in supersensible research. It may even happen that an investigator, able to perceive in supersensible domains, stumbles into errors in respect of logical description, and that a man who does not himself perceive supersensibly but has a good reasoning faculty, is subsequently able to correct him. As logic, however, no objection can be raised against the logic that is applied in supersensible research. Nor should it be necessary to emphasize that exception can never be taken to the facts themselves on merely logical grounds. Just as in the realm of the physical world one can never prove by logic whether or no a whale exists, but only by inspection, so it is with supersensible facts; they can be apprehended by spiritual perception and by that alone.

It cannot, however, be sufficiently stressed that for the student of supersensible realms it is a necessity, before he tries to approach the spiritual worlds with his own perception, to make sure that he is doing so from the right standpoint — the standpoint, that is, that he can reach through the above-mentioned logic and — what is no less important — through having come to recognize that, assuming the statements of Occult Science to be correct, the world wherever it is revealed to the senses appears intelligible. In effect, all conscious experience in the supersensible world remains uncertain, nay dangerous, a kind of groping in the dark, if the student disdains to undergo this preparation. And it is for this reason that the present book, before dealing with the actual path to supersensible knowledge, will communicate first the supersensible facts of Earth evolution.

One other point needs to be borne in mind in this connection. Someone who with pure thinking finds his way into what supersensible knowledge has to relate, is by no means in the same position as a man who listens to an account of some *physical* process which he is unable to witness for himself. Pure thinking is itself already a supersensible activity. True, inasmuch as it belongs to the life of sense, it cannot of itself take us to the supersensible events. But when applied to the supersensible events that are told out of supersensible perception, pure thinking does *of itself* grow into the supersensible world. Indeed one of the very best ways to attain perception of one's own in supersensible domains, is to grow into the higher world by thinking over what supersensible knowledge communicates. For with this way of entry the greatest clarity is ensured. Hence a certain school of spiritual-scientific research regards *pure thinking* as the soundest kind of first step in any spiritual-scientific training.

It will be readily understood that this book cannot set out to show, in connection with every detail of the Earth's evolution as perceived in the spirit, how the supersensible finds again and again its confirmation in the outwardly manifest. This certainly was not implied when we said that the hidden can everywhere be shown and proved in its manifest effects. Rather did we mean that everything man meets in life can become clear and intelligible to him, step by step, if he will but place the manifest events into the light that is made possible for him by Occult Science. Only in a few characteristic instances will reference be made in these pages to the confirmation of the hidden in the manifest, in order to show by a few examples how it is possible to find on every hand such confirmation in the practical pursuit of life, have we but the will to do so.

* * * * *

Following back the evolution of the Earth with spiritual-scientific research, we come to a spiritual condition of our planet. If however we pursue the investigation still further, we find that this spiritual has already been in a kind of physical embodiment before. That is to say, we encounter a past physical planetary condition which afterwards became spiritual and then, becoming material once more, was at length transformed into our Earth. Our Earth thus appears as the re-embodiment of a primeval planet. But spiritual science is able to go even farther back, and as it does so it finds the whole process repeated again twice over. Thus our Earth has passed through three previous planetary conditions, with intermediate states of spiritualization in between. The physical proves to be more and more fine and delicate, the farther back we trace the Earth's embodiment.

Against the descriptions that will now follow it may quite naturally be objected: How can any reasonable person entertain the postulate of world-conditions so immeasurably remote? The answer is, that to a man who can look with understanding at the spiritual that is there *now*, hidden within what is manifest to the senses, insight also into former states of evolution, however distant, cannot appear essentially impossible. If we do not recognize the hidden spiritual existence that is around us even at the present time, then it will indeed be meaningless to speak of an evolution such as is here in mind. But once we are able to recognize the presence of the spiritual here and now, we shall find the earlier condition given cr implied in the immediate vision of the present, just as the condition of the one-year-old infant is implied in the appearance of a man of fifty. Yes, someone may say, but in this instance we have among us, beside people of fifty, children of a year old — and all the intermediate stages too. That is quite true; but the same is also true of the evolution of the spiritual to which we here refer. Anyone possessing clear insight and discrimination will recognize that a complete observation of the present — which will necessarily include its spiritual part too — cannot but perceive there also evolutionary conditions of the past, preserved side by side with those stages of existence which have reached the present evolutionary level. Just as children of a year old are present side by side with men and women of fifty, so within all that goes on upon Earth at the present time we can still behold primordial happenings, if only we are able to hold distinct from one another the diverse stages of evolution.

Man, in the form and figure in which he is now evolving, does not emerge until the fourth of the above planetary embodiments — the Earth proper. The essential feature of man's present form is that he consists of the four members: physical body, life-body, astral body and Ego. This form however could not have emerged at all, had it not been prepared by the preceding facts of evolution. The preparation took place through the gradual evolution, during the earlier planetary embodiment, of beings who had already three of the four members of the present human being, namely physical body, life-body and astral body. These beings, whom we may call in a certain respect the ancestors of man, had as yet no I, but they evolved the other three members and the mutual connections of these three up to the point where they were ripe, subsequently to receive the I. Thus on the preceding embodiment of the planet, man's ancestor had reached a certain degree of maturity in three members. With this he passed into the state of spiritualization, out of which the new planetary condition — that of the Earth — subsequently arose. In this Earth were contained, like seeds, the thus far matured ancestors of man. By undergoing entire spiritualization and re-appearing in a new form, the planet could give the seeds it contained within it, with their physical body, life-body and astral body, not only the opportunity to evolve again up to the height which had been theirs before, but the further possibility, having attained this height, to go beyond it by receiving in addition the I. Earth evolution falls accordingly into two parts. In the first the Earth appears as a re-embodiment of the earlier planetary condition, although by virtue of the spiritualized condition it has meanwhile undergone, this recapitulation represents a higher stage than that of the former embodiment. Within it the Earth contains the seeds of the ancestors of man which have come from the earlier planet. To begin with, the seeds evolve up to the level on which they were before. When they have reached it, the first period is at an end. And now, since its own evolution is at a higher stage, the Earth can bring the seeds also to a higher level; it can make them capable of receiving the I. Thus the second period of Earth evolution is characterized by the unfolding of the I in physical body, life-body and astral body.

Through Earth evolution man is thus lifted a stage higher in his development. Now this was also the case in the former planetary embodiments. For something of the human being was already in existence on the very first of these. In order therefore to come to a clear understanding of man's present nature, we have to trace his evolution back to the far primeval past — to the above-mentioned first planetary embodiment. In supersensible research this first planetary embodiment may be called Saturn, the second may be designated Sun, and the third, Moon; the fourth is the Earth. One thing, however, must be strictly borne in mind in regard to these designations. They must not, *to begin with*, be associated in any way with the identical names as applied to the members of our present solar system. 'Saturn', 'Sun' and 'Moon' are here intended simply as the names for *past* evolutionary forms which the Earth has gone through. As to the relation of these pristine worlds to the heavenly bodies that constitute our present solar system — that will emerge in the further course of our studies. Then too the reason for the choice of the names will become evident.

The conditions on the four planetary embodiments will now be described. It can only be done in merest outline; for the events, the Beings and their destinies were truly no less manifold on Saturn, Sun and Moon than they are on Earth itself. Attention will be drawn to a few characteristic features that can help to illustrate how the present conditions of our Earth have evolved out of the former ones. The farther we go back in evolution, the less will the conditions be found to resemble those of the present time. Yet they can only be described by resorting to ideas and images derived from present conditions. Thus when we speak in this connection of light, warmth and the like, it must not be forgotten that what is thus referred to is not precisely the same as what we now call light and warmth. The notation is justified nevertheless, for the observer in the supersensible perceives in the earlier stages of evolution something from which the present light, warmth, etc. have come to be. And anyone who carefully follows the descriptions will be well able to gather, from the whole context into which things are placed, the kind of conceptions he will need in order to have pictures and images that truly convey the character of the events that took place in those remote ages of the past.

The difficulty is, however, undeniably great for those planetary conditions which precede the Moon embodiment. For the conditions of the Moon period still show a certain likeness to those of the Earth, and in attempting to describe them these similarities with the present day give one a point of contact and enable one to express in clear ideas what has been supersensibly perceived. It is a very different matter when we come to describe the Saturn and Sun evolutions. What confronts the clairvoyant observer here is as different as possible from the things and beings that now belong to the horizon of man's life. This makes it exceedingly difficult even to bring the corresponding facts into the domain of supersensible consciousness at all. But since the present human being cannot be understood without going back to the Saturn state, some description of it must none the less be given. And the description will not be misunderstood if it is borne in mind that the difficulty exists, and that many of the things here said are to be taken not so much as an exact description but more as a hint and indication of the facts.

What has just been said, as well as what will be said in the following pages, might not unnaturally be held to contradict the statement made previously as to the persistence of the earlier conditions within the present. Nowhere, it might be said, is there a former Saturn, Sun or Moon condition existing side by side with the present Earth condition, still less a form of human being such as is here described as having existed in those earlier conditions. It is quite true: there are no Saturn, Sun or Moon men running about among Earth men in the way that little children of three run about among the men and women of fifty. But *within* the human being as he is on Earth these earlier conditions of mankind are indeed perceptible — supersensibly. To recognize that this is so, we need only have acquired a power of discernment extending to the full horizon of the facts of life. As the child of three is present beside the man of fifty, so are present, beside the alive and waking man of Earth, the corpse, the man asleep, and the dreaming man. Granted that these various forms of manifestation of man's being do not immediately reveal, as we see them before us, the several stages of his evolution, nevertheless clear and objective contemplation will behold in them the corresponding stages.

*   *   *   *   *

Of the four present members of the human being the physical body is the oldest. Moreover it is the physical body which has attained the greatest perfection in its kind. Supersensible research shows that this member of the human being existed already in Saturn evolution. It is true, as will emerge in these descriptions, that the form it had on Saturn was utterly different from man's present physical body. The physical body of man as it is on Earth can only exist in its proper nature inasmuch as it is connected with a life-body, an astral body and an Ego, as has been described in earlier chapters of this book. On Saturn, there was as yet no such connection. The physical body was passing through its first stage in evolution without a human life-body or astral body or Ego being incorporated in it. During Saturn evolution it was only maturing towards the stage of receiving a life-body, and before this could happen, Saturn had first to pass into a spiritual state and then be re-incarnated as the Sun. In the Sun embodiment of the Earth, what the physical body had become on Saturn unfolded once more, as from a seed. Only then could it be permeated with an etheric body. Through receiving into it an etheric body, its nature was changed: the physical body was raised to a second level of its perfection. A like thing happened during the Moon evolution when the ancestor of man, having evolved from Sun to Moon, received into himself the astral body. The physical body was thereby changed again; this time it was raised to a third level of perfection. The life-body too was changed; henceforth it stood upon its second level of perfection. On Earth, into the ancestor of man consisting now of physical body, life-body and astral body, the Ego was incorporated. Therewith the physical body reached its fourth degree of perfection, the life-body its third, the astral body its second; while the Ego even now is only at the first stage of its existence.

If we really set out to consider man with an open mind, we shall have no difficulty in forming a right idea of the varying degrees of perfection of the several members. Compare, for example, the physical body with the astral in this respect. The astral body, it is true, being of the nature of 'soul', stands at a higher level in evolution than the physical; and when in future time the astral body has come to perfection, it will signify far more for man's whole being than the present physical body. Yet the latter *in its kind* has attained no mean height of development. Consider the structure of the heart, planned as it is in accordance with the highest wisdom! Or look at the miraculous structure of the brain; or at that of a single part only of some bone — the upper end of the thigh-bone, for example. We find there a network or scaffolding of tiny rods, arranged according to an inner principle. The structure of the whole is so compact as to produce with the minimum use of material the best possible effect at the joint-surfaces — the best distribution of friction, for example, hence affording the right kind of mobility. So do we find in different parts of the physical body arrangements that give evidence of the working of a deep wisdom. And if we go on to observe the harmony that prevails in the co-operation of the parts within the whole, we shall surely agree that this member of the human being has reached a certain perfection of its kind. The fact that here and there seeming inefficiencies appear, or that disturbances in structure or in function can occur, is unimportant in comparison. Nay more, we can even find that such disturbances are in a sense only the necessary shadows cast by the light of a wisdom which is poured out over the organism as a whole.

And now compare with this the astral body as the bearer of joy and sorrow, of cravings and passions. How full of uncertainty it is in its joy and sorrow! What manifold cravings and passions work themselves out in it that are adverse to the higher aims of man, and are often meaningless! The astral body is only on the way to the achievement of that harmony and self-containedness which we see already before us in the physical. So too it could be shown how the etheric body in its kind proves more perfect than the astral body, but less so than the physical. And the same line of thought will show with no less certainty that the real kernel of man's being, namely the I or Ego, is now only at the beginning of its evolution. For how much has the Ego yet accomplished of its task, which is to transform the other members until these become a revelation of itself?

For one acquainted with spiritual science, the insight arrived at in this way by external observation is intensified by something else. It might well be argued that the physical falls a prey to disease. Now spiritual science is able to show that a large proportion of illnesses are due to some fault or failing in the astral body being transmitted to the etheric, and, through the latter, disturbing the harmony of the physical body, which in itself is perfect. This deeper connection — which can here be no more than indicated — and with it the essential cause of many a disease, eludes that mode of science which would restrict itself to physical and sense-perceptible facts. More often than not, the connection is as follows. Injury to the astral body is followed by morbid symptoms in the physical, not in the same life in which the injury is done, but in a subsequent life. Consequently the laws that prevail here are significant only for those who are ready to admit the repetition of man's life on Earth. But even if one did not wish to concern oneself with these deeper realms of knowledge, common observation would reveal only too clearly that man gives himself up to cravings and enjoyments which undermine the harmony of the physical body. Now cravings, passions, enjoyment and the like have their seat not in the physical but in the astral body. In effect, the latter is in many respects still so imperfect that it can actually mar the perfection of the physical body.

Here again let it be emphasized that the connections indicated are by no means intended to prove the statements of spiritual science as to the evolution of the four members of man's being. The proofs are derived in every case from spiritual research, which reveals that the physical body has behind it a fourfold transformation to higher stages of perfection, and the other members less, as has been explained. It was only desired to point out that these communications from spiritual research are related to facts of which the consequences are even outwardly observable, in the degrees of perfection of physical body, life-body and the remaining members.

*　*　*　*　*

If we would form an idea — pictorial, but approximating to reality — of the conditions during Saturn evolution, we must bear in mind that of the things and beings now belonging to the Earth and included in the mineral, plant and animal kingdoms of Nature, virtually nothing was in existence then. The beings of these three kingdoms arose only in later periods of evolution. Of the beings of the Earth which are physically perceptible to-day man alone was present at that time, and of him only the physical body. But even now there are, belonging to the Earth, not only the beings of the mineral, animal, plant and human kingdoms, but other beings too, who do not manifest in physical corporeality. Such beings existed also in the Saturn evolution, and their activity upon the scene of Saturn resulted in the subsequent evolution of man.

If we turn, first of all, with spiritual organs of perception, not to the beginning or end but to the middle period of evolution of the Saturn embodiment of the Earth, we find a condition consisting essentially of 'warmth' alone. There is nothing to be found of gaseous or liquid, let alone of solid constituents. It is only in the later embodiments that these other states emerge. Let us assume that a human being with present-day sense-organs were to approach this Saturn as an observer. Of all the sense-impressions of which he is capable, nothing would meet him there, save the sensation of warmth. Imagine him approaching ever nearer and nearer. The most he would perceive as he reached it would be that the part of space occupied by Saturn was in a different warmth-condition from the remaining spatial environment. Nor would he find the Saturn space itself uniformly warm. Warmer and cooler portions would be alternating with one another in the most diverse ways. Along certain lines, radiant warmth would be perceived. Such lines would not simply go on and on in one direction; irregular figures would be arising from the differences of warmth. Thus he would have before him a kind of heavenly body, a being in the cosmos, inwardly organized and differentiated, appearing in manifold and constantly changing states, and composed of warmth alone.

It will be difficult for the man of to-day to imagine something that consists of warmth alone, for he is not accustomed to recognize heat or warmth as existing in itself; he is accustomed only to perceive it in connection with hot or cold gaseous, liquid or solid bodies. To one who has entirely adopted the physical conceptions of our time it will appear senseless to speak of 'warmth' in the way we have done. He may well reply that there are solid, liquid, and gaseous bodies, but 'heat' or 'warmth' denotes no more than a condition pertaining to one or other of these three. When the smallest particles of a gas are in motion, he will say we perceive this motion as warmth, but where there is no gas there can be no such motion, therefore no warmth.

The researcher in spiritual science sees the matter differently. Warmth, to him, is something of which he can speak in the same sense as of a gas, or of a liquid or solid body. It is only a yet finer substance than gas. Moreover, to him the gas itself is none other than warmth condensed, in the sense in which a liquid is condensed vapour or a solid body condensed liquid. Thus the spiritual scientist speaks of warmth-bodies, ` just as he speaks of gaseous and vaporous bodies.

To follow the spiritual researcher into this sphere, it is only necessary to admit the existence of a perception belonging entirely to the soul. In the world that is presented to the physical senses, warmth undoubtedly appears as a condition of what is solid, liquid or gaseous. But this is no more than the external side of warmth, or we may say, its effect. And it is really of this effect of warmth alone that physicists speak, not of its inner nature. Let us try for once to look away from the warmth-effects that we receive from outside and fix our attention purely on the inner experience we have when we say the words: 'I feel warm', or 'I feel cold'. It is this inner experience alone that can give an idea of what Saturn was in the above-described period of its evolution. We might have passed right through the part of space it occupied; there would have been no gas to exert pressure, no solid or liquid body from which impressions of light could be received. But at each point of space we should have felt, inwardly and without impressions from outside: '*Here* there is this or that degree of warmth.'

In a heavenly body of this kind there are not the conditions for the animal, plant or mineral creation of our present world. (Hence it can hardly be necessary to remark that the suggested assumption could not possibly take place in fact. A man of the present day could not, just as he is, confront Old Saturn as an observer. The suggestion had only an explanatory purpose.)

The beings of whom supersensible cognition becomes aware when observing Saturn were at a very different stage of evolution from the present, sense-perceptible beings of the Earth. Beings appear there, to begin with, who had not a physical body like the body man has to-day. When 'physical body' is spoken of, we must beware of thinking of man's present physical corporeality. For we have carefully to distinguish between physical body and mineral body. A physical body is one that is governed by the physical laws that are observable to-day in the mineral kingdom. The present physical body of man is not only governed by the physical laws; it is also permeated with mineral substance. On Saturn there can as yet be no question of a physical-mineral body of this kind. There, there is only a physical corporeality, governed by physical laws — which laws express themselves solely in warmth-effects. Thus the physical body on Saturn is a delicate, tenuous, ethereal body-of-warmth. And the entire Saturn consists of these warmth-bodies. They are the first beginnings of the present physical-mineral body of man, which has evolved out of the old warmth-body by receiving into it the gaseous, liquid and solid substances that developed only at a later stage.

Among the Beings who come before the supersensible consciousness in the moment when it is confronted by the Saturn stage of evolution, and of whom we may speak as dwellers upon Saturn in addition to man, there are for instance some who had no need of a physical body at all. The lowest member of their nature was an etheric body. On the other hand they had one member beyond the members of man's being. Man has the Spirit-Man as his highest member; these Beings have a still higher one, and between etheric body and Spirit-Man they have also all the other members that we find in man: astral body, Ego, Spirit-Self, and Life-Spirit. As our Earth is surrounded by an atmosphere, so too was Saturn, only with Saturn the atmosphere was of a spiritual kind.* For it consisted

* If one wanted to express more precisely the inner experience one has in spiritual investigation, one would have to say, not 'Saturn was surrounded by an atmosphere' but 'when the supersensible consciousness becomes aware of Saturn, there also appears before it an atmosphere of Saturn', or 'other Beings appear, of such and such kind'. To translate this into the wording 'this or that is there' is assuredly permissible, for in the last resort the very same change is made in applying the ordinary usages of speech to what the soul experiences in sense-perception. This point should nevertheless be borne in mind throughout the following description. It is indeed implicitly contained in the context.

of Beings — those already mentioned, and other Beings too. And there was a continual interaction between these Beings and the warmth-bodies of Saturn. The Beings let down the members of their nature into Saturn's physical warmth-bodies. And while in these themselves there was no life, the life of the Beings that dwelt in their encircling sphere expressed itself in them. The warmth-bodies might indeed be compared to mirrors; only it was not the above-named Beings themselves that were mirrored in them, but their life-conditions. In Saturn itself one could not have discovered anything that was alive, and yet Saturn had a vivifying influence on its environment in the heavenly spaces, for it rayed back — sent back, as it were — an echo of the life which was sent down to it. The whole of Saturn appeared like a mirror of the heavenly life. Certain sublime Beings, whose life Saturn rays back, may be called Spirits of Wisdom. (In Christian spiritual science they bear the name Kyriotetes, i.e. Dominions.) Their activity on Saturn does not by any means begin with the middle epoch of evolution which is here being described. Indeed in a certain sense it is by then already at an end. Before they could become conscious of the reflection of their own life, proceeding from the warmth-bodies of Saturn, they had first to make these bodies capable of bringing about such a reflection. Hence their activity began soon after the commencement of Saturn evolution, at a time when the Saturn corporeality was still chaotic substance which could not have reflected anything.

In setting out to contemplate this chaotic, undifferentiated substance, we have already transplanted ourselves in spiritual observation to the beginning of Saturn evolution. What can be observed there does not by any means bear the later character of warmth. To characterize it, we can only speak of a quality which may be compared to the human Will. Through and through, it is nothing else than Will. Here therefore we are dealing with a condition that is purely of the nature of soul. If we look for the source of this Will, we find that it arises from the outpouring of sublime Beings who had, by stages scarcely to be even dimly divined, brought their evolution to such a height that when the Saturn evolution began, they were able to let Will pour forth from Their own being. When the out-pouring has lasted for a certain time, the activity of the Spirits of Wisdom unites with the Will, with the result that the Will, which up to now might be said to have no inherent properties of its own, gradually acquires the property of raying forth Life, raying it back into the heavenly spaces.

The Beings who find Their blessedness in pouring out Will at the beginning of Saturn may be called 'Spirits of Will.' (In Christian esoteric science they are called the Thrones.)

When by the working together of Will and Life a certain stage of Saturn evolution has been reached, other Beings too begin to work. They also are in the surrounding sphere of Saturn. We may call them Spirits of Movement; in Christian terminology they are Dynamis or Mights. They have no physical body and no life-body; their lowest member is the astral body. When the Saturn bodies have attained the faculty of reflecting life, the life which is thus rayed back can become permeated with the properties which have their seat in the astral bodies of the Spirits of Movement. As a result, it appears as though expressions of emotion, feeling, and other soul-forces were being hurled out from Saturn into the heavenly spaces. The entire Saturn seems like a being that is ensouled, manifest-ing sympathies and antipathies. But these manifestations are not its own; they are but the reflection of the soul-activities of the Spirits of Movement.

When this too has lasted through a certain epoch, the activity of yet other Beings begins, whom we will call Spirits of Form. Their lowest member is also an astral body, but it is at a different stage in evolution from the astral body of the Spirits of Movement. The manifestations of feeling which the Spirits of Movement communicate to the life that is rayed back from Saturn are of a general kind, whereas the astral body of the Spirits of Form (in Christian language Exusiai or Powers) works in such a way that it seems as though manifestations are being hurled out into cosmic space from many single beings. The Spirits of Movement, we might say, make Saturn as a whole appear as an animate being endowed with soul. The Spirits of Form divide this life of Saturn into so many separate living entities, so that eventually it appears like a conglomeration of soul-beings.

Picture to yourself a mulberry or a blackberry, composed as it is of ever so many tiny berries. To the supersensible observer Saturn looks like this in the evolutionary epoch here described. It is composed of the single Saturn beings who have no life or soul of their own, but ray back the life and soul of the Beings that dwell around them.

And now at this stage in the evolution of Saturn certain Beings intervene, who again have the astral body for their lowest member, but have brought it on so far in its evolution that it works like a human I of the present time. Through them the I looks down from the surrounding spaces on to Saturn, and communicates its nature to the single 'live' beings. Hence something is sent forth from Saturn into the heavenly spaces, that resembles the impression made by human personality in our present cycle of life. The Beings who bring this about may be called 'Spirits of Personality' (in Christian terminology they are the Archai, First Beginnings, or Principalities). These Beings communicate to the particles of the Saturn body a semblance of the character of personality. Yet personality itself is not there on Saturn, but only its mirrored image — as it were, the shell or husk of personality. The Spirits of Personality have their real personality in the surrounding sphere. They cause their own being to be rayed back to them from the Saturn bodies, and this very process bestows upon the Saturn bodies the fine substantiality which was described above as 'warmth'. Throughout the whole of Saturn there is no inwardness; but the Spirits of Personality behold and recognize the image of their own inwardness, in that it streams out to them as warmth from Saturn.

While all this is happening, the Spirits of Personality are at the stage at which the human being is to-day. They are going through their 'human' epoch. To see this fact in its true light, we must be ready to conceive that a being can be a 'human' being without necessarily having the form and figure man has to-day. The Spirits of Personality are 'men' upon Saturn. Their lowest member is not the physical body but the astral body with the Ego. Therefore they cannot express the experiences of their astral body in a physical and an etheric body in the same way as can the man of to-day. Nevertheless they not only have an I or Ego but are *aware* of it, for the warmth of Saturn, by raying back this Ego, brings it home to their consciousness. They are, in effect, 'human beings' under conditions differing from the earthly.

In the further course of Saturn evolution, facts of quite another kind ensue. Hitherto it was all a reflection of life and feeling that were outside; henceforth there is a kind of inner life. A life of light begins, flickering here and there within the Saturn world and dying down again. At some places a quivering of glowing light will appear, at others something more like rapid lightning-flashes. The Saturn warmth-bodies begin to glimmer and glisten, even to radiate light. The attainment of this stage affords once more the possibility for certain Beings to unfold their activity. These are the Beings who may be designated 'Fire Spirits' (in Christian terminology, Archangeloi, Archangels). They have an astral body of their own at this stage of their existence but they cannot by themselves give it any stimulus. They would be quite incapable of arousing any feeling or sensation, were it not for the fact that they can work upon the warmth-bodies which have reached the stage here indicated. Working in this way makes it possible for them to perceive their own existence; they perceive it by the influence they exercise. They cannot say to themselves 'I am', rather would they have to say: 'My environment enables me to be'. They have perception; indeed their perceptions consist in the above-described light-effects on Saturn. These are in a certain sense their I . This gives them a peculiar form of consciousness. We may describe it as a picture-consciousness. It may be conceived as of the nature of man's dream-consciousness; only we must imagine it far more vivid, far more animated than human dreaming. Nor is it a mere meaningless ebb and flow of pictures; the dream-pictures of the Fire Spirits bear a real relationship to the play-of-light in Saturn.

In this interplay between the Fire Spirits and the warmth-bodies of Saturn, the seeds of the human sense-organs are first implanted in the stream of evolution. The organs whereby to-day man perceives the physical world, light up in their first, delicate, ethereal beginnings. Phantoms-of-man, revealing as yet no other outward sign than these 'light' archetypes of the sense-organs, become perceptible in Saturn to the faculty of clairvoyance. Man's sense-organs are thus the fruits of the activity of the Fire Spirits. But these are not the only Spirits concerned in their creation. Simultaneously with the Fire Spirits, other Beings appear upon the scene — Beings so far advanced in evolution that they are able to make use of the seeds of the sense-organs for witnessing the cosmic processes of Saturn's life. These are the Beings whom we may designate 'Spirits of Love' (in Christian language, Seraphim). Were it not for them, the Fire Spirits could not have the consciousness above described; for they gaze upon the processes taking place in Saturn with a consciousness that enables them to transmit pictures of these processes to the Fire Spirits. For themselves they forgo all the advantage they might have through witness-ing the Saturn events. They renounce every enjoyment it could afford them, every delight; they give that all up, so that the Fire Spirits may have it.

These events are followed by a new period in Saturn's existence. To the play of light another thing is added. It may well seem quite mad to many people when we tell what now confronts supersensible cognition. Within the Saturn body something like sensations of taste begin to go surging to and fro. Sweet, bitter, sour, etc., are perceived at diverse places in the interior of Saturn; while in the heavenly spaces without, all this gives the impression of sound, of a kind of music. And in these processes, once more, Beings find it possible to unfold their activity on Saturn. These Beings may be called the 'Sons of Twilight', or 'Sons of Life' (in Christian language they are the Angeloi or Angels). They begin to interact with the surging, eddying forces of taste in the interior of Saturn, and by this means their etheric or life-body develops an activity that we may designate as a kind of metabolism. They bring life into the interior of Saturn; processes of nutrition and excretion begin to take place there. Not that the Beings themselves bring about these processes directly; the processes arise indirectly, through their activity. And now this inner life makes it possible for yet other Beings to enter the heavenly body. Let them be called the 'Spirits of the Harmonies' (in Christian terminology they are the Cherubim). These Beings transmit to the Sons of Life a kind of dim consciousness, still more dull and dim than the dream-consciousness of man to-day. It is like the consciousness that belongs to man in dreamless sleep, which is of such a low degree that in a manner of speaking it does not 'come to consciousness' at all; man remains unaware of it. Yet it is there. It differs from day-consciousness in kind as well as in degree. Our present-day plants possess this 'dreamless sleep' consciousness. It affords no *perceptions* of an outer world in the human sense of the word, but it regulates the life-processes and brings them into harmony with those in the outer Universe. At the Saturn stage with which we are here dealing, the Sons of Life cannot perceive the regulation; but the Spirits of the Harmonies perceive it. They therefore are the real regulators.

All this life goes on in what we have described as the phantoms-of-man. These therefore appear to the spiritual eye as though they were alive; and yet their life is but a semblance of life. It is the life of the Sons of Life who as it were make use of these phantoms in order to live out their own life.

Let us now direct our attention to these phantoms-of-man with their semblance of life. During the period with which we have been dealing, they are of ever-changing form. Now they will resemble one shape, now another. In the further course of evolution the shapes become more definite, and sometimes even last for a while. This is due to their being now permeated by the influences of the Spirits who were at work in the very beginning of Saturn evolution, namely the Spirits of Will (the Thrones). As a result, the phantom-of-man appears to be endowed with the simplest, darkest form of consciousness. We must conceive it as being yet more dim than that of dreamless sleep. Under present-day conditions, the minerals possess this consciousness. It brings the inner nature of the object or being into unison with the physical external world. On Saturn it is the Spirits of Will who regulate this unison, with the result that man appears like an impress of the Saturn life itself. What the Saturn life is on a large scale, man is now at this stage on a small. And with this the first seed is given of what is still only in the seedling stage even in the man of to-day, namely Spirit-Man (Atma). Inwardly — within Saturn — this dull human will manifests itself to the faculty of supersensible perception by effects which may be compared to 'smells'. Outwardly — out into the heavenly spaces — there is a manifestation as of personality, a personality, however, that is not guided by an inner I, but regulated from outside like a machine. It is the Spirits of Will who regulate it.

Surveying the above, we see that from the middle condition onward the stages of Saturn's evolution could be characterized by comparing their effects with sense-impressions of the present time. Thus it was possible to say: Saturn evolution manifests as warmth; afterwards a play of light is added, then a play of taste and sound, until at length there appears what reveals itself inwardly — to the interior of Saturn — in sensations of smell, and outwardly like a human I working in a machine-like way. How is it then with the manifestations of Saturn evolution before the state of warmth is reached? They cannot be compared with anything whatsoever that is accessible to outer sensation. The warmth-condition is preceded by one which man to-day experiences only in his inner being. When he gives himself up to ideas which he forms for himself within his soul without the occasion being thrust upon him by any impression from outside, then he has within him something which no physical senses can perceive — something which is accessible, as a perception, to higher spiritual sight alone. The warmth-condition of Saturn is in effect preceded by manifestations which exist only for one who can perceive the supersensible. Three such conditions may be named: pure warmth-of-soul, not outwardly perceptible; purely spiritual light, which outwardly is darkness; and spiritual being which is complete in itself, needing the presence of no outer being to make it conscious of itself. Pure inner warmth accompanies the appearance on Saturn of the Spirits of Movement, pure spiritual light that of the Spirits of Wisdom, whilst pure in-ward being is connected with the first outpouring of the Spirits of Will. Thus with the appearance of the Saturn warmth, our evolution first emerges from an inner life of pure spirituality, to an existence manifesting outwardly.

One more thing must be added, with which the present consciousness may find it still more difficult to come to terms. With the warmth-condition of Old Saturn there also first emerges what we call Time. The previous conditions are in fact not temporal at all. They belong to the realm which, in spiritual science, may be named Duration. All that is said in this book of conditions in the Realm of Duration must therefore be understood in this sense. It must be borne in mind that any expression implying time-relationships is used only for the sake of comparison and exposition. In human language even those things which, in a manner of speaking, precede time, can only be characterized with words in which the time-conception is implicit. We must remember that though the first, second and third Saturn states did not take place 'one after the other' in the present-day sense of the words, we cannot, after all, avoid describing them in sequence. Moreover, in spite of their dura-tion or simultaneity, they depend on one another, and the dependence is such as to be comparable with a succession in time.

With this reference to the earliest evolutionary states of Saturn, light is also thrown on all further questionings as to the 'whence' of these conditions. In a purely intellectual way it is possible, of course, in the case of every given origin, to ask again after *its* origin. But in relation to facts this will not do. We can easily bring it home to ourselves by a comparison. If we see ruts in a road we may ask, 'Whence do they come?' We may receive the answer, 'From a carriage.' Then we can ask again, 'Where did the carriage come from, and where was it going?' Here again an answer founded on facts is possible. We can still go on to ask, 'Who was in the carriage? What were the intentions of the person using it? What was he doing?' But we shall at length reach a point where our questioning is brought to a natural conclusion by the facts themselves. And if we go on asking questions beyond this point, we are departing from the purpose of the original question; we only prolong the questioning, as it were, mechanically. In cases like the one here cited as an illustration, we can readily see where the facts themselves will put a natural end to questioning. With the great questions of the Universe it is not so easy. None the less, if we think it over carefully, we shall recognize that all questions of 'whence' must come to an end with the Saturn conditions we have been describing. For we have here reached a sphere where the beings and processes are no longer to be accounted for by reference to that from which they take their origin, but by what they are in themselves.

The eventual result of Saturn evolution is to be seen in the fact that the seed of man has grown and developed to a certain point. It has attained the low, dim state of consciousness which was described above. We must not imagine that this began to evolve only in the last stage of Saturn. The Spirits of Will are working throughout all the conditions, but it is in the last period that the result of their activity is most apparent to supersensible perception. Altogether, no hard and fast line can be drawn between the activities of the several groups of Beings. When it is said: First the Spirits of Will are active, then the Spirits of Wisdom, and so forth — it does not mean that they are active at that stage only. They work throughout the whole of Saturn evolution; their working is, however, most readily observed in the times thus indicated, when the several Beings have as it were their periods of leadership.

The whole of Saturn evolution thus appears as an elaboration, by the Spirits of Wisdom, Movement, Form, etc., of that which was poured out in the beginning by the Spirits of Will. The spiritual Beings themselves undergo evolution in the process. The Spirits of Wisdom, for example, after having received their life rayed back to them from Saturn, are at another stage than before. Their own faculties have advanced to a higher level, and there follows for them something not unlike what sleep is for the human being. Periods of activity on Saturn are followed by times when they are living as it were in other worlds; and then their activity is turned away from

Saturn. Consequently, supersensible perception sees in the Saturn evolution here described, a rise and fall. The former lasts until the state of warmth has developed and matured. Then, with the play of light, a waning process begins. And when through the working of the Spirits of Will the phantoms-of-man have taken shape and form, the spiritual Beings have by then all gradually withdrawn. Saturn evolution dies away into itself, and disappears as such. A kind of interval of rest begins. The germ or seed of man passes as it were into a state of dissolution; not that it vanishes entirely — rather is it in the condition of a plant seed which, resting in the Earth, will ripen by and by into a new plant. So does the seed of man rest in the bosom of the world, there to await a new awakening. And when the time for its awakening has come, then the spiritual Beings have on their part acquired — under different conditions — the faculties to work still further upon the seed of man. The Spirits of Wisdom have in their etheric body attained the power to do more than enjoy the reflection of Life — as on Saturn; they are now able to pour Life out of themselves, endowing other beings with it. The Spirits of Movement are now as far advanced as were the Spirits of Wisdom upon Saturn. Their lowest member upon Saturn was the astral body; henceforth they have in addition an etheric or life-body of their own. And the other spiritual Beings too have reached a further stage in their evolution. Hence in the further evolution of the seed of man these spiritual Beings can all work in quite another way than they did upon Saturn.

But now at the end of Saturn evolution the seed of man had, as it were, dissolved; and in order that the Spirit-beings — more highly evolved as they now are — may continue where they left off before, it must briefly recapitulate the stages it went through on Saturn. And this is precisely what shows itself to supersensible perception. Emerging once more from its hidden state, the seed of man begins to unfold by its own inherent faculty — by virtue of the forces with which it was imbued on Saturn. It comes forth out of the darkness as a being-of-will, and raises itself to the semblance of life, of soul-likeness and so forth, until it reaches the manifestation of machine-like personality which belonged to it at the close of Saturn evolution.

*　*　*　*　*

The second of the great evolutionary periods — the Sun stage — uplifts the human being to a higher level of consciousness than he attained on Saturn, although compared with man's present consciousness, his condition on the Sun might still be called unconsciousness. For it is well-nigh equivalent to the state in which he now finds himself in absolutely dreamless sleep. We might also compare it with the low degree of consciousness in which our world of plants is slumbering to-day. For supersensible perception there is, as a matter of fact, no such thing as unconsciousness; there are but differing degrees of consciousness. Everything in the world is conscious.

Man attains this higher state of consciousness in the course of Sun evolution through the fact that the etheric or life-body is now incorporated in him. But this cannot take place until the Saturn conditions have been recapitulated. Such recapitulation has a quite definite meaning. When the interval of rest is over, what was previously Saturn emerges from the 'cosmic sleep' as a new world-entity — as Sun. But the whole situation within which evolution takes place is now changed. The Spirit-beings whose working upon Saturn we described have progressed to new conditions. The seed of man, however, as it emerges on the newly formed Sun, appears, to begin with, just as it became on Saturn. It has accordingly first of all to transmute the several evolutionary stages it underwent on Saturn, in order to adapt them to the conditions on Sun. Hence the Sun epoch begins with a repetition of the Saturn events, but a repetition adapted to the changed conditions. Then, when the human being has reached this point — when the degree of evolution that he attained on Saturn has been completely adapted to the Sun conditions — the Spirits of Wisdom begin their work of pouring the etheric or life-body into the physical. The higher stage that man attains upon Sun may be characterized as follows. The physical body, formed already upon Saturn in its germinal beginnings, is raised to a second level of perfection, in that it now becomes the bearer of an etheric or life-body. The etheric or life-body itself attains, during Sun evolution, the first degree of its perfection. But for these stages of perfection to be achieved — the second for the physical and the first for the life-body — the intervention of other Spirit-beings too is needed, just as it was for the Saturn stage.

When the Spirits of Wisdom begin with their inpouring of the life-body, the Sun entity, which until now was dark, begins to radiate light. Simultaneously the first signs of an inner quickening appear in the seed of man: life begins to be. What on Saturn had to be described as a mere semblance of life, is now becoming real life. The inpouring goes on for a time, and then an important change comes over the seed of man; it differentiates into two parts. Hitherto, the physical body and life-body have been in intimate union as a single whole; now, the physical begins to separate off as a distinct part, — although it still remains permeated with the life-body. Thus we now have to do with a twofold human being. One part of man is physical body, permeated through and through with life-body: the other consists of life-body alone. This severance takes place during an interval of rest in the Sun life, when the light-radiance which had begun to appear dies down again. It happens during what may be called a 'cosmic night'. This interval of rest is however far shorter than the aforesaid interval between the Saturn and Sun evolutions. When it is over, the Spirits of Wisdom continue for a while to work upon the two-fold human being, just as they worked on him before, when he was single and undivided. Thereafter, the Spirits of Movement come in with their activity; they permeate with their own astral body the life-body of the human being. The life-body thus attains the faculty to carry out certain inner movements in the physical — movements that are comparable to those of the saps and fluids in a plant of the present day.

The whole of Saturn consisted of warmth alone. During Sun evolution this warmth-substance condenses to a state which may be likened to that of our present gas or vapour. It is the condition we can denote as Air. The first beginnings of it show themselves after the Spirits of Movement have come in with their activity. To supersensible consciousness the following appears. Within the warmth-substance delicate, tenuous structures emerge, which are brought into regular movement by the forces of the life-body. These structures make manifest the physical body of the human being as it is at this stage in its evolution. They are permeated through and through with warmth, and are also enveloped as if by an integument of warmth. Warmth-creations with air-forms incorporated in them, the latter engaged in regular and constant movement — so may we describe the human being, physically speaking, at this stage. If we want to maintain the suggested comparison with the plant of the present day, we must remember that we are not dealing with a compact plant but with a form consisting of air or gas, the movements of which are not unlike those of the sap in the present plant.*

This evolution is then carried further. After a time an interval of rest once more ensues; and when this is over, the Spirits of Movement continue with their work, until it is supplemented by that of the Spirits of Form, as a result of whose activity the gaseous structures, hitherto constantly changing, now assume more permanent shape. This too is brought about through the Spirits of Form pouring their forces in and out of the life-body of the human beings. Previously, when the Spirits of Movement alone were working upon them, the gaseous bodies were in incessant motion; only for a moment did they ever maintain their shape. Henceforward they will now assume, for a time, distinguishable forms.

Once more, after a certain time, comes an interval of rest; and when that is over, the Spirits of Form resume their activity. Then, however, altogether new conditions appear within Sun evolution.

For now the point is reached where Sun evolution has attained its middle epoch. It is the time when the Spirits of Personality, who reached their human level upon Saturn, rise

* The gas appears to supersensible consciousness through the light-effects which it sends forth. Hence we might also speak of forms of light presenting themselves to spiritual vision.

to a higher stage of perfection, thus transcending the stage of humanity. They attain a consciousness which, in the regular course of evolution, present-day man does not yet possess. He will attain it when the Earth — the fourth of the planetary stages in evolution — has reached its goal and the next planetary period will have begun. At that time, man will no longer perceive around him merely what the present physical senses communicate to him; he will be able to observe in pictures the inner soul-condition of the beings that surround him. He will have picture-consciousness, still however retaining full self-consciousness. For in his picture-vision, there will be nothing dim or dreamlike. He will perceive things of the soul — in pictures it is true, yet so that the pictures will express realities just as physical colours and tones do to-day. In our time it is only by spiritual-scientific training that man can raise himself to this kind of seership. The training will be dealt with in a later chapter.

Such seership the Spirits of Personality attain as their normal gift of evolution in the middle of the Sun stage. And it enables them, during Sun evolution, to work upon the newly formed life-body of the human being in the same way as they worked upon his physical body during Saturn. As upon Saturn the warmth rayed back to them their own personality, so now the gaseous forms ray back to them in shining light the picture-visions of their seership. They behold — supersensibly — what is now taking place on Sun. Nor is their seeing by any means mere observation. For in the pictures that stream outward from the Sun, it is as though something of that force which man on Earth denotes as Love were making itself felt. And as we look — in soul — more closely, we find the cause of this. Into the light as it rays outward from the Sun, sublime Beings have mingled their activity. These are the 'Spirits of Love' (in Christian language, Seraphim) already named in the preceding pages. Henceforth they work upon the human etheric body (or life-body) in co-operation with the Spirits of Personality. The combined activity of these Beings enables the life-body to take a further step on its path of evolution. It becomes capable not only of transforming the gaseous structures which are within it, but of so working upon them that the first suggestions of a reproductive process appear in the living human entities. Secretions are as it were driven forth — or we might say, 'perspired' — by the already-formed gaseous organisms, and assume form in their turn in the likeness of their mother-organism.

Before we can go on to describe the further evolution of the Sun, we must point to a fact which is of the greatest importance in the whole cosmic process. In the course of a given epoch not all the beings attain the goal of their evolution. Some fall short of it. During Saturn evolution, for example, not all the Spirits of Personality attained the 'human' stage appointed for them. Nor did all the human physical bodies that developed upon Saturn reach the degree of maturity which could enable them to become the bearers on Sun of an independent life-body. As a result, beings and structures are present on the Sun, unsuited to the conditions that obtain there. These must now make good what they have missed on Saturn. During the Sun stage spiritual perception can therefore observe the following. When the Spirits of Wisdom begin with their in-pouring of the life-body, the whole body of the Sun becomes as it were clouded. For it is interspersed with structures which belong essentially to Saturn — warmth-structures that are unable to condense in the proper way to air. These are the human entities which have remained behind at the Saturn stage. They cannot become bearers of a normally developed life-body.

What is thus left behind of Saturn's warmth-substance, divides on the Sun into two portions. One is as it were absorbed by the human bodies, and constitutes henceforth, within the human being, a kind of lower nature. Thus on Sun the human being receives something into his bodily nature that corresponds in reality to the Saturn stage. Now as the Saturn body of man made it possible for the Spirits of Personality to rise to their 'human' level, so on the Sun does this Saturn part of man render a like service to the Fire Spirits. These rise to their human stage by pouring their forces in and out of it, just as the Spirits of Personality did on Saturn. This too takes place during the middle epoch of Sun evolution, for then the Saturn part of the human being is sufficiently mature for the Fire Spirits (the Archangeloi) to pass through their human stage with its assistance.

Another portion of the Saturn warmth-substance separates off and comes to an independent existence alongside of and among the Sun human beings, constituting thus a second kingdom, developing a fully independent, but purely physical body — a body of warmth. There is therefore in this second kingdom no independent life-body to receive the activity of the fully evolved Spirits of Personality. But now certain Spirits of Personality have also stopped short at the Saturn stage; they did not attain there the level of humanity. Between them and this second kingdom of the Sun, there is a bond of attraction. They must now relate themselves to this retarded kingdom in the same way as their more advanced companions related themselves upon Saturn to the human beings. For upon Saturn these too had developed only a physical body. But on the Sun itself there is no possibility for this work to be done by the backward Spirits of Personality. They therefore separate themselves from the Sun and form an independent heavenly body outside it. From this heavenly body that has left the Sun, the retarded Spirits of Personality work upon the creatures of the second Sun kingdom. The single cosmic entity that Saturn was before, has thus become two. Henceforth the Sun has a second heavenly body in its environment, representing a kind of re-birth of Saturn — as it were, a new Saturn. From this new Saturn the second kingdom of the Sun is endowed with the character of personality. Its beings have no personality upon the Sun itself; but they reflect to the Spirits of Personality on the new Saturn *their* personality. In among the human beings on the Sun, supersensible consciousness can observe forces of warmth, whose working intermingles with the regular evolution of the Sun. Herein we have to perceive the Spirits of the new Saturn wielding their power.

Observation of the human being during the middle epoch of Sun evolution reveals it to be divided into a physical body and a life-body. The latter is the scene of activity for the more advanced Spirits of Personality, in unison with the Spirits of

Love. The physical body is now intermingled with a portion of the retarded Saturn nature, and here the activity of the Fire Spirits is at work. In what the Fire Spirits achieve in this retarded Saturn nature, we have to recognize the forerunners of the present sense-organs of Earth man. (It will be remembered that already upon Saturn the Fire Spirits were concerned in elaborating within the warmth-substance the seeds of the human senses.) On the other hand, in that which is accomplished by the Spirits of Personality in union with the Spirits of Love (the Seraphim), we have to perceive the first beginnings of man's present glandular organs.

But now the work of those Spirits of Personality who dwell on the new Saturn is not exhaustively described in what was said above. Their activity goes beyond the second kingdom of the Sun; they also establish a kind of connection between this second kingdom and the human senses. The warmth-substances of this second kingdom stream through the human senses in their germinal condition, pouring continually in and out of them. In this way the human being rises on Sun to a kind of perception of the lower kingdom that is there beside him. It is, in the nature of the case, a very dim perception — corresponding in all respects to the dull Saturn consciousness of which we spoke before. And it consists essentially in varying effects of warmth.

All that has here been described as pertaining to the middle epoch of Sun evolution, lasts for a certain time; and then, once more there is an interval of rest. After the interval, things go on for a while in the same way as before, until a point is reached in evolution when the human etheric body is mature for a united working of the Sons of Life (the Angeloi) and the Spirits of Harmony (the Cherubim). To supersensible consciousness manifestations now appear within the human being which may be likened to perceptions of taste, and which reveal themselves outwardly as sounds. It will be remembered that we resorted to a similar comparison in our description of Saturn evolution. Here however, on Sun, all that goes on in the human being is far more inward, is full of a more independent life.

The Sons of Life hereby attain the dim picture-consciousness which the Fire Spirits reached on Saturn. The Spirits of Harmony (Cherubim) are their helpers in this. They behold in spirit what is now taking its course in Sun evolution; but they deny themselves all the fruits of this their contemplation, all feeling of the Wisdom-filled pictures that arise there, and pour them like wondrous magic scenes into the dream-consciousness of the Sons of Life. These in turn weave the forms they behold into man's etheric body, which rises thereby to higher and higher stages in its evolution.

Again there is an interval of rest. Again the whole arises out of the 'sleep of worlds' and, after it has continued its course for a time, the human being is mature enough to be able to arouse within him forces of his own. These are the forces which were poured into his being by the Thrones during the last epoch of Saturn evolution. The human being now continues his evolution in an inner life which, in its manifestation to consciousness, may be likened to an inward sensation of smell. Outwardly, over against the heavenly spaces, he reveals himself as a personality — albeit one that is not directed by an inner I, but seems more like a plant that gives the impression of personality. We have already seen how at the end of Saturn evolution, personality manifested like a machine. Moreover, as at that time the first seed was developed of what is still in a seedling state even in the man of to-day, namely Spirit-Man or Atma, so now and in like manner the first seed is formed of Life-Spirit or Budhi.

After all this has gone on for a certain time, there is once more an interval of rest. And, as has happened before, after the interval the former activity of the human being is resumed for a while. Then new conditions enter in, arising out of a fresh intervention on the part of the Spirits of Wisdom. Through this the human being becomes able to feel the first traces of sympathy and antipathy with his environment. It is as yet not real feeling; nevertheless, it is a forerunner of feeling. For the inner activity of life, the manifestations of which could be described as resembling perceptions of smell, reveals itself outwardly as if in a kind of primitive speech. When an agreeable smell or taste, glimmer of light, or other manifestation is inwardly perceived, the human being makes it known outwardly by a sound. Similarly too with an inwardly distasteful perception. And now, as a result of all these developments, the true meaning of Sun evolution for the being of man has been attained. He has reached a higher level of consciousness than was his on Saturn. It is the consciousness of sleep.

After a while the point has also been reached when the higher Beings connected with the Sun stage must pass to other spheres, there to assimilate the potentialities they have implanted in themselves by the work they have done on the human being. A greater interval of rest supervenes, such as there was between Saturn and Sun. All that has been evolved on Sun passes into a condition like that of a plant when its forces of growth are resting in the seed. But as these come forth again to the light of day in a new plant, so after the interval of rest is over, all that was life upon the Sun emerges again out of the bosom of the worlds and a new planetary existence begins. We shall well understand the meaning of such an interval of rest or 'sleep of worlds' if we turn our thought for a moment to some one of the above-named groups of Beings — the Spirits of Wisdom, for example. On Saturn, these Beings were not yet so far advanced as to be able to pour forth from themselves an etheric body. The experiences they underwent there served however to prepare them for this **activity**. During the interval they transmuted what had been prepared in them, into the actual faculty, with the result that on Sun they were ready to let the life stream out from them and so endow the human being with a life-body of his own.

* * * * *

When the interval of rest is over, what formerly was Sun comes forth again from the 'sleep of worlds'. That is to say, it becomes perceptible once more to those powers of spiritual sight which had formerly been able to observe it but from which it vanished in the interval of rest. The planetary being emerging now in its new form shall be designated 'Moon' — but we must not confuse it with that fragment of it which constitutes the present Moon, the satellite of the Earth. Two things are to be noted, as it re-emerges. In the first place, the new Saturn, which separated off during Sun, is now again within the planetary being. During the interval of rest, it has re-united with the Sun. The whole content of the original Saturn comes forth again to begin with as a single cosmic entity. Secondly, the life-bodies of the human beings, that were formed upon Sun, have been absorbed during the interval of rest by the planet's spiritual envelope — for such, in a sense, it is. Hence at this point of time the life-bodies do not appear in union with the human physical bodies; these emerge, to begin with, by themselves. Though bearing in their nature all that has been achieved in them on Saturn and on Sun, they are still without the etheric or life-body. Nor indeed would they be able to receive it at once, for in the interval of rest the etheric body itself has undergone an evolution to which they are not yet adapted. And so now, at the beginning of Moon evolution, another repetition of the Saturn events takes place, in order to achieve this adaptation.

The physical life of man passes in recapitulation through the stages of Saturn evolution, but under altogether changed conditions. For on Saturn the forces of a warmth-body alone were at work in it, whereas now there are also those of the gaseous body which it has assimilated. The latter do not however emerge at once. In the beginning of Moon evolution it is as though the human being consisted of warmth-substance alone, with the gaseous forces still asleep within it. Then follows a period when these emerge in their first indication. And at length, in the last period of the Saturn repetition, the human being has already the *appearance* he had when he was alive on Sun. Yet all 'life' at this stage proves to be no more than a mere semblance of life. For there must first be an interval of rest, like the short intervals of rest during Sun evolution. Then begins once more the inpouring of the life-body, for which the physical body has now made itself mature. This inpouring takes place, as did the Saturn repetition, in three distinct epochs. In the second of these, the human being is so far adapted to the new Moon conditions that the Spirits of Movement can bring into action the faculty they have acquired.

Out of their own nature they can now pour the astral body into the human beings. For this work they prepared themselves during Sun evolution, and in the interval of rest between Sun and Moon they have transmuted what they had prepared into the actual faculty. This inpouring of the astral body lasts for a certain time, and then again one of the smaller intervals of rest ensues; after which the inpouring is continued, until the Spirits of Form enter with their activity. Through the Spirits of Movement pouring into him the astral body, the human being acquires his first qualities of soul. The processes that take place in him by virtue of the life-body — which in Sun evolution were still of a plant-like character — these he now begins to follow with sensation, feeling pleasure in them or disliking them. But the sympathies and antipathies thus aroused remain in ever-changing ebb and flow, until the Spirits of Form come in and play their part. Thereupon the ever-changing feelings become so transformed that there emerges in the human being what we may regard as a first sign of wish and craving. He strives for a repetition of what gave enjoyment, and seeks to avoid what roused a feeling of antipathy. Since however the Spirits of Form do not communicate their own nature to the human being but only cause their forces to pour in and out of him, this craving is without inwardness or independence. It is guided by the Spirits of Form, and gives the impression of being purely instinctive.

On Saturn the physical body of the human being was a body of warmth; on Sun there was a condensation to the gaseous condition, to 'air'. Now, in Moon evolution, when the Astral is poured in, the moment is reached when the physical attains a further stage of condensation. It comes into a condition comparable to that of a liquid in our time. This new state may be designated 'water', meaning however not our present water but any liquid form of existence. The human physical body comes now gradually to assume a form composed of three organic structures, distinct from one another in their substance. The densest is a 'water body'; this is permeated through and through by airy currents, and warmth effects continue also to pervade the whole.

But now, as on Saturn, so in the Sun stage too, not all the forms attain the corresponding maturity. Hence we find upon Moon, forms which are even now still at the Saturn stage, and some also which have reached but remain at the stage of Sun. Two other kingdoms thus emerge, beside the properly developed human kingdom. One consists of beings which, having remained at the Saturn stage, have physical body alone; and this physical body is not yet able, even now on Moon, to become the bearer of an independent life-body. These beings form the lowest kingdom. A second kingdom is composed of beings who have stopped short at the Sun stage, and are accordingly not ready on Moon to incorporate within them an independent astral body. They constitute an intermediate kingdom, between the aforesaid and the normally advanced human kingdom.

A further event has now to be noted. The substances with forces of warmth alone, those also that have stopped short at forces of air, permeate the human beings too. These, therefore, on Moon, bear within them a Saturn and a Sun nature. Thereby a kind of split has come about in human nature, and in consequence of this, an event of great significance takes place in Moon evolution. Soon after the Spirits of Form have come in with their activity, a severance begins to be prepared for in the heavenly body of the Moon. A portion of the substances and beings is split off from the remainder. Out of the single heavenly body, two separate ones evolve. The first is taken for their dwelling-place by certain higher Beings, hitherto more intimately united with the heavenly body in its single state. The second is occupied by man, together with the two lower kingdoms above-mentioned and also certain higher Beings who do not pass over to the first. The former heavenly body, with the higher Beings, appears now as a Sun re-born and at the same time refined; the latter is henceforth the essentially new creation — 'Old Moon', as it has to be called — the third planetary embodiment of our Earth, following on the Saturn and Sun embodiments.

Of the substances that have come into existence on Moon, the new-born Sun, as it goes forth, takes with it only warmth and air; while on the remainder which is left behind as Moon, beside these two the watery state is also to be found. In consequence of the severance, the Beings who have gone forth with the new-born Sun are no longer hampered in their evolution by the denser beings of the Moon. They are now able to progress untrammelled in their own becoming, and they attain thereby the greater strength to work — now from without, from their dwelling-place, the Sun — upon the beings of the Moon. Thus do the Moon beings too attain new possibilities of evolution. What is for them particularly significant is that the Spirits of Form have remained united with them. These establish more firmly the desire-nature of the human being, and by degrees this comes to find expression in a further condensation of the physical body. Where hitherto it has been but watery, it begins to assume a more viscous form, and the structures of air and of warmth are densified to correspond. Similar changes take place also in the two lower kingdoms.

In consequence of having separated from the Sun, the Moon is now related to the Sun in the same way as once was Saturn to the whole of the surrounding cosmic evolution. Saturn was formed out of the body of the Spirits of Will (Thrones). From the Saturn substance rayed back into cosmic space all that was experienced in consciousness by the Spirit-beings in its environment. And through the events that followed, this raying-back gradually awoke to independent life. Such is the essence of all evolution. Independent being is first separated out from the life of the environment, then the environment engraves itself — as it were, by reflection — upon the separated being, and then the latter evolves further, independently.

So did the Moon body sever itself from the Sun, and, to begin with, simply reflect the life of the Sun body. If, therefore, nothing else had happened, the situation in the cosmos would have been as follows. There would have been a Sun body, where spiritual Beings well adapted to its nature had their experiences in the elements of warmth and air. Over against it would have been a Lunar body, wherein other Beings were evolving, living a life of warmth and air and water. And the progress from the Sun to the Moon embodiment would have meant for the Sun Beings that in what was happening on Moon they would have beheld their own life as in a mirror, and would in this way have been able to receive it and enjoy it, which during the Sun embodiment had not yet been possible. But evolution took another turn. Something took place which was of the very deepest significance for all succeeding evolution. Certain beings, who were adapted to the Moon body, possessed themselves of the element of Will (a heritage from the Thrones) which stood at their disposal, and evolved therewith a life of their own, that grew up independently of the Sun life.

Alongside the experiences on Moon which were entirely subject to the Sun's influence, independent experiences now arose — states of rebellion, as it were, or of opposition to the Sun Beings. And the various kingdoms that had arisen on Sun and Moon — above all, the kingdom of the forefather of man — became involved in these new conditions. Spiritually and materially, the Moon body contained now within it two kinds of life — one that was in intimate union with the Sun's life, and another which, having 'fallen' from this, went on its own independent way. This division into a twofold life comes to expression in all the succeeding events of the Moon embodiment.

That which presents itself to supersensible consciousness at this epoch in evolution, can be described in the following picture. The ground mass of the Moon was formed of a semi-live substance, which was in constant movement, sometimes sluggish, sometimes quick and lively. There is as yet no solid mineral mass like the rocks and other constituents of the Earth on which man treads to-day. We might describe it as a kind of plant-mineral kingdom. Only, we have to imagine the whole ground and body of the Moon consisting of this plant-mineral substance, just as the Earth to-day consists of rocks and stones, arable soil, etc. As here and there rocks protrude from the Earth to-day, so in the Lunar mass, harder portions also were embedded. These might be likened to forms made of hard wood or of horn. Moreover, as plants to-day spring from the mineral soil, so was the ground of the Moon bedecked, and also penetrated, by a second kingdom, consisting of a kind of plant-animal. The substance of this kingdom was softer than the ground and more mobile in itself. It spread over the lower kingdom like a turgid sea. And as for man himself, he might be described as animal-man. He had in his nature the constituents of the two other kingdoms; but his being was permeated through and through by a life-body and an astral body, upon which the forces of the higher Beings on the Sun were working, thereby ennobling his form and figure. The Spirits of Form gave him a form and figure that adapted him to the Moon life; the Sun Spirits, on the other hand, made him a being that was lifted beyond this life. With the faculties bestowed on him by these Spirits, man had the power to ennoble his own nature; he could even lift up on to a higher level that within him which was akin to the lower kingdoms.

Seen in their spiritual aspect, these developments may be described as follows. Man's ancestor had also been ennobled by beings who had fallen away from the Sun kingdom. Their ennobling influence extended, above all, to everything that could be experienced in the watery element. Upon this element, the influence of the Beings of the Sun was not so great; they were rulers in the elements of warmth and air. The outcome of all this was that a twofold nature began to declare itself in man's organism. One part of it was permeated through and through by the influence of the Sun Beings; while in the other, the fallen beings, the Moon beings, were working. The latter part was thus more independent. In the former, no other states of consciousness could arise than those in which the Beings of the Sun were living, while in the latter there lived a kind of cosmic consciousness, such as had belonged to the Saturn state, but on a higher level. Through it man's ancestor saw himself as an 'Image of the Universe', while in the 'Sun' part of his being he would feel himself only as an 'Image of the Sun'.

These two natures in man began now to come into a kind of conflict. And for this conflict a balance was established by the influence of the Sun Beings making transient and frail the more material part of man's organism whereby he was enabled to have the independent World-consciousness. Henceforth this part had to be thrown off from time to time. During the process and for some while after, man's ancestor was a being subject to the Sun influence alone. His consciousness became less independent; he lived in utter devotion to the Solar life. Thereupon the independent — Moon — part would be renewed once more; and after a while the whole process be repeated. This happened time and again. Thus did the ancestor of man live on the Moon in alternating states of consciousness — now duller, now clearer; and the alternation was accompanied by a changing and renewal of his being in its material aspect. From time to time he would lay aside his Moon body, then after a while put it on once more.

Seen in their physical aspect, the aforesaid kingdoms of the Moon show great variety. The mineral-plants differ from one another, group by group; so do the plant-animals and the animal-men. This we shall readily understand if we recall that certain structures have remained behind at each of the preceding stages. Forms very varied in quality will thus have been embodied. Some there are which still reveal the initial properties of Saturn; others, those of its middle epoch; others again, those of its end. So too for all the successive evolutionary stages of the Sun.

Nor is it only the forms and structures belonging to the heavenly body that remain behind as it goes forward in its evolution. The same applies to many of the Beings connected with it. With the advance of evolution to Moon, a number of different ranks of such Beings are to be found. There are Spirits of Personality who even on Sun did not attain their human level, while there are others who made good there what they had missed before, and rose to the human stage. The same with the Fire Spirits who should have become human beings on Sun: a number of these have also remained behind. And as in Sun evolution certain Spirits of Personality, having remained behind, withdrew from the Sun and made Saturn arise anew as a distinct heavenly body, so too in the course of Moon evolution do the Beings aforesaid remove themselves on to separate heavenly bodies. So far, we have spoken only of the separation into Sun and Moon, but in the same manner other heavenly forms were also separated from the Moon body which emerged after the great interval between the Sun and Moon stages of evolution; so that we have in time a whole system of heavenly bodies, the most advanced of which, as will readily be seen, must be the new Sun. And now, as in Sun evolution there was a bond of attraction between the backward Saturn kingdom and the Spirits of Personality on the new Saturn, so, in like manner, bonds of attraction now arise between the several heavenly bodies and the corresponding Moon beings. It would lead us much too far afield to trace here in detail all the heavenly bodies that emerged. Let it suffice to have pointed out the reason why, as time went on, from the single heavenly body which arose as Saturn in the beginning of human evolution, a whole number of heavenly bodies detached themselves, one after another.

After the Spirits of Form have come in with their activity, Moon evolution continues for a time along these lines. Then there is once more an interval, during which the coarser parts of the three Moon kingdoms remain in a kind of quiescent state, while the finer parts — and notably the astral bodies of the human beings — free themselves from these coarser structures. They come into a condition where the higher forces of the sublime Beings of the Sun can work upon them with peculiar intensity.

After this interval of rest, the finer portions penetrate once more into the parts of the human being that are of coarser substance. What with the strength they have acquired in their free condition during the interval, they can now make these coarser substances ready to receive the influence which, after a time, the normally progressive Spirits of Personality and the Fire Spirits will bring to bear on them.

The Spirits of Personality have risen meanwhile to a stage at which they have the consciousness of Inspiration. Not only can they, as in their former picture-consciousness, perceive in picture form the inner states of other beings; they can behold their very inwardness, expressed in a language as it were of spiritual music. Meanwhile the Fire Spirits have risen to the consciousness which the Spirits of Personality possessed on Sun.

145

Both kinds of Spirits are thus able to enter, and play their part in, the now more ripened life of the human being. The Spirits of Personality work on his astral body, the Fire Spirits on his etheric body. The astral body receives thereby the character of personality. Henceforth it not only experiences pleasure and pain, it also relates them to itself. Not yet does it rise to the full consciousness of 'I' which says to itself 'I am'; rather does it feel sustained and sheltered by other beings in its environment. Turning its gaze upward, as it were, to these, it can exclaim: 'This my environment upholds me in existence.'

Meanwhile the Fire Spirits work upon the etheric body. Under their influence the motion of the forces in this body becomes gradually more and more of an inward life activity. It finds physical expression in a movement of the saps and fluids and in phenomena of growth. The gaseous substances have been condensed to watery, and we may now begin to speak of a kind of nutrition — in the sense that what is received from without is inwardly transmuted and assimilated. If we imagine something intermediate between the nutrition and the breathing of to-day, we shall have a fair idea of what was taking place in this direction. The human being derived his 'food-stuffs' from the animal-plant kingdom. These animal-plants we must imagine hovering and floating in a surrounding element (or sometimes also loosely rooted in the ground), rather as the lower animals of to-day live in the water, or the terrestrial animals in the air. But the element in which the animal-plants lived was neither water nor air in the present sense; it was something intermediate between the two — a kind of dense vapour wherein the most diverse substances, being as it were dissolved in it, moved hither and thither in manifold currents. The animal-plants seemed like forms within this element that were only rather more regular and condensed. Physically they were often but little different from their surrounding element. Besides the process of nutrition, there was also a breathing process. But it was not as it is on Earth; it was more like an in-drawing and out-pouring of warmth. To the supersensible observer of these processes, it is as though organs were opening out and drawing to again, while a warmth-giving stream pours in and out of them, and air and water substances are conveyed inwards and outwards. And since the human being has already at this stage an astral body of his own, both breathing and nutrition are accompanied by inner feelings. A kind of pleasure is experienced when substances that are helpful for building the human being, are absorbed; discomfort is felt when harmful substances flow in, or even when they only come too near.

Now as the breathing process was during Moon evolution nearly related to that of nutrition, so was the process of ideation — the forming of mental images — to the reproduction process. The things and beings in Moon man's environment exercised no immediate effect on any human senses. Man's mental life was rather of the following character. In his dim twilight consciousness, pictures were called up by the presence of these things and beings; and the pictures were far more intimately related to the real inner nature of the environment than are our sense-perceptions, which reveal — in colours, sounds, smells, etc. — merely its outer aspect. To gain a better idea of Moon man's consciousness we should imagine him steeped in the vapour-like environment above described. Manifold processes are taking place within it. Substances are combining, substances are separating; some parts grow more condensed, others thin out, become more tenuous. All this goes on in such a way that though the human beings do not directly see or hear it, it calls forth pictures in their consciousness. These may be likened to the pictures of our dream-consciousness to-day. Let us say, an object falls to the floor. The sleeper does not perceive the real process, but instead some arbitrary picture — for example, he thinks a shot is being fired. The pictures of Moon consciousness, however, unlike our dream-pictures, are not arbitrary. Though they are not copies but symbols only of outer processes, nevertheless they correspond to them. For a particular outer process one picture will arise and no other. Moon man is thus in a position to order his conduct according to the pictures, just as to-day man orders his conduct according to his perceptions. Only, observe the difference: conduct based on our perceptions is subject to free

147

choice, whereas action under the influence of these pictures takes place as though impelled by a deep inner urge.

We must not however imagine that in this picture-consciousness we have no more than a symbolization of outer physical processes. Through the pictures, the spiritual Beings holding sway behind the physical facts — these spiritual Beings and their activities are also presented to consciousness. Thus in the creatures of the animal-like kingdom the Spirits of Personality are as it were made visible, while the Fire Spirits appear behind and within the mineral-plant beings. Other beings too appear, whom man can conceive without connection with anything physical; he beholds them rather as ethereal and soul-like forces. These are the Sons of Life.

The mental pictures of Moon consciousness being not copies but symbols of the outer things, their influence on the inner life of the human being was on this very account all the greater; it was far greater than that of the mental pictures man has to-day, that are communicated by external perception. The pictures of Moon consciousness were capable of arousing his whole inner life to movement and action. The inner processes took shape to accord with them, they were formative forces in the true sense of the word. The human being became even as they formed him. He became, so to speak, the image of his own processes in consciousness.

But now the farther evolution goes on in this way, the more does it entail a deeply incisive change for the human being. The power proceeding from the pictures in consciousness grows gradually less and less able to extend over his whole bodily nature. The latter separates into two parts, into two natures. Some members are subject in their formation to the formative plastic influences of the picture-consciousness, and become to a large extent an image of the mental life in the way that has been indicated; but there are other organs that withdraw themselves from this influence. In part of his being, man is as it were too dense — determined too much by other laws — for him to follow the pictures he has in his consciousness. These organs withdraw from his influence. But they come under another; they come under the influence of the sublime Sun Beings themselves. This stage in evolution is however seen to be preceded by

148

an interval of rest, wherein the Sun Spirits gather up their forces, in order to work upon the beings of the Moon under these quite new conditions.

After the interval of rest, the human being is seen to be divided into two natures. One is withdrawn from the independent working of his picture-consciousness. It takes on a more definite shape and comes under the influence of forces which, though they proceed from the body of the Moon, can only arise there through the influence of the Sun Beings. This portion of man's being partakes increasingly in the life that is kindled by the Sun. The other rises out of this one, like a kind of head. It is mobile and pliable, shaping itself so as to express and sustain the dream-like consciousness in which man lives. The two portions are however intimately bound up with one another. They send each other their respective fluids, and the members of each extend into the other.

While all this has been taking place, a relationship of Sun and Moon has arisen, which accords with the trend of this evolution. A significant harmony is thereby brought about.

It has already been shown how the spiritual Beings, as they go forward through the stages of their evolution, detach from the great cosmic mass various heavenly bodies, to be their dwelling-places. It is the Beings who radiate the forces by which the cosmic substances are organized and differentiated. The separation of Sun and Moon was thus a necessary event, to lead up to the provision of proper dwelling-places for the several spiritual Beings. But this determination of substance and of its forces by the Spirit goes still farther. For it is the spiritual Beings who give rise to certain movements of the heavenly bodies, revolutions one about another, with the result that the heavenly bodies change their relative positions; and every change in the relative position of one heavenly body to another means a change in the mutual influences of the Beings.

This is what happened with regard to Sun and Moon. A movement of the Moon about the Sun is induced, which at certain times brings the human beings more into the sphere of the Sun's influence, while at other, alternating times they are enabled to turn away from it and so be thrown more upon their own resources. The movement is an outcome of the above-mentioned 'fall' of certain beings of the Moon, and of the balance established in settlement of the conflict which ensued. It is simply the physical expression for the spiritual relationship of forces that was engendered by the 'fall'. Through the one heavenly body moving around the other, there arise in the Beings who inhabit them such alternating states of consciousness as were described above. It can indeed be said that the Moon alternately turns her life towards the Sun and away from it. There is a Sun time and a planetary time. During the latter the Moon Beings grow and evolve on a side of the Moon which is turned away from the Sun. It must however be added that something else comes into play on the Moon, beside this motion of the heavenly bodies. Supersensible consciousness, as it looks back, can see the Moon Beings themselves migrating round their planet at regular intervals of time. Sometimes they seek the regions where they can give themselves up to the Sun's influence, at other times they journey to regions where they are not subject to it — where they can, as it were, muse upon their own life and being.

To complete the picture, it is moreover to be observed that in this epoch the Sons of Life attain their human stage. We have seen how the first beginnings of the human senses came into being upon Saturn. Even now on Moon, man cannot yet use these senses for his own perception of external objects; at this stage, however, they can become instruments for the Sons of Life. The Sons of Life use them in order through them to have perception. Thus these senses, that belong to the physical body of man, enter into mutual relation with the Sons of Life. For the Sons of Life do not merely make use of them; they also work upon them and perfect them.

Through these alternating relations to the Sun, recurring changes arise, as we have seen, in the life-conditions of man himself. It happens in the following way. Each time that he is subjected to the influence of the Sun, man devotes himself to the Sun life and its manifestations rather than to himself. At such times he feels the greatness and majesty of the Universe as expressed in the shining of the Sun. He inhales, as it were, sublime and cosmic greatness. It is then that the lofty Beings, who have their dwelling on the Sun, are exerting their influence upon the Moon. And the Moon, in turn, is working — not upon the whole human being, but chiefly upon those parts of him which have withdrawn from the influence of the pictures he has in his consciousness. The physical body and the life-body especially attain at these times a certain magnitude and a certain perfection of form. In the manifestations of consciousness, on the other hand, there is a decline. But when the life of the human being is turned away from the Sun, he occupies himself more with his own nature. Then inner life and mobility begin in the astral body, while the outer figure grows less comely, less perfect in formation.

There are therefore during Moon evolution two alternating states of consciousness, quite distinct from one another. The one during the Sun period is more dim; the other — in the epoch when life is thrown more on its own resources — is clearer. The former condition, while it is dimmer, is at the same time more selfless, for man then lives more in devotion to the outer world — to the Universe as reflected in the Sun. This alternation in states of consciousness may be compared, in the man of the present day, both to the alternation of sleeping and waking, and also to that of life between birth and death on the one hand and, on the other, the more spiritual existence between death and a new birth. Man's awakening on Moon, when the Sun time draws to a close, might thus be described as something intermediate between the awakening of present-day man each morning, and his birth. So too the gradual dimming of consciousness as the Sun time approaches is like an intermediate state between our dying and our falling asleep; for it must not be supposed that on Old Moon there was as yet a consciousness of birth and death such as man has to-day. In the Sun time the human being abandoned himself to the enjoyment of a kind of Sun-life. He was lifted away from his own life and lived more spiritually. We can do no more than attempt an approximate and comparative description of what he then experienced. He felt as if the very forces of the

Universe, as if all their influences were streaming in upon him, throbbing through his being. He felt intoxicated by the cosmic harmonies in which his life participated. At such times his astral body was in a way freed from the physical, and with it part of the life-body too was drawn away; and this entity of astral body and life-body was like a delicate and wonderful musical instrument, upon the chords of which the cosmic Mysteries resounded. And the members of that part of man on which his consciousness had little influence were then shaped and moulded in accordance with the harmonies of the Universe. For in these harmonies the Beings of the Sun were working. This part of man was thus in very truth shaped and formed by the tones of spiritual, cosmic sound.

The transition from the brighter state of consciousness to the duller one was not so marked as is the transition from the waking condition to the dreamless sleep of man to-day. The picture-consciousness was not, indeed, as bright as waking consciousness to-day, neither was the other state of consciousness as dull as our dreamless sleep. Man had a certain apprehension, though a dim one, of the playing of the cosmic harmonies in his physical body and in that part of his etheric body which had remained united with the physical. And when the Sun was, as it were, no longer shining for him, the mental pictures came into his consciousness in place of the cosmic harmonies. Life was then kindled more in those members of the physical and etheric bodies which were subject to the direct influence of his own consciousness, while the other parts of man — the formative, creative forces no longer working on them from the Sun — went through a kind of withering and hardening process. And as the Sun time drew near once more, the old bodies fell away. They detached themselves from the human being, and out of his old bodily nature, as though out of a grave, man came forth once more — new-formed within, though crude as yet in outer shape and stature. The life-process in him had undergone renewal. After this, the new-born body — under the influence of the Sun Beings with their cosmic harmonies — grew and unfolded to its perfect state once more, and then the whole process was repeated.

Man felt this renewal like the putting-on of a fresh garment. He had not, with the kernel of his being, gone through an actual birth or death. He had but passed from a spiritual consciousness of cosmic Sound — when he was in a state of devotion to the outer Universe — to a consciousness that was directed upon his own inner being. He had cast his skin. The old body having grown unfit for use had been laid aside — and renewed.

Herewith we have also indicated more precisely what was characterized above as a kind of reproduction that was closely related to the life of ideation — the forming of mental images. In respect of certain parts of the physical and etheric body it is true to say that the human being brought forth his kind. But this does not mean that we have then a daughter-being fully distinct from the parent-being. The kernel of the latter passes over to the former, thus bringing forth — not a new being — but itself in a new shape.

Such then is the alternation in consciousness that Moon man experiences. When the Sun time draws near, his mental pictures grow fainter and fainter, a sense of blissful devotion fills him, and in the peace and silence of his inner being the universal harmonies resound. Towards the end of this period the pictures in the astral body become alive again; man begins to be increasingly aware of himself. He feels as though he were awakening from the blissful rest in which he has been immersed during the Sun time. Another significant experience meets him here. With the renewed lighting-up of the pictures in consciousness, the human being sees himself enshrouded as it were within a cloud, which has descended on him like a Being from the great Universe. This Being, he feels, belongs to him, is a kind of completion of his own nature. He it is, he feels, that grants him his existence, that grants him his I. The Being is one of the Sons of Life. Man's feeling towards him can be expressed somewhat as follows — 'In him I lived, even in the Sun time when I was given up to the sublime glory of the Universal All. Only, then he was not visible to me; now he is becoming visible.' And it is this Son of Life from whom the force proceeds that enables man to work upon his own bodily

153

nature during the Sun-less time. Then, when the Sun time draws near once more, man feels as though he himself were becoming one with the Son of Life. Even then he does not see him, but he feels deeply and inwardly united with him.

The relation of the human beings to the Sons of Life was not such that each single human being had his Son of Life to himself, but a whole group would feel that a Son of Life belonged to it as a group. Men lived, on Moon, separated in this way into groups, and each group felt its common 'group-Ego' in a Son of Life. The difference between the groups made itself felt notably in the etheric body, which had a special form in each group. Since however the physical body takes its form from the etheric, the differences in the latter were impressed upon the former, and the several groups may be regarded as so many human species. When the Sons of Life looked down upon the human groups belonging to them, they saw themselves manifolded, as it were, in so many single human beings. And that gave them the feeling of their own Ego-hood. They saw the reflection of themselves in the human beings. Herein too lay the function of the human senses at that time. We have already seen that the senses did not yet transmit any perceptions of external objects, but at this stage they reflected the being of the Sons of Life. What the Sons of Life perceived through this reflection, gave them their 'I' consciousness. And what was kindled in man's astral body by the same reflection — was none other than the picture-content of his dim Moon consciousness. The effect of this activity of man in mutual interaction with the Sons of Life finds expression in the physical body in the beginnings of the nervous system. The nerves make their appearance there like prolongations of the senses into the inward parts of the body.

From all this a clear picture emerges of how the three kinds of Spirits — the Spirits of Personality, the Fire Spirits and the Sons of Life — worked upon Moon man. Fixing our attention on the main period — the middle epoch — of Moon evolution, we may say: The Spirits of Personality implant independence, the character of personality, in the human astral body. It is due to this that man is able, in the times when — so to speak —

the Sun is not shining for him, to turn in upon himself and labour at his own formation. The Fire Spirits are at work in the etheric body, in so far as the same independent character becomes impressed upon it too. It is owing to their influence that after each renewal of his body man feels himself still the same being. This is because the etheric body is endowed by them with a kind of memory. The Sons of Life work on the physical body. They make it possible for the physical body to become an expression of the new independent astral body — to become, as it were, a physiognomical image of it. On the other hand, higher spiritual Beings are also working into the physical and etheric bodies in so far as in the Sun periods these bodies grow and develop apart from the independent astral body. This applies especially to the Spirits of Form and the Spirits of Movement. Their intervention takes place from the Sun, as has been described.

Amid all these various influences, the human being matures to the point where he begins to develop within him the seed of Spirit-Self, just as the seed of Spirit-Man arose in the second half of Saturn evolution and the seed of Life-Spirit on Sun. And now all the conditions on Moon undergo change. Through the successive metamorphoses and renewals the human beings have been growing ever nobler, purer and finer in their nature; at the same time they have also gained in strength. Hence they are able increasingly to preserve the picture-consciousness even on into the Sun periods, with the result that this consciousness gains influence on the formation of the physical and the etheric bodies, which formerly was effected through the working of the Sun Beings alone. All that happens upon Moon through the agency of the human beings and the Spirits connected with them, comes more and more to resemble what was formerly brought about by the Sun and the higher Beings that belong to it. In consequence of this, the Sun Beings are able to apply their forces more and more to their own evolution. The Moon too grew ready after a time to be united again with the Sun.

Spiritually regarded, these processes reveal themselves as follows. Little by little, the 'fallen' Moon Beings have been overcome by the Sun Beings and must henceforth come into line with them. The deeds of the Moon Beings must become part and parcel of the deeds of the Sun Beings, to whom they are now subordinate. This change requires long epochs of time, during which the Moon periods grow ever shorter and shorter and the Sun periods longer and longer. And then there comes once more a period of evolution during which Sun and Moon form a single cosmic entity. The physical human body has now become entirely ethereal. When this is said, it must not however be imagined that under such conditions there is no physical body. That which has been evolved as physical body during the times of Saturn, Sun and Moon, remains as such. The fact is, we must not limit our recognition of the physical to where it manifests in an outwardly physical form. The physical can also exist in such a way as to present outwardly the form of the etheric, nay even of the astral. We must distinguish here between outward appearance and inner law and principle. A physical can become ethereal and astral, while still retaining the physical laws in its inner nature. And this is what happens when on the Moon the physical body of man has reached a certain stage in its perfection. It becomes ethereal in form. But when the supersensible consciousness that can perceive such things, turns its attention to this body, then, although ethereal in form, it shows itself to be imbued with the laws, not of the etheric but of the physical. In effect, the physical has then been received into the etheric, to rest in it as in a mother's womb and to be nurtured there. Afterwards it will emerge in a physical form once more, but on a higher level. If the human beings of Moon had had to maintain their physical bodies in gross physical form, the Moon could never have been reunited with the Sun. By assuming etheric form, the physical body becomes more akin to the etheric body, and is thus able to be imbued again more intimately with those portions of the etheric and astral bodies which had to be withdrawn from it in the Sun-time epochs of Moon evolution. Man, having appeared like a twofold being during the severance of Sun and Moon, now grows once more into a single whole. The physical takes on more of the quality of soul; and

156

the soul-life is at the same time more bound up with the physical.

Upon this human being, single and coherent, the Spirits of the Sun into whose realm he has now entered can work quite differently than they could before, when they were sending their influences to the Moon from without. Man is now living in an environment that is more of the soul and spirit. This enables the Spirits of Wisdom to come in with an activity of deep significance. They imbue man with Wisdom — ensoul him with Wisdom. Thereby he becomes in a sense an independent soul. Then to their influence is added that of the Spirits of Movement, who work above all upon the astral body. Under the influence of these high Beings, the astral body develops within it quickness of soul and a Wisdom-filled life-body. This Wisdom-filled etheric body is the germ of what was described in an earlier chapter — in respect of the man of present time — as intellectual soul, while the astral body, animated as it now is by the Spirits of Movement, is the seed and beginning of the sentient soul. And since all this is brought about in the human being at a time when his independence is enhanced, these beginnings of intellectual soul and sentient soul appear as the expression of the Spirit-Self. We must not make the mistake of imagining the Spirit-Self to be, in this period of evolution, a separate entity beside the intellectual and the sentient souls. The latter are only the expression of the Spirit-Self, which in its turn signifies their higher union and harmony.

The intervention of the Spirits of Wisdom in this epoch is of peculiar significance. For they intervene not only for the human beings but for the other kingdoms too, which have developed upon Moon. When Sun and Moon are joined again, these lower kingdoms are also drawn into the realm of the Sun. All that was physical in them is etherealised. So now there are in the Sun not only human beings, but also mineral-plants and plant-animals. These other beings still maintain however their own nature, their own laws of being. Consequently they feel themselves strangers in their new surroundings. For they emerge there with a nature which is scarcely in accord with their environment. Since, however, they are etherealised, they too are accessible to the influence of the Spirits of Wisdom. Indeed, all that has come over from Moon into Sun is now permeated with the forces of these Spirits. That which the Sun-Moon entity has become during this time in evolution may accordingly be called 'Cosmos of Wisdom'.

When after an interval of rest the system of our Earth emerges as the successor to this Cosmos of Wisdom, and the created beings that have come over from Moon as seeds come alive again on Earth, then all these beings reveal themselves as filled and permeated with Wisdom. And now we see how it is that Earth man, as he contemplates the things around him, is able to discover Wisdom in their very nature. We can admire the Wisdom in every leaf, in every bone of animal or man, or again in the marvellous construction of the brain and the heart. If man needs Wisdom to understand the things — if, that is, he can examine them and draw forth Wisdom from them — it proves that Wisdom is inherent in them. Try as he will to understand the things of the Earth with Wisdom-filled ideas, man could extract no Wisdom from them if Wisdom had not first been implanted in them. Anyone who would presume to grasp by Wisdom things of which he thinks that they have not first received that Wisdom, may just as well suppose that he can draw water from a glass into which water has not first been poured. Earth — as will be shown later — is Old Moon reborn. And it manifests as a creation filled with Wisdom, because in the epoch here described the Spirits of Wisdom imbued it with their forces.

It will readily be understood that in the above account of Moon conditions it has only been possible to depict a few transient forms of this whole stage of evolution. Out of the whole course of events we have had to lay hold, as it were, on certain elements, singling them out for description. One might feel dissatisfied with a method of exposition that can give no more than isolated pictures, and regret that Moon evolution had not been brought into a nexus of well defined concepts. If objection is taken on this ground, all one can say is that these descriptions have purposely been given in concepts less sharp and definite. For the intention here is not so much to provide speculative concepts and built-up schemes of thought, but a mental picture of what can actually appear before the spiritual eye when supersensible vision is directed to the facts. And for Moon evolution this has far less of sharp and clear-cut outline than have our perceptions on Earth. In the Moon epoch we have to do much more with changing, varying impressions, with fleeting, mobile pictures and their transitions from one to another. It must moreover be borne in mind that we are considering an evolution that continues through long, long ages, and in any description of it we can after all do no more than hold fast momentary pictures here and there.

The culminating point of the Moon epoch is reached at the moment when the human being, through the astral body which has been implanted in him, has advanced so far in evolution that his physical body gives to the Sons of Life the means to attain their human stage. For at this point the human being has also attained all that the Moon epoch can give him for himself, for his own inner being, on his forward path. The ensuing time — the second half of Moon evolution — may therefore be described as a waning period. Yet in this time, as we have seen, something of great importance is nevertheless achieved, both for man's environment and also for man himself. Wisdom is implanted into the heavenly body of Sun-Moon. Moreover it is in this declining period that the seeds are sown of the intellectual and the sentient souls. Their unfoldment, however, and that of the spiritual soul — and withal, the birth of the I in free self-consciousness — does not take place until the Earth. At the Moon stage the intellectual and sentient souls do not by any means appear as though the human being were already expressing *himself* through them; rather do they seem like instruments for the Sons of Life who are associated with Man's being. If one wanted to describe how man felt in this respect on Old Moon, one would have to express his consciousness in some such words as these — 'In me and through me lives the Son of Life. Through me he beholds the Lunar environment, the Moon; in me he thinks upon the things and beings that Moon contains.' Moon man, in fact, feels himself overshadowed by the Son of Life. He feels himself as the tool or instrument of this higher Being. During the severance of Sun and Moon, in the times when he is turned away from the Sun, he feels, it is true, more independent; he also feels as though the I belonging to him — which in the Sun times vanished from his picture-consciousness — were now becoming visible. This alternation in consciousness — for so we may describe it — gives the human being on Moon the feeling: 'In the Sun time my Ego soars away with me to higher realms, to Beings lofty and sublime; then it descends with me, when the Sun vanishes, into deeper worlds.'

Moon evolution proper was preceded by a preparatory stage; a kind of repetition of Saturn and Sun evolutions took place. And now, in this declining period, after the reunion of Sun and Moon, we can similarly distinguish two epochs, during which there were to some extent even physical condensations. So do physical and soul-spiritual conditions of the Sun-Moon body alternate with one another. In the physical epochs the human being, and also the beings of the lower kingdoms, appear as though foreshadowing, in 'set' forms that are without independence, what they will afterwards become in a more independent way during the Earth time.

Thus we have two preparatory epochs of Moon evolution and again two epochs in the declining time. Such epochs may be called 'cycles' or 'rounds'. In the intervening time, after the two preparatory epochs but before the epochs of decline — in the time, that is to say, when Moon and Sun are severed — we shall be able to recognize three distinct epochs. The middle one is the time when the Sons of Life reach their human stage. It is preceded by an epoch when the conditions are all leading up to this central event, and it is followed by another, wherein the Sons of Life enter more fully into the new creations and carry their development further. These three epochs when taken together with the two of preparation and the two of decline, make seven rounds in all. Moon evolution as a whole may therefore be said to take its course in seven rounds. Between the rounds are intervals of rest, such as we have already had frequent occasion to describe. But if we want to have a true picture of what happens, we must not imagine an abrupt transition from activity to interval of rest. The Sun Beings, for example, gradually withdraw from their activities on the Moon. A time begins for them which, seen from without, appears as their interval of rest, while on the Moon itself, quick, independent activity continues. In this way the period of activity for one kind of Being will often extend into the period of rest for another. Taking this into account, we may speak of a rhythmic waxing and waning of forces in cyclic epochs. Nay more, a similar division is also recognizable within each of the seven Moon cycles above indicated. The whole of Moon evolution may be described as one great — or planetary — cycle; the seven divisions within it as small cycles, and their sub-divisions as still smaller ones. This seven times sevenfold division can be observed also in Sun evolution, and even in the Saturn epoch there is a suggestion of it. It should however be borne in mind that the dividing lines are to some extent obliterated in the Sun epoch and still more so in Saturn. They grow increasingly distinct, the farther evolution proceeds towards the Earth epoch.

* * * * *

At the close of the Moon evolution that has been described in outline in the foregoing pages, all the forces and Beings connected with it pass into a more spiritual form of existence, that is on an entirely different level both from the form of existence during the Moon period and also from that during the Earth evolution which follows. A being with faculties sufficiently highly developed to be able to perceive all the details of Moon and Earth evolutions, will not necessarily be able to see what takes place in the interval between the two. For him, the Beings and forces would, at the close of the Moon period, vanish as it were into the void, and then after a lapse of time emerge again from the dim twilight of the cosmic womb. Only a being with far higher faculties could trace the spiritual events that are enacted in the intervening time.

When the interval is over, the Beings who took part in the evolutionary processes on Saturn, Sun and Moon reappear, endowed with new faculties. By their former deeds, the Beings who stand above man have attained the power to bring his evolution so far forward that in the Earth epoch which follows on the Moon he will be able to develop a new mode of consciousness, that stands at a stage higher than the picture-consciousness he had in the Moon epoch. But man must first be prepared to receive this new gift. During the Saturn, Sun and Moon evolutions he has incorporated into his being the physical body, the etheric body and the astral body. But these members received only those faculties and forces which enabled them to live for a picture-consciousness. The organs, and also the whole form and figure which would enable them to perceive a world of external objects are lacking. Just as a new plant will unfold no more than is contained, as potentiality, in the seed that comes from the old one, so too, at the beginning of the new stage in evolution, the three members of man's nature emerge with forms and organs such as allow of the development only of a picture-consciousness. For the unfolding of a higher stage in consciousness they will have first to be prepared.

The preparation takes place in three stages. During the first, the physical body is lifted to a height of development such as enables it to undergo the necessary change into a form and figure which can provide the basis for objective consciousness. This preliminary stage of Earth evolution may be described as a repetition of the Saturn period on a higher level. For in this period, as in the Saturn time, higher Beings are working upon the physical body alone. When the evolution of this physical body is far enough advanced, all the Beings have to pass once more into a higher form of existence, before the life-body can advance in its turn. The physical body has, as it were, to be re-cast, in order to be able to receive, when it unfolds again, the more highly evolved life-body. After this interval devoted to a higher form of existence, there follows a kind of recapitulation of Sun evolution on a higher level, for the further development of the life-body. And then — after a further interval — the like is done, in a recapitulation of Moon evolution, for the astral body.

Let our attention now be turned to the events of evolution after the close of the third of these repetitions. All the Beings and forces have become spiritualized once more, rising during the process of spiritualization into far higher worlds. The lowest of the worlds where something of them is still to be perceived is the very world where man now sojourns between death and new birth — the several regions, namely, of Spirit-land. Thereafter the Beings gradually descend once more into lower worlds. Before the physical evolution of the Earth begins, they have come down so far that their lowest manifestations can be beheld in the astral or soul-world.

All that exists of man during this period is still in astral form. For a right understanding of this stage in his develop-ment it is important to realize that although man has in him physical body, life-body and astral body, the physical body is not yet present in a physical form. What makes the physical body physical at this stage is not physical form but the fact that while possessing astral form it bears within it physical laws. It is an entity with physical laws and principles in a form that is of the nature of soul — and the like holds good of the life-body.

To the eye of the spirit the Earth at this stage in its evolution appears at first as a world-entity which is all soul and spirit — that is to say, in which even the physical and living forces show a soul-like form. In this world-entity is potentially contained all that is destined subsequently to metamorphose into the, crea-tures of the physical Earth. It radiates light; but the light is not yet such as physical eyes could have perceived — even if they had existed then. It shines only for the opened eyes of the seer, shines for him in the light that is of the soul.

Within this soul-entity there now takes place what may be described as a condensation, with the result that after a time in the very midst of the soul-entity a form of fire makes its appear-ance, even such a fiery form as Saturn was in its densest state. This form is woven-through with the influences of the various Beings who are partaking in the evolution. Like a surging forth and a diving down into the fiery sphere of the Earth — such is the interplay we can observe between the Beings and the heavenly body. We are not therefore to think of this fiery sphere of the Earth as being of the same substance throughout. Rather is it like an organism that is permeated with soul and spirit. As to those beings who are destined to become on Earth human beings in their present form, they can take very little share in this diving down into the fire-body. They are still in a condition that obliges them to remain almost entirely in the uncondensed surrounding sphere, where they are within the womb of higher spiritual Beings. At this stage they touch the fire-Earth with a single point only of their soul-form, with the result that the warmth condenses a portion of their astral form. Thereby Earth life is kindled in them. For the most part, their being still belongs to worlds of soul and spirit; only through this contact with the earthly fire does warmth of life begin to play around them. If therefore we would make us a picture — at once sensible and supersensible — of man at this beginning of the physical Earth, we must conceive a soul-form of egglike shape, contained in the encircling sphere of Earth, and surrounded at its lower surface in the way an acorn is by a cup; only, the substance of this 'cup' consists entirely of warmth or fire. Now as a consequence of this envelopment by warmth, not only is life kindled in the human being, but at the same time a change takes place in his astral body. Into it is implanted the first beginning of that which afterwards becomes the sentient soul. We may say therefore that, at this stage, man consists of sentient soul, astral body, life-body, and of a physical body that is woven of fire. In the astral body are surging up and down the spiritual Beings who partake in his existence. Through the sentient soul man feels himself bound to the Earth. He has in this time a predominating picture-consciousness where the spiritual Beings in whose womb he lies reveal themselves; and only like a point within this consciousness is the sensation man has of the body that belongs to him. It is as though he were looking down from the spiritual world upon an earthly possession, of which he feels: 'That is thine.'

Stage by stage the condensation of the Earth continues, and the above-described differentiation in man grows gradually more distinct. Then comes a moment in evolution when the

Earth is so far condensed that only a part of it remains fiery, while another part has assumed a form of substance that may be described as 'gas' or 'air'. With man too a change is brought about. Henceforth not only is he touched by the warmth of Earth, but air-substance too begins to be imparted to his fire-body. And as the warmth kindled the life in him, so does the air as it plays around him evoke within him what can be described as — spiritual — sound. His life-body rings forth with sound. Simultaneously, a portion of his astral body becomes separated out as the first germinal beginning of the intellectual soul that emerges later.

To envisage what is going on at this time in the soul of man, we must remember that the higher Beings are continuously surging up and down in the air-and-fire body of the Earth. In the fire-Earth it is, to begin with, the Spirits of Personality that are of importance for man. And while he is being called to life by the Earth-warmth, his sentient soul says to itself: 'These are the Spirits of Personality.' In the air too, higher Beings are in like manner making themselves known. They are the ones we have already named, following Christian esoteric usage, the Archangels; and it is their influence that man feels as inward sound when the air is wafted round him. Then does his intellectual soul say to itself: 'These are the Archangels.' For what man perceives at this stage through his connection with the Earth does not yet consist of so many physical objects. He lives in the sensations of warmth that rise up to him, and in sounds; and within these streams of warmth and surging waves of sound he feels the presence of the Spirits of Personality and the Archangels. He cannot yet perceive these Beings directly, only through the veils, as it were, of warmth and sound. While the perceptions of warmth and sound are penetrating into his soul, pictures of the higher Beings in whose sheltering care he feels himself to be, are continually rising and falling within him.

And now evolution continues, its progress finding expression once again in a further condensation. Watery substance is incorporated into the Earth-body, which consists now of three members: the fiery, the airy and the watery. But before this, an important event takes place. Out of the fire-air Earth an independent heavenly body splits off, which will in its further course become the present Sun. Hitherto Earth and Sun have been a single body. After the severance of the Sun, Earth still contains within it, to begin with, all that is in and on our present Moon. The separation of the Sun takes place because higher Beings — for their own evolution and for that which they have yet to do for the Earth — can no longer endure the matter which is now condensed as far as water. Out of the whole Earth-mass they separate the substances which alone are suited to their use, and take their departure to make themselves a new dwelling-place in the Sun. Henceforth they work on to the Earth from without, from the Sun. Man, on the other hand, needs for his further evolution a scene of action where matter will condense still more.

Hand in hand with the incorporation of watery substance into the Earth-body, once again a change is wrought in man himself. Henceforth not only does the fire pour into him, and the air play around him, but watery substance too is incorporated into his physical body. Simultaneously his etheric part undergoes a change; he now begins to perceive it as a delicate body-of-light. Formerly, man felt streams of warmth rise upward to him from the Earth, while tones made him conscious of air being wafted towards him; now, his body is penetrated also by the watery element, whose inpouring and outpouring he beholds as waxing and waning light. Moreover, in his soul too a change has taken place. To the first beginning of sentient and then of intellectual soul, that of the spiritual soul has been added. In the element of water work the Angels; they are the real kindlers of light. For man it is as though they were appearing to him in light.

Certain higher Beings who were formerly in the Earth-body itself now act upon it from the Sun. In consequence of this, all influences that are at work on the Earth are changed. Man, fettered to the Earth, would no longer have been able to feel within him the influences of the Sun Beings, were his soul turned perpetually towards the Earth from which his physical body is derived. Henceforth he is brought into alternating states of consciousness. At certain times the Sun Beings tear his soul away from the physical body; so that he is now alternately in the lap of the Sun Beings in a pure life of soul, and then again in a condition where, united with the body, he receives the influences of the Earth. When he is in the physical body, the streams of warmth flow up towards him, the airy masses resound around him, the waters pour in and out of him. When he is outside the body, the pictures of the higher Beings, in whose womb he is, go surging through his soul.

Earth at this stage of evolution lives through two alternating times. At one time it can play around the human souls with its substances and enwrap them with bodies; at another, the human souls have withdrawn from it and only the bodies are left. Earth with its human beings is then in a state of sleep. It is by no means out of keeping with the facts to say that in those pristine ages the Earth underwent a day-time and a night-time. (In terms of physical space this can be expressed as follows. Through the mutual influence of the Beings of Sun and Earth, the Earth comes into movement in relation to the Sun, and in this way the alternation of the above-described periods of night and day is brought about. It is day when the surface of the Earth where man is evolving is turned towards the Sun; when it is turned away it is night — that is, the time during which man's life is entirely a life of soul. But we must not imagine that the movement of the Earth around the Sun in that primeval age was like the movement it describes to-day. Conditions were altogether different. Nevertheless, it is good already at this point to begin to sense that the movements of the heavenly bodies come about as a consequence of the relation the spiritual Beings who inhabit them have to one another. Spiritual causes bring the heavenly bodies into such relative movements and positions as enable the spiritual conditions to work themselves out in the physical.)

Turning our gaze upon it during its nocturnal time, the body of the Earth would look to us like a corpse. For it is largely composed of the disintegrating bodies of human beings whose souls are in another form of existence. The watery and aeriform organic structures of which the human bodies consist disintegrate in the night and are dissolved in the remaining mass of the Earth. That part alone of the human body which was formed from the very beginning of Earth evolution by the interaction of fire with the human soul, and which then in course of time grew ever denser and denser — that part alone remains, but quite inconspicuous, like a seed. It will easily be seen that we must not imagine the 'periods of day and night' here described as bearing very much resemblance to what these terms denote for the present Earth. When at the beginning of the day-time the Earth again comes under the immediate influence of the Sun, the human souls press forward into the region of physical life. Touching the seeds, they cause these to sprout and grow into an outer form which looks like an image of the human being such as he is in his soul-nature. Something not unlike a tender act of fertilization takes place here between man's soul and the seed-like body. Then do the souls thus incarnated begin once more to draw to themselves the air- and water-masses and incorporate them into their bodies. The differentiated body expels and inhales the air — a first beginning of the later breathing process. The water too is absorbed and expelled; nutriment in a primeval form begins. These processes, however, are not yet perceived as outward happenings. Only in the case of the above-described 'fertilization' do we find the soul engaged in a kind of external perception. As it touches the seed which the Earth is holding out towards it, the soul is dimly aware of awakening to physical existence. What it then perceives may be conveyed approximately in the words: 'That is my form.' This feeling — we might also describe it as a dawning sensation of I — remains with the soul throughout the time of its union with the physical body. The absorption of the air on the other hand is still experienced in an entirely spiritual way. It appears in the form of sound-pictures surging and dying away, which 'form' the seed that is undergoing differentiation. Surrounded on all hands by surging waves of sound, the soul feels how it is forming and shaping its own body according to the forces of these sound-tones. At this stage in evolution, human forms and figures begin to take shape, the like of which cannot be observed by present-day consciousness in any outer world. They evolve like plant- and flower-forms of the most delicate texture; being inwardly mobile they give rather the appearance of waving, fluttering flowers. During his time on Earth, man lives through a blissful feeling of being fashioned into such forms as these. The absorption of the watery parts of the Earth is felt in the soul as an access of force, as an inner strengthening. Outwardly it appears in the physical entity of man as growth. As the direct working of the Sun declines, the human soul loses the power to control these processes. Little by little, they are cast aside. Only those parts remain, which bring about the maturing of what we described as the seed. Man himself deserts his body and returns into the spiritual form of existence. (Not all the parts of the Earth are used up in the construction of the human bodies. We must not imagine that the Earth in its nocturnal time consists entirely of disintegrating corpses and seeds which await their re-awakening. These are embedded in other forms, fashioned out of the substance of Earth, the nature of which will be revealed later.)

And now the condensation-process goes still further. To the watery element is added the solid — we may call it the element of 'earth'. Man too begins during his Earth time to incorporate the earth-element into his body. And then it immediately becomes evident that the forces which his soul brings with it from the body-free condition no longer have the same power as heretofore. Formerly the soul fashioned its body from the fiery, airy and watery elements, according to the tones that rang out from them and the pictures of light that they set playing all around. Now that the form is solidified, the soul can no longer do this. Other powers enter into the forming process. That which remains behind when the soul departs from the body is no longer merely like a seed, to be kindled to life by the returning soul. Henceforth it actually contains within itself the quickening power. The soul at its departure leaves not merely its image behind on Earth but, implanted in the image, a portion also of this quickening power. At its re-appearance upon Earth, it is no longer able on its own to awaken the image to life. The calling-to-life must take place within the image itself. Henceforth the spiritual Beings who work on to the Earth from the Sun maintain the quickening force in the human body even when man himself is not upon the Earth. Now therefore the reincarnating soul is aware not only of the sounds and pictures-of-light that surge around, wherein it feels the higher Beings who are immediately above it; in receiving the earth-element the soul experiences the influence of those still higher Beings who have established their scene of action on the Sun.

Formerly, man felt himself belonging to the Beings of soul and spirit with whom he was united when free of the body. His I was still sheltered within their womb. From now on, the I confronted him during physical incarnation, along with all the other things that were around him. Independent images of man's soul and spirit existed henceforth on Earth. Compared to the present human body they were fine and delicate in substance. For only in a very rarefied state did 'earth' enter into their composition — rather as when the man of to-day receives into his organ of smell the finely distributed substances of some outer object. The human bodies were like wraiths, like shadows. Distributed as they were over the whole Earth, they came under different kinds of Earthly influence at different parts of the Earth's surface. While the bodily images, being in accordance with the soul of man that quickened them, were heretofore essentially alike over the whole Earth, diversity began now to appear among the human forms. Thus was the way prepared for what afterwards showed itself in variety of race.

Now that the bodily man had grown more independent, the former intimate union between the Earthly human being and the world of soul and spirit was to some extent dissolved. Henceforth, when the soul left the body, the latter experienced something like a continuation of life.

Had evolution gone on in this way, the Earth would needs have hardened under the influence of its solid element. Supersensible cognition, looking back upon these conditions, sees the human bodies, when their souls depart from them, growing more and more solid. After a time, human souls returning to Earth would no longer have found any suitable material with which to unite. It would all have been used up in filling the Earth with the lignified relics of their incarnations.

At this juncture an event took place which gave to the whole of evolution a new turn. Everything that could conduce to a permanent hardening in the solid substance of the Earth was eliminated. This was the time when our present Moon left the Earth. The influences that contributed to permanence of form and had hitherto worked *directly* from within the Earth, worked henceforth *indirectly* in a weakened manner from the Moon. The higher Beings upon whom this 'forming of form' depends, had resolved to let their influences come no longer from within the Earth but from without. As a result, there now appeared in the human bodily organisms a diversity which may rightly be regarded as the beginning of the separation into male and female. The delicately constituted human forms that previously inhabited the Earth had brought forth the new human form, their descendant, by the interaction within them of two forces — the seed-force and the life-giving, quickening force. These descendants now underwent a change. In one group of them worked more of the seed-force of the soul and spirit; in the other, more of the quickening seed-force. This was due to the fact that with the departure of the Moon from the Earth the earth-element had toned down its power. The working of the two forces one upon the other now became more gentle, more tender than it had been when it took place within a single living body. Consequently the descendant organism too was more tender, more delicate. Entering upon its life on Earth in this tender condition, it only gradually assimilated the more solid parts. Thus, for the human soul returning to Earth, the possibility of union with the body was restored. The soul no longer called the body to life from without, for now the quickening process took place on Earth; but it united with the body and made it grow — although a certain limit was set to the body's growth. Owing to the separation of the Moon the human body became plastic for a while; but the longer it continued to grow on Earth, the more did the hardening forces gain the upper hand, until at length the soul could partake but feebly in its organisation. Thereupon the body fell into decay, while the soul ascended to other — spiritual — modes of life.

Stage by stage, while this configuration of the Earth is proceeding, the forces man has been acquiring during Saturn,
Sun and Moon evolutions, begin gradually to partake in his
further development. First, the astral body — still containing
the life-body and the physical body dissolved within it — is
kindled by the Earthly fire. Then it separates into a finer,
specifically astral part — the sentient soul — and a coarser,
etheric part which will from now on be touched also by the
earth-element. The etheric or life-body, hitherto latent, makes
its appearance. And while in the astral man the intellectual and
the spiritual soul are developing, the coarser parts, receptive to
sound and light, are separated out in the etheric body.

Finally, in the moment when the etheric body condenses
still more, so as to become — from a 'light' body — a fire body,
or body-of-warmth, the stage in evolution is reached when the
solid earth-element begins to be incorporated in the human
being. Having condensed to fire, the etheric body can now
unite — by virtue of the forces of the physical body that have
been implanted in it — with the substances of the physical
Earth which are rarefied to the stage of fire. But it is no longer
able by itself to introduce the airy substances into the body,
which has in the meantime grown more solid. And this is
where the higher Beings come in who dwell on the Sun. They
breathe into man's body the air. Whereas by virtue of his past,
man has within him the power to permeate himself with the
Earth's fire, higher Beings have to guide the breath of air into
his body. Before the hardening took place, the life-body of
man, as the receiver of sound, guided the stream of air and
permeated the physical body with life. Now man's physical
body begins to receive a life that comes from outside. The
consequence is that this life grows independent of the soul part
of man. The soul of man, when withdrawing from Earth,
leaves behind not a mere seed of his form, but a complete
living image of himself. The Spirits of Form remain united
with the image; they carry over to the descendants, when the
soul has left the body, the life which they have bestowed. In
this way what we may call 'heredity' develops. And when the

soul of man appears again on Earth, he feels himself within a body whose life has been transmitted from the ancestors. To such a body he feels especially attracted. Something like a *memory* evolves of the progenitor with whom the soul feels at one. Through the sequence of the descendants this memory continues like a common consciousness. The I flows downward through the generations.

At this stage in his evolution man felt himself an independent being during his time on Earth. He felt the inner fire of his life-body united with the outer fire of the Earth. The warmth, as it flowed through him, he could feel as his own I . Here in these streams of warmth, woven through and through with life, we have the first beginnings of the circulation of the blood. But in the air that streamed into him man did not altogether feel his own being. For in the air the forces of higher Beings were at work. Nevertheless, part of the forces and influences within the air that poured through him still remained his own, namely, that portion which had already become his own through the etheric forces he had formerly developed. Man had, therefore, a portion of the airy currents under his command. Inasmuch as this was so, not alone higher Beings but he himself was working at his formation and configuration. He shaped the airy parts within him in accordance with the pictures in his astral body. While air was streaming into his body from without, to become there the foundation of his breathing life, a portion of the air was differentiated off within him, into an organism inherent in his own nature. This became the basis of the later nervous system. Thus through warmth and air did man at this time have his connection with the surrounding world of the Earth.

On the other hand he was not sensible at all of the assimilation of the solid earth-element. Though this element also played its part at his incarnation, he could not perceive its introduction directly but only in a dimly conscious picture of the higher Beings working in it. Formerly too, man had perceived — but then also in picture form, as a manifestation of Beings far above him — the entry into his body of the fluid element of Earth. Now that his earthly form has become denser, these pictures have undergone a change in his consciousness. The solid element being now mingled with the fluid, the introduction of that too must needs be felt as proceeding from higher Beings, working from without. Man can no longer have the power in his own soul to guide this assimilation, for the body which it has now to serve has been built up from outside. He would indeed spoil its form if he attempted to do so. Thus what he assimilates from without appears to him as guided by edicts proceeding from the higher Beings who work at the formation of his body. Man feels himself as an Ego; he has within him, as a part of his astral body, his intellectual soul, through which he experiences inwardly in pictures what is going on outside him, and with which he permeates his delicate nervous system. He feels himself as a descendant of forefathers, by virtue of the life streaming through the generations. He breathes — and feels his breathing as brought about by the higher Beings who have been described as the Spirits of Form. To these he also feels beholden for all that through their impulses is brought to him from without, as nourishment. Darkest of all to him is his origin as an individual. The nearest he comes to any feeling of it is a sense of having an influence from the Spirits of Form, as they manifest in the forces of the Earth. Man is guided and directed in his relation to the outer world. This comes to expression in that he is conscious of activities of soul and spirit that are going on behind his physical world. He does not perceive the spiritual Beings in their own form, but he experiences sounds and colours and the like within his soul and knows that in this world of ideal images live the deeds of spiritual Beings. What they communicate sounds forth to him; what they reveal appears to him in pictures of light. The most inward feeling Earth man has of himself comes to him through the conceptions he gains of the element of fire or warmth. He can already distinguish his own inner warmth from the streams of warmth in his environment. In the latter the Spirits of Personality reveal themselves. But man has no more than a dim consciousness of what is there behind these outer streams of warmth. He feels in them the influence of the Spirits of Form. When mighty activities of warmth manifest in his environment, then the feeling arises in the soul: 'Now, glowing through this Earth's horizon are the spiritual Beings, a spark of whose fire has detached itself to become the warmth that fills my inner being.'

In the workings of light, man does not yet distinguish in quite the same way an outer and an inner. When pictures of light emerged in his environment, they did not always give rise to the same feeling in the soul of man. There were times when he felt them as coming from outside. This was when he had descended from the body-free condition and entered into incarnation — periods, that is, of his growth on Earth. But as the time drew near, when the seed of the new Earth man was taking shape, the pictures faded and man retained no more than something like inner memories of them. In these pictures of light the deeds of the Fire Spirits (Archangels) were contained. The Fire Spirits appeared to man as ministering spirits of the Warmth-Beings who planted a spark of fire in his inner nature. When these outer manifestations faded, man experienced them as mental images (as memories) within him. He felt united with their forces; and so indeed he was. For by virtue of what he had received from them he was able to work upon the sphere of air that surrounded him. Under his influence it began to ray forth light. That was a time when Nature forces and human forces were not yet separate from one another as they afterwards became. Whatever took place upon Earth proceeded still to a large extent from the forces of human beings. An observer, looking from beyond the Earth upon the events of Nature that were taking place there, would not have seen in these mere outer processes, independent of man; he would have recognized in them the influence also of human beings.

The perceptions of sound took yet another form for Earth man. From the very beginning of his Earthly life, he perceived them as coming from without. And whilst the light-pictures were so perceived only until the middle period of his existence on Earth, external sounds could still be heard even after this middle period. Only towards the end of his life did Earth man become insensitive to these; and then there remained to him still the inner memories of them. The sounds bore within them the manifestations of the Sons of Life (the Angels). When towards the end of his life man felt himself inwardly united with these forces, he could then, by imitating them, call forth mighty activities in the water-element of the Earth. Under his influence arose a surging of the waters — within the Earth and over its surface.

Only in the first quarter of his Earthly life did man have any conscious experience of taste, and even then it appeared to his soul like a memory of experiences in his body-free condition. So long as he had the sense of taste, the solidification of his body by the absorption of outer substances continued. In the second quarter of his Earthly life, though growth might still continue, man's form and figure was already fully developed. At this period, he could only perceive other living beings beside himself through the warmth, light and sound effects that they produced. For he was not yet able to form any conception of the solid element. Of the watery he received only, in the first quarter of his life, the taste effects above mentioned.

A reflection of this inner soul-condition of man could be seen in his external, bodily form. Those parts which contained the beginning of what afterwards became the form of the head, were the most perfectly evolved. The remaining organs appeared only as appendages, and were shadowlike and indistinct. But not all Earth men were alike in form and figure. Some there were in whom, according to the conditions under which they lived, the 'appendages' were more, or less, developed — the variation depending upon their dwelling-place on Earth. Where they became more deeply involved in the Earth world, the appendages appeared more prominent. There were also human beings who at the beginning of the physical development of Earth had, by virtue of their preceding evolution, been the most mature and had accordingly experienced the contact with the fire-element at the very outset, when Earth had not yet condensed to air, and who were now able to develop more perfectly the beginnings of the head. These were, in their inner life, of all human beings the most harmonious. Others had not been ready for contact with the fire-element until the Earth had evolved within it also the air; they were more dependent on external conditions The former kind were clearly aware, through the warmth, of the Spirits of Form, and their feeling of themselves in Earthly life was as though they retained a memory of belonging to the Spirits of Form, of having been united with them in the body-free condition. The others had the memory of the body-free condition only to a lesser degree; they were chiefly aware of their membership of the spiritual world through the light-effects of the Spirits of Fire (Archangels).

There was in addition a third kind of human being, still more deeply entangled in Earthly existence. These had not been able to be touched by the fire-element until such time as the Earth, already separated from the Sun, had received into it the element of water. The feeling they had of belonging to the spiritual world was slight, notably at the beginning of their Earthly life. Only when the working of the Archangels, and more especially of the Angels made itself felt in their inner mental life, did they become aware of it. On the other hand, at the beginning of their Earthly time they were full of eager impulse for action — for such actions, namely, as could be performed within the conditions of the Earth itself. In such human beings the other organs (the appendages) were especially developed.

In the time when, before the separation of the Moon, the Moon forces were bringing about in the Earth a constantly increasing measure of solidification, it befell that among the descendants of the 'seeds' left behind by men on Earth, there were some in whom the human souls returning from the body-free condition could no longer incarnate. Their form was much too hardened, and under the influence of the Moon forces had grown all too unlike the human figure to be able to receive the soul. This meant that certain human souls no longer found it possible to return to Earth. Only the most mature, only the strongest felt themselves equal to the task of so transforming the Earthly body during its growth that it could blossom forth into the true human form. Hence but a portion only of the human bodily descendants became vehicles for Earth men. Another portion, owing to their hardened form, could only receive souls that were at a lower level than the souls of men. Some of the human souls, on the other hand, being thus compelled to cease partaking in Earth evolution during that epoch, were brought into a different kind of life-history. Even at the time of the separation of the Sun, there had already been souls who could no longer find a place on Earth. These were transplanted for their further evolution to another planet. Under the guidance of cosmic Beings, this planet wrested itself free of the general World-substance which had been united with the physical evolution of Earth at its beginning, and out of which the Sun itself had also separated. This was the planet whose physical expression is known to external science as Jupiter. (Here we are speaking of heavenly bodies and planets, and of their names, in precisely the same way as was customary in a science of former times. The meaning will be clear from the context. The physical Earth is but the physical expression for an organism of soul and spirit, and the same is true of every other heavenly body. He who perceives the Supersensible does not mean by the name 'Earth' the mere physical planet, nor by 'Sun' the mere physical fixed star. And in like manner, when he speaks of Jupiter, Mars, etc., he is referring to far-reaching spiritual complexes. Naturally, the heavenly bodies have since the times of which we are here telling undergone fundamental changes in their form and purpose — in a certain respect, even in their position in the heavenly spaces. Only one who is able to follow back their evolution into far distant ages, can recognize the connection of the present planets with their forebears.)

It was thus on Jupiter that such souls continued their evolution. Later on, when the Earth was inclining still more to the solid state, another dwelling-place had to be created for souls who, though able for a time to inhabit the hardened bodies, could no longer do so when the hardening had gone too far. For these, there arose in Mars a dwelling suited to their further evolution. Then again there were souls who at a still earlier time, when the Earth was united with the Sun and was incorporating in itself the air element, proved unadapted to partake in its evolution. These souls were affected too strongly by the Earthly corporeal form. They had therefore to be withdrawn, already at that time, from the immediate influence of the Sun forces. The Sun forces must work upon them from without. They found on Saturn a place for their further evolution. Thus in the course of its evolution the number of human forms on Earth steadily decreased. Forms began to appear in which human souls were not incarnated — forms which were able to receive only astral bodies, even as man's physical body and life-body had done on Old Moon. While Earth was growing waste and void as to human inhabitants, these beings now established themselves upon it. In the last resort, all human souls would have had to leave the Earth — had it not been for the severance of the Moon. This made it possible for human forms which at that time could still be humanly ensouled, to withdraw the human seed or embryo during their Earthly life from the Moon forces emanating directly from the Earth, and let it mature within themselves up to the point where it could safely be exposed to these forces. This meant that, while the seed or embryo was taking shape within the human being, it came under the influence of those Beings who, guided by the Mightiest among them, had severed the Moon from the Earth, so as to carry Earth's evolution forward over a critical point.

When the Earth had developed the air-element within it, there were astral beings in the sense of the above description — as relics from Old Moon — who had remained farther back in evolution than the lowest of human souls. These became the souls of the forms which had to be deserted by man even before the separation of the Sun, and were the forefathers of the animal kingdom. In course of time, they evolved especially those organs which in man existed only as appendages. Their astral body had to work upon the physical and the life-body in the same way as was the case with man on Old Moon. This, then, is how the animals originated; and they had souls which could not dwell in the single creature. The soul extended its being to the descendant of the parent form. Animals that are in the main descended from a single form, have one soul together. Only when, as a result of special influences, the descendant departs from the parent form, does a new animal-soul come into incarnation. And it is in this sense that in spiritual science we speak of specific (or generic) souls, or 'group souls' of the animals.

Something not unlike this took place at the time of the separation of the Sun from the Earth. Out of the watery element forms emerged which were no farther on in their development than man had been before his evolution on Old Moon. Such forms were only able to receive an astral influence when it worked upon them from without; and this could not happen until after the departure of the Sun from the Earth. Each time that the Sun period of the Earth set in, the Astral of the Sun roused up these forms to build themselves their life-body from out of the Ethereal of the Earth. Then, when the Sun was turned away from the Earth, this life-body was dissolved once more in the common body of the Earth. As a result of this working together of the Astral of the Sun and the Ethereal of the Earth, physical forms arose out of the watery element which were the forebears of the present plant kingdom.

Man has become on Earth an individualized soul-being. His astral body, poured into him on Old Moon by the Spirits of Movement, has been organized on Earth into the sentient, the intellectual and the spiritual soul. When his spiritual soul was so far developed as to be able, during Earth life, to build itself a body well adapted to contain it, the Spirits of Form endowed him with a spark of their own fire. The I was kindled in him. Every time he left the physical body, man was in the spiritual world, where he encountered the Beings who had given him his physical body, his life-body and his astral body during the Saturn, Sun and Moon evolutions, and had perfected these up to the Earth level of development. But now that the spark of fire of the I had been kindled in his life on Earth, a change had come about in the body-free life as well. Before this moment in his evolution, man had no independence in relation to the spiritual world. He did not in that world feel himself as a separate, single being, but as membered into the sublime organism composed of higher Beings above him. Now, however, the 'I' experience on Earth began to work on into the spiritual world; there too, man began to feel himself as a single unit. Yet at the same time he also felt he was eternally united with that world. In the body-free condition he found again in a higher aspect the Spirits of Form whom he had perceived in their manifestation upon Earth through the spark of his own I .

The severance of the Moon from the Earth involved also new experiences for the body-free soul in the spiritual world. For it was only through the transference from the Earth to the Moon of a portion of the form-building forces that it was made possible still to develop upon Earth such human forms as could receive a soul's individuality. Thereby the individuality of man was brought into the realm of the Moon Beings. And even in the body-free condition, the after-echo of Earthly individuality could only be effective inasmuch as there too the soul remained within the realm of those mighty Spirits who had brought about the separation of the Moon. It happened in the following way. Immediately after leaving the Earth, the soul could only see the sublime Beings of the Sun as it were in a reflected radiance cast by the Beings of the Moon. Not until it had been sufficiently prepared by beholding this reflected radiance, did the soul come face to face with the sublime Sun Beings themselves.

The mineral kingdom of the Earth also arose by being thrust out from the evolution of mankind. Its structures represent what was still left in a hardened condition when the Moon was separated from the Earth. The soul-nature that felt drawn to these structures was of a kind which, having remained at the Saturn stage, was fitted to create only physical forms. All the events of which we are speaking here — or will be speaking in the sequel — are to be thought of as taking place in the course of immense epochs, the precise determination of which is beyond our present scope.

The above descriptions have given a picture of the evolution of the Earth from its external aspect. Seen from the aspect of the Spirit, the following emerges. The spiritual Beings who drew the Moon away from the Earth and bound up their own existence with it — becoming in this way Beings of the Earth's

Moon — sent down their forces from that heavenly body to Earth and thereby determined the form and structure of man's organization. Their influence was directed to the I or Ego which man had by then acquired; it made itself felt in the interplay of the I with the astral, etheric and physical bodies. It was due to these Beings that the possibility arose in man, consciously to mirror in himself the wisdom-filled configuration of the World, and to portray it, as by reflection, in an act of knowledge. Let the reader recall here the description that was given of how in the Old Moon time, through the Moon's severance from the Sun, man had attained a certain independence in his organization — a freer state of consciousness than could proceed directly from the Sun Beings themselves. During the period of Earth evolution we are now describing, this free and independent consciousness appeared again — a heritage from Old Moon evolution. Under the influence of the Moon Beings, it could have been harmonized once more with the great Universe, and made into a faithful image of it. And this would indeed have come to pass had no other influence intervened. Man would have become a being with a consciousness whose content mirrored back the Universe in the pictures of the life of knowledge, as by natural necessity, not by his own free intention. But it did not happen so. At the very time of the Moon's severance, certain spiritual Beings intervened in human evolution, who had retained so much of their own Moon nature that they could not partake in the departure of the Sun from the Earth, while on the other hand they were also excluded from the influences of the Beings who worked on to the Earth from the Moon. These Beings with an Old Moon nature were banished, as it were by an abnormal evolution, to the Earth. In their Moon nature was contained precisely that quality which had rebelled against the Spirits of the Sun during Old Moon, and had at that time been of real benefit to man, inasmuch as it had brought him to a free and independent consciousness. As a consequence of their peculiar evolution during the Earth epoch, they now became the opponents of those who, working from the Moon, desired to make man's consciousness an infallible knowledge-mirror of the World.

The very same thing which on Old Moon had helped man to a higher level, proved itself now a factor of resistance to the new conditions that had been made possible in the course of Earth evolution. The opposing powers had brought with them from their Old Moon nature the faculty to work upon the human astral body in such manner as to make it — in the sense of the above descriptions — independent. This faculty they used; they gave the astral body — for the Earth epoch too — a certain independence, as against the unfree consciousness determined by necessity, that was being induced in it by the Beings of Earth-Moon.

It is not easy to express in ordinary language what the influence of these spiritual Beings was like in that primeval time. We must not conceive it to have been like the present-day influences of Nature, nor yet like the influence of man on man, when by his words one man awakens in another forces of inner consciousness, whereby the other learns to understand something or is moved to some virtue or vice. The primeval influence to which we here refer was not a 'natural' influence at all, but a purely spiritual one. It worked also in a spiritual way: it was transmitted, as a spiritual influence, from the higher Spirit Beings to the human being in a manner that accorded with his state of consciousness at that time. If we imagine it like an influence of Nature, we completely fail to perceive its real essence. If on the other hand, we say that the Beings with the Old Moon nature approached man with intent to win him over for their aims by 'tempting' him, then we are using a symbolical expression, which is all right, so long as we are aware of its symbolic nature and realize that behind the symbol lies a spiritual fact.

This influence on man, proceeding from Spirit-beings who had remained behind in the Old Moon condition, entailed for him a twofold consequence. His consciousness was divested of the character of a mere mirror of the Universe, for there was kindled in the human astral body the power to regulate and control the pictures in consciousness. Man became the master of his own faculty of cognition. On the other hand, since it was the astral body which was made the source of this control, the

Ego, in spite of being in reality above the astral, fell into a state of perpetual dependence on it. This meant that for the future man was exposed to the constant influence of a lower element in his own nature. It was now possible for his life to sink beneath the high level on which the Earth-Moon Beings had placed him in the cosmic process. And in the sequel there remained the constant influence upon his nature of the abnormally developed Beings of the Moon. These latter may be called — in contrast to those who from Earth-Moon formed man's consciousness to be a mirror of the Universe, yet gave him no free will — the Luciferian Spirits. They brought man the power to unfold a free activity in his own consciousness, but brought him at the same time the possibility of error and of evil.

As a result of these events, man came into a different relation to the Sun Spirits than was predestined for him by the Earth-Moon Beings. The latter wanted to evolve the mirror of his consciousness in such a way that the influence of the Sun Spirits would predominate in his entire life of soul. But this intention of theirs was frustrated, and in the human being an opposition was set up between the influence of the Sun Spirits and the influence of the Spirits who were undergoing an irregular Moon evolution, with the result that man was rendered incapable of recognizing the physical influences of the Sun for what they were; they remained hidden from him behind the earthly impressions of the outer world. Filled with these impressions, the astral in man was drawn into the domain of the I. Had it not been for this, the I of man would have been content simply to feel the spark of fire bequeathed him by the Spirits of Form, remaining subject to their commands in all that appertained to the outer fire. But now the I began to use the fire-element, with which it had itself been informed, to influence the phenomena of warmth in the surrounding world. Thus a bond of attraction was established between the I and the Earth fire, and man became entangled, more than had been predestined for him, in the realm of earthly matter. Previously he had had a physical body, consisting as to its main parts of fire, air and water, with only a shade or, as it were, a phantom of earth substance added. Now the body became more densely compact of earth. Previously, man had moreover been living — as a being rather delicately organized — in a kind of floating, soaring movement above the solid ground of Earth; now he had to descend from the surrounding sphere to the parts of Earth which were already more or less solidified.

That such physical effects were possible as a direct outcome of spiritual influences, is explained by the fact that these influences were of the kind we have described. They were not Nature influences nor were they like the influences of soul that work from man to man. The latter do not extend their effects so far into the bodily as did the spiritual forces with which we are dealing here.

Because man exposed himself to the influences of the outer world under the guidance merely of his own ideas, subject as these were to error, because moreover he lived by cravings and passions which he did not allow higher spiritual influences to regulate, the possibility of illness arose. And another marked effect of the Luciferian influence was the following. Henceforth man was unable to feel his single life on Earth as a continuation of body-free existence. He now received such Earthly impressions as he could experience through the astral element with which he had been inoculated, and these impressions joined themselves on to the forces that destroy life. Man experienced this as the doing away of his Earthly life. Death, brought about by human nature itself, now made its appearance. Here we touch a significant secret of man's nature — the connection of the human astral body with illness and death.

Peculiar conditions now arose for the life-body of man. It was placed in such a position between the physical and astral bodies as to be withdrawn to a certain extent from the faculties man had acquired through the Luciferian influence. A portion of the life-body remained outside the physical body, and was accordingly controllable by higher Beings alone, and not by the human Ego. These were the Beings who, under the leadership of one of their sublime number, had left the Earth at the separation of the Sun, to occupy another dwelling-place. Had this portion of the life-body remained united with the astral body, man would have seized on supersensible forces which had belonged to him before, and put them to his own use; he would have extended the Luciferian influence to these supersensible forces. In so doing man would in time have severed himself completely from the Beings of the Sun, and his Ego would have become an entirely Earthly Ego. For at the death of the physical body (or even during its disintegration) the Earthly Ego would have been obliged to take up its abode in another physical body — in a descendant body — without first passing through a time of union with higher spiritual Beings in a body-free condition. Man would thus have attained the consciousness of his I, but only as an Earthly I.

This result was averted by the special development described above in connection with the life-body, a development that was brought about by the Earth-Moon Beings. The true individual Ego was thereby loosed from the merely Earthly Ego, so that man during his earthly life felt himself only partly as his own I, while at the same time he felt that his Earthly Ego was a continuation of the Earthly Ego of his forefathers through the generations. Thus during life on Earth the soul felt a kind of Group Ego reaching back to distant ancestors, and the individual man felt himself a member of the group. It was only on entering into the body-free condition that the individual Ego could feel itself a single being. And even this individualization was impaired inasmuch as the Ego was still burdened with the memory of the Earthly consciousness — the consciousness, that is, of the Earthly Ego. This memory clouded man's vision of the spiritual world, which began to be veiled over between death and birth, as it was already for man's physical vision upon Earth.

The many changes that took place in the spiritual world while human evolution was passing through these conditions, found physical expression in the gradual regulation of the mutual relationships of Sun and Moon and Earth — and, in a wider sense, of other heavenly bodies too. *One* consequence of these relationships may here be singled out: the alternation of day and night. (The movements of the heavenly bodies are regulated by the Beings who inhabit them. The movement of the Earth whereby day and night arise, was brought about by the mutual relations of the higher Spirit-Beings above humanity. And it was in like manner that the Lunar motion came about; for after the severance of Moon from Earth, the rotation of the former about the latter enabled the Spirits of Form to work upon the physical body of man in the right way — in the proper rhythm.) By day the Ego and astral body of man were working in the physical body and the life-body. By night this work ceased; the Ego and astral body left the physical and the life-body. During this time they were entirely within the domain of the Sons of Life (Angels), the Fire Spirits (Archangels), the Spirits of Personality and the Spirits of Form. The physical body and life-body were also received into their sphere of influence by the Spirits of Form, and in addition by the Spirits of Movement, the Spirits of Wisdom and the Thrones. In this way the harmful influences which had been brought to bear on man during the day through the aberrations of the astral body could be made good again.

Human beings now began to multiply again on Earth, and there was no longer any reason why human souls should not proceed to incarnate in the descendants. For the way in which the Earth-Moon forces were now working enabled the human bodies to take such shape as adapted them perfectly for the embodiment of human souls. Now therefore the souls, formerly translated on to Mars, Jupiter, etc., were guided once more to the Earth. For every human descendant born in the sequence of the generations, a soul was thus made available. And so it went on for a long time: the coming of fresh souls to settle on the Earth corresponded to the increase in the population. And when these souls left the body through Earthly death, they retained like a memory, in the body-free condition, the echo of their Earthly individuality. This memory worked in such a way that when a body proper for its habitation was born again on Earth, the soul would incarnate in it once more. Thus it came about that among the progeny of men, there were some with souls coming from outside — appearing again on Earth for the first time since the primeval ages of its evolution — and others with souls that were now reincarnating. As evolution

187

continued, the 'young' souls appearing for the first time grew ever less and the reincarnated more in number. Nevertheless, for long ages of time the human race still consisted of these two kinds of human beings.

On Earth man now felt himself more united with his forefathers through the common Ego of the group. The experience of the individual I was correspondingly more intense in the body-free condition between death and a new birth. The souls who came fresh from heavenly spaces to take up their abode in human bodies were in a different situation from those who had one or more Earthly lives behind them. The former brought with them to physical life on Earth only those conditions of soul which they owed to the influence of the higher spiritual world and to the experiences they had undergone outside the Earth's domain. The others had, in earlier lives on Earth, added conditions of their own making. The destinies of the former souls were determined entirely by facts that lay outside the new Earth conditions, while those of the reincarnated souls depended also on what they themselves had done in their former lives under the conditions that prevailed on Earth. And so it came about that along with reincarnation, individual human Karma began to show itself.

Through the withdrawal of the human life-body from the influence of the astral body — in the way indicated above — the relationships of reproduction remained outside the horizon of man's consciousness, and were subject to the guidance of the spiritual world. Whenever a soul had to descend into the Earth sphere, the impulses for reproduction arose in man on Earth. For Earthly consciousness the whole process was veiled to some extent in mystery and darkness.

But now also during Earthly life this partial separation of the life-body from the physical had its results. Spiritual influence was able to effect a notable enhancement of the faculties inherent in the life-body, which manifested in a peculiar development of the power of memory. Independent logical thinking was only in its very first beginnings in that period of man's existence. But the power of memory was almost unlimited. Another effect showed itself in a more outward manner in the fact that man had an immediate 'feeling' knowledge of the potent virtues of all living things. He could enlist in his own service the forces of life and reproduction inherent in animal, and more especially in plant natures. He could withdraw from the plant the force that impels it in its growth, and use this force, just as nowadays forces are taken from lifeless nature — the latent force of coal, for instance — and used to set machines in motion. (Further details on this subject will be found in my book on Atlantis and Lemuria.*)

Man's inner life of soul was also altered in diverse ways through the Luciferian influence; many kinds of feelings and emotions could be cited which owed their origin to it. Mention may here be made of a few of these changes. Previously the human soul, in whatever it had to do and create, worked in accordance with the aims of higher spiritual Beings. The plan for what had to be achieved was settled in advance. And in the measure in which his consciousness was evolved, man could even foresee how, in pursuance of the preconceived plan, things must necessarily develop in the future. This forward-seeing consciousness was lost when a veil of earthly perceptions was woven across the revelations of the higher Beings and hid from man's view the real forces of the Sun Beings. The future now became uncertain, and this meant that the possibility of feeling fear was implanted in the soul. Fear is a direct consequence of error.

At the same time we see how with the Luciferian influence man became independent of certain forces to which he had hitherto been entirely subject. Henceforth he could make resolves — quite on his own. Freedom is thus the result of this influence. Fear, and feelings akin to fear, are but concomitant phenomena of man's evolution towards freedom.

There is a spiritual aspect to this emergence of fear. Within the forces of the Earth, under whose influence man had been brought by the Luciferian powers, other powers were at work

* See the volume entitled *Cosmic Memory: Prehistory of Earth and Man*, published in 1959 by Rudolf Steiner Publications Inc., Englewood, New Jersey, U.S.A. The title of the corresponding volume in German is *Aus der Akasha Chronik*. (Note by Translators.)

— powers which had begun to evince irregularity far earlier in evolution than the Luciferian. Along with the Earth forces, man began now to receive into his being the influences of these other powers. They instilled into feelings which without them would have worked quite differently, the quality of fear. We may name them here the Ahrimanic beings; they are the same as are called by Goethe, Mephistophelian.

Now although at first the Luciferian influence made itself felt only in the most advanced human beings, it soon began to extend over others too. The descendants of the more advanced mingled with those of the less advanced, with the result that the Luciferian force penetrated also to these. Moreover the life-body of the souls returning from the planets could not be protected to the same extent as the life-body of the descendants of those who had remained on Earth. The protection of the latter was the work of a sublime Being who had the leadership in the Cosmos at the time when the Sun separated from the Earth. In connection with the development we are here considering, this Being appears as the Ruler in the kingdom of the Sun. With Him there journeyed to the Solar dwelling-place such sublime Spirits as had attained the necessary maturity in their cosmic evolution.

But there were also Beings who at the separation of the Sun had not reached this height of development. They had to look for other scenes of action. And these are the Beings through whom it had come to pass that Jupiter and other planets split off from the common World-substance which was in the physical organism of the Earth in the beginning. Jupiter became the habitation of Beings who had not matured to the level of the Sun. The most advanced among them became the leader of Jupiter. As the leader of the Sun evolution became the higher Ego, working in the life-body of the descendants of the human beings who had remained on Earth, so did the Jupiter leader become the higher Ego which passed like a common consciousness through other human beings — those, namely, who traced their descent to a mingling of the offspring of the men who had remained on Earth with those who had only appeared on Earth at the time of the air element and had then gone off to Jupiter. The latter may accordingly be named in spiritual science 'Jupiter men'. They were those human descendants who in that ancient time had still been receiving human souls — souls, however, which at the beginning of Earthly evolution had not yet been mature enough to partake in the first contact with the fire-element. These were souls between the human and the animal kingdoms.

And there were still other Beings, who — once more under the leadership of a Highest among them — had separated Mars out of the common World-substance as their dwelling-place, and they exercised their influence upon a third kind of human being who had also arisen by intermingling, the 'Mars men'. (This kind of knowledge throws light on the fundamental causes and origins of the planets in our solar system. All the heavenly bodies of this system have come into being through the varying degrees of maturity of the Spirits who inhabit them. Naturally, we cannot enter here into all the details of these cosmic differentiations.)

Those human beings on the other hand, who beheld the presence in their life-body of the high Being of the Sun Himself, may be called 'Sun men'. The Being who lived in them as a higher Ego — only in the generations, needless to say, not in the single individuals — is the One to whom diverse names were subsequently given, when men acquired conscious knowledge of Him. To the men of the present time He is the One in whom the relation of the Christ to the Cosmos is revealed.

We can also distinguish 'Saturn men'. In them there appeared as higher Ego a Being who, with his companions, had to leave the common substance of the World even before the separation of the Sun. The Saturn men were a type of human being in whom, not only in the life-body but in the physical body too, there was a portion which remained withdrawn from the Luciferian influence.

But now it was so, that in the lower kinds of human beings the life-body was after all too little protected, and could not sufficiently resist the encroachments of the Luciferian nature. Such human beings could so far extend the arbitrary power of the fiery spark of the I which was within them as to be able to call forth in their environment mighty workings of fire, of a harmful nature. This led eventually to a stupendous Earth catastrophe. A great portion of the then inhabited Earth was destroyed in these fire-storms, and with it perished also the human beings who had fallen into error. Only a very small number of them, having remained comparatively untouched by error, could save themselves by taking refuge on some region of the Earth that had so far been protected from the harmful influence of men. One land in particular proved suitable as such a dwelling-place for the new humanity. It was situated at the part of the Earth's surface which is now covered by the Atlantic Ocean. The portion of mankind that had remained most pure from error migrated thither. Other parts became inhabited only by stray remnants. The continent which then existed between the present Europe, Africa and America may be called in spiritual science, Atlantis. (The above-described period of human evolution, preceding the Atlantean, is dealt with from a certain aspect in the relevant literature. It is there called the Lemurian epoch of the Earth, whereas the time when the Moon forces had not yet unfolded their most powerful effects may be called the Hyperborean age. This epoch was preceded by yet another, which coincides with the very earliest time of physical Earth evolution. In Biblical tradition the time before the entry of the Luciferian beings is referred to as the time of Paradise, and the descent on to the Earth — man's entanglement in the world of the senses — as the expulsion from Paradise.)

It was during evolution in the region of Atlantis that the actual separation of humanity into the men of Saturn, Sun, Jupiter and Mars took place. Previously, no more than the initial tendencies in this direction had shown themselves. The division also into the waking and the sleeping state now entailed yet other important consequences, which came strongly into evidence in Atlantean humanity. During the night, man's astral body and Ego were in the realm of the Beings above him, reaching as far as to the Spirits of Personality. Through the portion of his life-body which was not united with the physical he could have perception of the Sons of Life (the

Angels) and the Fire Spirits (the Archangels). For he could remain united, during sleep, with this portion of the life-body. His perception however of the Spirits of Personality remained indistinct, and this was directly due to the Luciferian influence. But with the Angels and Archangels, other beings also became visible to man in this condition. These were beings who, having remained behind on Sun or Moon, had not been able to enter upon Earth-existence at all; they had had perforce to remain in the world of soul and spirit. Under the Luciferian influence, however, man drew them into the realm of his own soul when it was separated from the physical. Thus he came into touch with beings whose influence upon him was in the highest degree seductive. They multiplied in his soul the impulses that led him astray, especially the impulse to misuse the forces of growth and reproduction, which now stood at man's disposal owing to the partial separation of the physical body from the life-body.

Now there were individual human beings of the Atlantean epoch who were to a large extent enabled to avoid entanglement in the world of the senses. Through them the Luciferian influence was changed from a hindrance in man's evolution into a means for his higher progress. For with its help they were enabled to unfold a knowledge of the things of Earth sooner than would otherwise have been possible, and in so doing, they strove to remove error from their mental life and to bring to light from out of the world's phenomena the primal intentions of the Spirit-Beings. They kept themselves free from impulses and cravings of the astral body directed merely to the world of the senses. Thus they became less and less liable to error, and were brought in this way into conditions of consciousness whereby they had perception purely in that part of the life-body which was separated from the physical. At these times it was as though the physical body's power of perception were extinguished and the body itself dead. But through the life-body these human beings were wholly united with the kingdom of the Spirits of Form, and could learn from them how they were led and guided by the sublime Being who had been the Leader in the severance of Sun and Earth, and through whom the understanding for the 'Christ' was subsequently revealed to man. Such men were Initiates. But because the human individuality had now, as we have seen, come into the domain of the Moon Beings, even the Initiates could not, as a rule, be touched directly by the Sun Being. He could be revealed to them only, as it were in reflection, through the Moon Beings. Thus they beheld not the Sun Being Himself, but His reflected radiance. These Initiates became the leaders of the rest of mankind, to whom they were able to communicate the secrets they saw. They trained up disciples, teaching them the paths to the attainment of the condition that leads to Initiation. The knowledge of what had formerly manifested through 'Christ' was attainable only by such as belonged to the Sun humanity in the sense above described. These cultivated their secret knowledge, and the ministrations which led up to it, at a special sanctuary which shall here be named the Christ — or the Sun — Oracle. ('Oraculum' meaning a place where the intentions of spiritual Beings are perceived.)

What is here said in reference to the Christ will be misunderstood unless the following is borne in mind. Supersensible knowledge has to recognize, in the appearance of Christ on Earth, an event to which those men of earlier ages who knew the meaning and purpose of Earth evolution could point, as to an event that was to come in the future. It would be a mistake to presume in those Initiates a relationship to Christ which has only been made possible by the event they prophesied. This much they could prophetically understand and bring home to their disciples: 'Whoso is touched by the might of the Sun Being, sees the Christ coming towards the Earth.'

Other Oracles were called into life by the members of Saturn, Mars and Jupiter humanity, whose Initiates carried their vision no farther than to those Beings who could be revealed to them — as 'higher Egos' — in their life-bodies. Thus there arose the adherents of the Saturn, the Jupiter and the Mars Wisdom. Beside these modes of Initiation, there were again still others, for human beings who had received into themselves too much of the Luciferic nature to permit of so great a part of the life-body being separated from the physical as was the

194

case with the Sun humanity; more of the etheric body was held back in the physical by the astral body than with the Sun humanity. Human beings of this type were not able, even in their more advanced states of consciousness, to reach through to the prophetic Christ Revelation. Their astral body being more under the influence of the Luciferian principle, they had harder experiences to undergo in preparation, before they could receive, in a less body-free condition than the others, not indeed the revelation of the Christ Himself, but that of other sublime Beings; for there were Beings who, though they had left the Earth at the time of the separation of the Sun, were not upon so high a level as to be able to partake continuously in the Sun's evolution. After the severance of Sun and Earth they went forth again from the Sun, taking with them another separate dwelling-place — and this was Venus. Their leader was the Being who now became the 'higher Ego' for the above-described Initiates and their followers. A similar thing happened with the leading Spirit of Mercury in connection with still another kind of human being. And so there arose the Venus and the Mercury Oracles.

There was moreover a further class of human beings who had absorbed most of all of the Luciferian influence. They could only reach up to a Spirit-Being who with his associates had been thrust forth again soonest of all from the evolution of the Sun. This Being has no special planet in the cosmic spaces but lives to this day in the surrounding sphere of the Earth itself, with which he re-united after his return thither from the Sun. The human beings to whom he revealed himself as their higher Ego may be called adherents of the Vulcan Oracle. Their vision was more directed than that of all the other Initiates to the phenomena of Earth. They laid the first foundation for what afterwards arose among men as arts and sciences. The Mercury Initiates, on the other hand, founded the science of things more supersensible; and to a still higher degree the Venus Initiates did the same. The Vulcan, Mercury and Venus Initiates differed from the Saturn, Jupiter and Mars Initiates in the following way. The latter received their secrets more as a revelation from above, more in a finished state, while the former were already receiving knowledge more in the form of thoughts and ideas that were their own. The Christ-Initiates stood between the two; together with the direct revelation, they received at the same time the faculty to clothe their secrets in the form of human concepts. The Saturn, Jupiter and Mars Initiates had to express themselves more in symbolic pictures; the Christ, Venus, Mercury and Vulcan Initiates could make their communications more in the form of ideas and thought-pictures.

All that was given to Atlantean humanity in this way, came to them through their Initiates, but the rest of mankind also received special faculties through the working of the Luciferian principle, inasmuch as the great cosmic Beings turned to good what might otherwise have been quite detrimental. One such faculty is that of speech. Speech came to man through his condensation into physical materiality and through the separation of a part of his life-body from the physical body. In the times that followed the separation of the Moon, man, to begin with, felt himself united with his physical forefathers through the Ego of the group. But in course of generations this common consciousness, uniting descendants with their forefathers, was gradually lost. Thus with the later descendants the 'inner memory' reached back only to a fairly recent ancestor, not any longer to the more ancient forefathers. It was only in conditions resembling sleep, where men came in contact with the spiritual world, that the memory of this or that ancestor would emerge. Then would a man often deem himself one with some such ancestor, whom he believed to have reappeared in himself. This was, in fact, a mistaken idea of reincarnation, which arose especially in the last period of Atlantis. The true teaching about reincarnation was to be found only in the schools of the Initiates. For the Initiates were able to behold how the human soul passes in the body-free condition from incarnation to incarnation. They alone could impart the truth to their pupils.

In the far distant past of which we are here speaking, the physical form and figure of man was as yet very different from what it is to-day. It was still to a great extent the expression of qualities of soul. The human being was of a finer, softer materiality than he afterwards became. Where his members are now quite rigid, they were plastic, soft and pliable. A man more filled with soul and spirit was of gentle build, mobile, expressive. One who was less spiritually developed had coarser bodily forms, immobile, not so plastic. Improvement in the life of the soul tended to draw man's members together; such a man would remain small in stature. Backwardness of soul, entanglement in sensuality, came to expression in gigantic bodily proportions. While man was still in his period of growth, the body took shape according to what was growing in the soul — and this to an extent which must seem fabulous, indeed quite fantastic, to present-day ideas. Depravity of passion, or of instinct or desire brought with it a monstrous enlargement of the material in man. The present human form has arisen by the contraction, condensation and rigidification of Atlantean man. Before the time of Atlantis, man had presented a faithful image of his soul, of his inner being, but the very events and processes that took place in Atlantean evolution contained the inner causes which led to the human being of post-Atlantean time, who in his physical form and stature is firm and well-established, comparatively little dependent on his qualities of soul. (The animal kingdom grew dense in its forms, in far earlier epochs than man.) The laws which at the present time underlie the moulding and shaping of forms in the kingdoms of Nature can certainly not be extended to the more remote ages of the past.

Towards the middle of the Atlantean period of evolution, a great calamity began gradually to overwhelm mankind. The secrets of the Initiates *should* have been carefully protected from those human beings who had not by due preparation purified their astral bodies from error. For if such attained insight into the hidden knowledge — into the laws whereby the higher Beings guided the forces of Nature — they might enlist these laws in the service of their own mistaken needs and passions. The danger was all the greater, since, as we have seen, men were coming into the realm of lower spirit-beings who were themselves unable to partake in the regular evolution of the Earth and therefore worked against it. These beings were perpetually influencing men, imbuing them with interests which worked against the true welfare of mankind. And then too, the men of that time still had the faculty to place at their own disposal the forces of growth and reproduction in animal and human nature.

Nor was it only the ordinary run of human beings, but some of the Initiates too succumbed to the temptations of lower spirit-beings, and even went so far as to employ the above-named supersensible forces for an end that was directly opposed to the evolution of mankind. For this purpose they gathered round them as associates men who were uninitiated and who applied the secrets of the supersensible working of Nature for decidedly lower ends. A widespread corruption of humanity ensued. The evil grew to greater and greater dimensions.

Now the forces of growth and reproduction, when torn from their mother-soil and independently employed, stand in a mysterious relationship to certain forces that work in air and water. Mighty and ominous powers of Nature were thus let loose by the deeds of men, leading eventually to the gradual destruction of the whole territory of Atlantis by catastrophes of air and water. Atlantean humanity — the portion of it, that is, which did not perish in the storms — was compelled to migrate. As a result too of the great storms, the whole face of the Earth was changed. Europe, Asia and Africa on the one hand, and America on the other, began gradually to assume their present shape. Vast numbers of human beings migrated into these countries. For us in our time those above all are of importance who went eastward from Atlantis. Europe, Asia and Africa gradually became colonized by descendants of the Atlanteans. Peoples of many kinds took up their abode in these countries, peoples that stood at many different levels of evolution — and also of corruption. And in their midst went the Initiates, the Guardians of the secrets of the Oracles. In various regions the Initiates established holy places where the services of Jupiter, Venus, etc. were cultivated in a good — or in an evil — sense. Most detrimental of all was the betrayal of the Vulcan secrets. For the adherents of the Vulcan Mysteries had their attention concentrated upon the things of Earth. By this betrayal mankind was brought into a state of dependence upon spiritual beings who in consequence of their preceding evolution were disposed to reject all that came from the spiritual world that had evolved through the separation of the Earth from the Sun. Such was the tendency they had developed, and they worked in accordance with it, precisely in that element which was arising in man inasmuch as he had sense-perceptions in the physical world — perceptions behind which the spiritual remained hidden. These beings now attained great influence over many of the human inhabitants of Earth, and the immediate outcome of it was to deprive man more and more of any feeling for things spiritual.

In those times, the size, form and plasticity of man's physical body were still largely determined by qualities of soul. Hence the results of the betrayal appeared in changes of this very kind in the human race. Where supersensible forces were placed in the service of lower instincts, passions and desires — where, that is, the prevalent corruption took this particular form — human figures would arise that were monstrous and grotesque in size and shape. These could not, however, survive beyond the Atlantean epoch; they died out. Physically speaking, post-Atlantean humanity evolved from Atlantean forebears whose bodily figure had already become firm enough not to give way to the soul-forces which had grown to be so contrary to their true nature. There was a period in Atlantean evolution when the laws prevailing in and around the Earth were such as to subject the human figure precisely to those conditions under which it had to grow firm. Human racial forms which had hardened before this time could continue to propagate themselves for a good while to come, but by degrees the souls incarnating in them found themselves so restricted that these races too had to die out. Many of the forms were nevertheless able to maintain themselves right into post-Atlantean times; indeed, some of them that had remained mobile enough, survived in a somewhat altered condition for a very long time. On the other hand, the human forms which had retained their plasticity beyond the above-mentioned period, became bodies for those souls in particular who had suffered in a high degree the harmful influence of the betrayal. Such forms were destined to die out early.

In consequence of these developments, other beings had, since the middle of the Atlantean time, been making themselves felt in the realm of human evolution, owing to whose influence man was induced to enter the world of the physical senses in an unspiritual manner. So much so that in place of the true form of this world, hallucinations could appear to him, phantasms, and delusions of all kinds. Man was thus exposed not *only* to the Luciferian influence but also to that of these other beings, to whose existence we have already alluded. The leader of them may be called, after the name he received later on in the ancient Persian civilisation, Ahriman. (Mephistopheles is the same being.) Through this influence man came after his death among powers which caused him to appear even there as a being whose inclination was entirely towards the things of Earth and of the life of the senses. The free and open outlook into all that was going on in the spiritual world — of this he was deprived more and more. He had to feel himself in the grip of Ahriman and to a certain extent excluded from community with the spiritual world.

One Oracle sanctuary was of peculiar importance. Amid the general decline this sanctuary had preserved the ancient service in the purest form. It belonged to the Christ Oracles, and was accordingly able to preserve not only the secret of the Christ Himself but those of the other Oracles as well. For in the manifestation of the supreme Spirit of the Sun, the leaders of Saturn, Jupiter, etc. were also unveiled. In the Sun Oracle was known the secret of producing, in one or other human being, life-bodies such as the best of the Initiates of Jupiter, Mercury, etc. had possessed. By means which they had in their power, but into which we cannot enter in further detail here, the Initiates of the Sun Oracle caused the impress of the best life-bodies of the old Initiates to be preserved, and then stamped on chosen human beings of a later time. The Venus, Mercury and Vulcan Initiates could also do the like with astral bodies.

A time came when the leader of the Christ-Initiates saw

himself left alone with a few associates, to whom he could, to a very limited degree, impart the secrets of the world. For they were men in whom, owing to their natural endowment, there was least of all of the separation between physical body and life-body. In that age of time such men were altogether the best suited for the further progress of mankind in those times. Conscious experiences in the realm of sleep were coming to them less and less. More and more did the spiritual world become closed to them. They also lacked understanding for all that had been revealed in more ancient times when man was not in his physical but only in his life-body. These men in the immediate vicinity of the leader of the Christ Oracle were the farthest advanced as regards the reunion with the physical body of that part of the life-body which had formerly been separated from it. This reunion was now gradually taking place in mankind as a whole, as a result of the transformation which their Atlantean dwelling-place and the Earth in general had undergone. The physical body and the life-body of man were tending more and more to coincide. This meant that the formerly unlimited powers of memory were being lost, and the life of thought was beginning. The portion of the life-body that had now united with the physical transformed the physical brain into the essential instrument of thought. And now at last did man really begin to feel his I within the physical body; now at last did self-consciousness awaken there. To begin with, this happened with a small portion only of mankind, first among whom were the companions of the leader of the Sun Oracle. The remaining masses of mankind, spread over Europe, Asia and Africa, preserved in varying degrees remnants of the ancient states of consciousness. They had therefore immediate experience of the supersensible world.

The companions of the Christ-Initiate were men of highly developed intellect, whilst of all the people of that time they had the least experience in the supersensible domain. The Christ-Initiate journeyed with them from West to East, to a region of central Asia. He wanted to protect them as far as possible from contact with men who were less advanced than they in the evolution of consciousness. He educated them according to the hidden things that were to him open and visible, and worked in this way especially on their descendants. Thus did he train up a group of human beings who had received into their hearts the inner impulses that responded to the secrets of the Christ-Initiation. Out of this group he chose the seven best, that they might be able to have life-bodies and astral bodies corresponding to the impressions of the life-bodies of the seven best Atlantean Initiates. In this way he trained up a successor to each of the Christ, Saturn, Jupiter, etc., Initiates. These seven Initiates became the teachers and guides of those who in the time after Atlantis had settled in the South of Asia, more particularly in ancient India. Endowed as they were with after-images of the life-bodies of their spiritual predecessors, what these great teachers had in their astral bodies — namely, the knowledge and understanding which they had themselves assimilated and made their own — did not come up to what was revealed to them through their life-bodies. For these revelations to speak to them, they had to silence their own faculty of cognition. Then did there speak, from them and through them, the sublime Beings who had also spoken for their spiritual forebears. Save in the times when these great Beings were speaking through them, they were simple, unassuming men, endowed merely with such culture of intellect and heart as they had themselves acquired.

In India there was living at this time a type of human being that had preserved to a marked degree a living memory of the ancient Atlantean soul-condition that permitted of conscious experience in the spiritual world. In very many of them remained also a strong urge of heart and mind towards such experiences in the supersensible world. By a wise guidance of destiny the main portion of this type of mankind, who were from the best of the Atlantean population, had found their way into Southern Asia. They were then joined by others who migrated thither at different times. Such was the complex of humanity to which the Christ-Initiate assigned his seven great disciples to be their teachers. These gave their wisdom and their commandments to this ancient Indian people. In many a one among these ancient Indians only slight preparation was required to kindle in him the scarcely extinct faculties that could lead to observation in the spiritual world. Indeed the longing for that world was to the Indian a fundamental, ever-present mood of soul. Within that world, he felt, was the primeval home of mankind. Man had been transplanted from it into this world which can endow him with external sense-perception and the intellect connected with it; but he felt the supersensible world as the true one and the sense-world as a fallacy of man's perception — an illusion, a maya — and strove by every means in his power to gain insight into the true world. In the illusory world of the senses he could summon up no interest — or only in so far as it manifests as a veil of the supersensible.

The power that could go out from the seven great Teachers to human beings such as these was tremendous. All that could be revealed through them entered deeply and livingly into the Indian soul. Gifted moreover as the Teachers were, by virtue of the life-bodies and astral bodies that had been bequeathed to them, with high spiritual forces, they were able also to work magically on their pupils. They did not really teach; they worked as though by magic from man to man. Thus arose a civilization permeated through and through with supersensible Wisdom. What is contained in the Wisdom-books of the Indians (the Vedas) reproduces, not the lofty Wisdom-teachings in their primal form — guarded as these were and cared for by the great Teachers in those ancient times — but only a faint echo of the same. The eye of seership alone, as it looks back, can detect behind the written, an unwritten, pristine Wisdom. One feature which especially emerges in this primal Wisdom is the harmonious sounding-together of the diverse Wisdoms of the Oracles of Atlantean time. Each of the great Teachers could unveil the Wisdom of one of these Oracles, and the different aspects of Wisdom gave together a perfect harmony, for behind them stood the fundamental Wisdom of the prophetic Christ-Initiation. The Teacher who was the spiritual successor of the Christ-Initiate did not, it is true, show forth what the Christ-Initiate himself had been able to unveil. The latter remained in the background of evolution. He could not, to begin with, transmit his high office to any member of post-Atlantean mankind. The Christ-Initiate who was with the seven Indian Teachers differed from him in this respect: *he* had been able, as we know, completely to assimilate to human concepts and ideas his vision of the Mystery of Christ; whereas the Indian Christ-Initiate could but present a reflected radiance of this Mystery in signs and symbols, such power of ideation as he had been able to attain by his own effort being inadequate to comprehend it. Nevertheless, out of the union of the seven Teachers there arose in a sublime Wisdom-picture a knowledge of the supersensible world, only single parts of which had been able to be revealed in the ancient Atlantean Oracle. The Guiding Powers of the great cosmic world were unveiled; men learned, as it were in whispered tones, of the one great Sun Spirit, the Hidden One, enthroned above the Spirits who manifested through the seven Teachers.

What is here to be understood by the term 'ancient India' is not coincident with what the words are generally taken to mean. Of the time of which we are speaking no outer document-ary records exist. The people now commonly known as Indians belong to a stage of historic evolution which developed long afterwards. We have thus to recognize a first post-Atlantean period of the Earth, in which the civilization here described as Indian was dominant. After it a second post-Atlantean period took shape, in which the civilization hereafter referred to as the ancient Persian became dominant. Still later, there evolved the Egypto-Chaldean civilization, also to be described in the following pages. During the development of these second and third post-Atlantean culture-epochs, ancient India lived through a second and a third epoch of its own, and the third is the one usually spoken of as 'ancient India'. We must accord-ingly not confuse it with the description given here.

Another feature of the ancient Indian culture was what subsequently led to the division of men into castes. The dwellers in ancient India were descendants of Atlanteans who belonged to the diverse kinds of humanity — Saturn men, Jupiter men, etc. The supersensible teachings they received made it quite plain to them that a soul has not been placed by chance into this or that caste, but by its own self-determination.

Nor was it difficult for the men of ancient India to accept this teaching, inasmuch as in many of them what has been described as 'inner memory' of their ancestors could still be called to life. Such memories were, however, also apt to lead all too easily to a mistaken idea of reincarnation. As in the Atlantean age it had been through the Initiates alone that the true idea of reincarnation could be attained, similarly in ancient India it was attainable only by direct contact with the great Teachers. And it is undeniable that the erroneous idea became widely prevalent among the peoples who were scattered over Europe, Asia and Africa in consequence of the downfall of Atlantis. The Initiates who had gone astray during the Atlantean evolution had communicated this secret too to immature persons, and so it came to pass that men tended increasingly to confuse the true idea with the mistaken one. It must not be forgotten that a kind of dim clairvoyance had remained to these people as a heritage from Atlantean time. As the Atlanteans had in sleep entered into the region of the spiritual world, so did their descendants experience the same spiritual world in abnormal states, intermediate between sleeping and waking. Pictures then arose in them of that olden time to which their ancestors had belonged; and they believed themselves reincarnations of human beings of that time. Teachings on reincarnation, that were incompatible with the true ideas possessed by the Initiates, spread over the whole Earth.

As a result of the prolonged migrations from West to East ever since the beginning of the Atlantean catastrophe, a group of peoples had settled in the regions of Western Asia, the descendants of whom are known to history as the Persians and kindred races. Supersensible knowledge must however look back to far earlier times than those of which history tells. We are here concerned with very early forefathers of the later Persians. Among these arose, following upon the Indian, the second great civilization-epoch of post-Atlantean evolution. The peoples of this epoch had a different task. Their longings and inclinations were not directed solely to the supersensible world. They were a people well fitted for the physical world of the senses. They learned to love the Earth. They valued what man can win for himself on Earth and what he can then also acquire by making use of its forces. Their achievements as a warlike nation and the means they invented to possess themselves of the treasures of the Earth, correspond with this trait in their character. Theirs was not the danger of yearning so intensely for the supersensible as to turn right away from the 'illusion' of the physical world. Rather were they in danger of cherishing so strong a feeling for this physical world that their souls might lose all connection with the world of the supersensible. The Oracle-sanctuaries too, which had been transplanted hither from the ancient land of Atlantis, shared in the general character of the people. Of all the forces which men had once been able to acquire by conscious experience in the supersensible world and which — in certain lower forms — were still at their command, this people cultivated the power so to direct the phenomena of Nature that these may serve the personal interests of man. They still possessed great power over Nature-forces that subsequently withdrew from the control of human will. The Guardians of the Oracles were in command of inner forces connected with fire and other elements. They may indeed rightly be called magicians. The heritage of supersensible knowledge and supersensible forces which they had preserved from ancient times was feeble, no doubt, compared with what men had been able to attain in the far distant past. Nevertheless, it found expression in a multitude of forms, from noble arts which had in mind only the true weal of man, down to the most abominable practices. The Luciferian nature worked in these men in a peculiar way. It had brought them into connection with all that can divert man from the intentions of those higher Beings who, had Lucifer not intervened, would have had the sole guidance of human evolution. Some of them, who were still gifted with relics of the old clairvoyance that belonged to the condition between waking and sleeping, felt themselves strongly attracted to the lower beings of the spiritual world. A strong spiritual impulse needed to be given to this whole people, to counteract these qualities in their character. From the same fountain-head from which the ancient Indian spiritual life had proceeded, a leader was-given them by the Keeper of the secrets of the Sun Oracle.

The leader, whom the Guardian of the Sun Oracle assigned to the ancient Persian spiritual culture, may be called·by the name that is familiar to us in history as Zoroaster or Zarathustra. It must however be emphasized that he belonged to a far earlier time than history attributes to the bearer of the name. Here, as you know, we are not concerned with outer historical research, but with spiritual science. Whoever feels bound to associate the bearer of the name Zarathustra with a later date, will be able to find himself in harmony with what spiritual science tells, when he realizes that he is thinking of a successor of the first great Zarathustra — one who took his name and laboured in the spirit of his teaching.

The impulse Zarathustra had to give to his people may be described as follows. He showed them that the world of the physical senses is not void of spirit, as it appears to be when man allows himself to fall exclusively under the influence of the Lucifer Being. To this Being man owes his personal independence and his sense of freedom, but Lucifer has to work in him in harmony with the opposite spiritual Being. For the ancient Persians it was of first importance that they should keep alive their feeling for this opposite spiritual Being. Owing to their inclination to the physical world they were in danger of merging altogether into the Luciferian beings. Now Zarathustra had received from the Guardian of the Sun Oracle an Initiation that made it possible for the revelations of the sublime Beings of the Sun to be vouchsafed him. In special states of consciousness, to which he had been brought by his training, he could behold the Leader of the Sun Beings, who had taken the human life-body under His protection in the way that has been described. He knew that this Being had charge of the spiritual guidance of the evolution of mankind, but that the right time must be awaited before He would be able to descend from cosmic space on to the Earth. To this end it was necessary that He should be able to live in the astral body of a human being, even as He had worked in the life-body since the entry of the Luciferic influence. A human being must appear on Earth who had restored the astral body to a stage of development such as it would have attained, had it not been for Lucifer, at an earlier point of time — namely, at the middle of the Atlantean evolution. Had Lucifer not come, man would have attained this stage more quickly, but without personal independence and without the possibility of inner freedom. Now he was to reach it even with the possession of these qualities.

Zarathustra in his moments of vision foresaw that a time would come in man's evolution when there would be a human being possessing an astral body of this kind. He knew also that until that time the spiritual forces of the Sun could not be found on Earth, but that supersensible vision could perceive them within the spiritual realm of the Sun; he himself could behold them when he looked upward to the Sun with the eye of seership. And he proclaimed to his people the nature of these forces which, although in the meantime they are discoverable in the spiritual world alone, are yet destined in the future to descend to Earth. Such was Zarathustra's prophecy of the great Sun Spirit or Spirit of Light (Ahura Mazdao, Ormuzd, the Aura of the Sun). To Zarathustra and his disciples the Spirit of Light revealed Himself as the Being who from the spiritual world inclines His countenance to man and works within mankind, preparing the future. It was the Spirit revealing the future Christ before His appearance upon Earth, whom Zarathustra proclaimed as the Spirit of Light. In Ahriman (Angra mainyu) on the other hand, he described a Power whose influence, if man blindly gives himself up to it, works harmfully upon the life of soul. This Power is none other than the one described above, who had attained particular dominion on the Earth since the betrayal of the Vulcan secrets.

Together with his message of the God of Light, Zarathustra taught also of those spiritual Beings who are revealed to the pure vision of the seer as the companions of the Light-Spirit, in contrast to the tempters who become manifest to the unpurified remnants of the clairvoyance preserved from Atlantean time. For it had to be made clear to the Persian people of that olden time, how in the soul of man, in so far as he directs his energy to doing work in the physical world, a battle is raging between the power of the God of Light and the power of His Opponent; and man had to be shown how he must bear himself, so that the Adversary may not lead him down to the abyss, but on the contrary his evil influence be turned to good by the forces of the God of Light.

A third civilization-epoch of post-Atlantean time was born among peoples who in the great migrations had eventually come together in Asia Minor and Northern Africa. It evolved among the Chaldeans, Babylonians and Assyrians on the one hand, and among the Egyptians on the other. In these peoples the feeling for the physical world was developed in still another way than in the ancient Persians. They had received far more than other peoples of the spiritual predisposition which provides the right foundation for the development of thought, of that gift of intelligence that had begun to manifest in man since later Atlantean times. It is, as we know, the essential task of post-Atlantean mankind to unfold those faculties of soul which can be gained through awakened forces of thought and mind and feeling, forces not stimulated directly by the spiritual world, but arising out of the fact that man observes the world of sense, lives his way into it and works upon it. The conquest of the physical world by his own human faculties must be regarded as the mission of post-Atlantean man. Stage by stage the conquest advances. Even in ancient India the condition of man's soul was already such as to direct his attention to this world; but he still regarded it as illusion, and his spirit inclined towards the supersensible world. The ancient Persian people made the endeavour to conquer this physical world of the senses. To a large extent, however, they still relied on forces of soul that remained to them as heritage from a time when man was able to reach right up into the supersensible world. In the peoples of the third epoch, these supersensible faculties were by then in great measure lost to the soul. Man had now to search out in the world of sense that lay around him the manifestations of the Spiritual and continue his soul's development by discovering and inventing the means of civilization in what this world provides.

As man learned to elicit from the physical world of sense the laws of the Spiritual that underlies it, the sciences came into being; and as he came to recognize and manipulate the forces of this world, arts and crafts arose; man began to have his tools and his technique. To a man of the Chaldean and Babylonian peoples the world of the senses was no longer an illusion. In its various kingdoms, in mountain and ocean, in wind and water, it was a revelation of the spiritual deeds of Powers that were there behind it, whose laws he was studying to apprehend. To the Egyptian, the Earth was a field for his labour, given to him in a condition which it was his task so to transform by his own faculties of intelligence, that it might bear the stamp of man's ascendancy. The sanctuaries which had been transplanted from Atlantis into Egypt came chiefly from the Oracle of Mercury. There were, however, also others — Venus Oracles for instance. Into all that could be nurtured in the Egyptian people from these sacred places, a new seed of civilization was implanted. This was the work of a great leader, who had been trained within the Persian Mysteries of Zarathustra. (He was the reincarnation of a disciple of the great Zarathustra.) We may call him Hermes, taking once more an historic name. What he received from the Zarathustra Mysteries, enabled Hermes to find the right way of giving guidance to the Egyptian people. In their life on Earth between birth and death they had been turning their minds towards the physical world so as to recognize in it the laws and workings of the underlying Spirit-world, but their immediate vision of the latter was decidedly restricted. The spiritual world could not therefore be described to them as a world into which they might find their way while living on Earth. In place of this, however, they could be shown how in the body-free condition after death man would be living in the world of Spirit-beings who during his time on Earth appear through their counterparts in the physical and sense-perceptible realm. Hermes taught them: In so far as man employs his forces upon Earth to work in it in accordance with the aims of the Spirit Powers, he fits himself to be united with these Powers after death; and those who between birth and death have worked the most zealously in this direction, will be united with Osiris, even with the sublime Being of the Sun.

On the Chaldean and Babylonian side of this stream of civilization, the inclination of men's minds towards the physical and sensible was stronger than it was on the Egyptian. They investigated the laws of this world; and although they turned their gaze from the sense-perceptible images or proto-types to the spiritual archetypes, these peoples remained in many ways entangled in the world of sense. Instead of the Spirit of the star, the star itself was placed in the foreground; instead of other Spirit-beings, their earthly images or idols. It was only the leaders who attained genuine and deep know-ledge of the laws of the supersensible world and of its connection with the sensible. More so than anywhere else did a contrast make itself felt here between the wisdom of the Initiates and the mistaken beliefs of the people.

Utterly different were the conditions that prevailed in those regions of Southern Europe and Western Asia where the fourth post-Atlantean epoch of civilization grew and blossomed. We may define it as the Graeco-Latin epoch. In these countries, descendants of human beings from the most diverse regions of the more ancient world had come together. Here were Oracle-sanctuaries, successors to the various Atlantean Oracles. Here too were men who inherited as a natural gift fragments of the old clairvoyance, and others who by special training could with comparative ease attain the same. At select places not only were the traditions of the old Initiates preserved, but worthy successors to them arose, and the disciples who were trained by these were able to rise to high levels of seership. Moreover these peoples had in them an impulse to create within the world of sense a realm which should express the spiritual in the physical in perfect form. Among many other things, Greek Art was an outcome of this impulse. We have only to look with the eye of the spirit at a Grecian temple, and we can perceive how in this wonder-work of Art the sense-perceptible material has been so formed and fashioned by man that in its every detail it gives expression to the spiritual. The Grecian temple is a veritable 'home of the spirit'. In its forms we behold what can otherwise be apprehended only by the spirit-vision of one who sees the supersensible. A temple of Zeus (or Jupiter) was so formed as to present to the outer eye a visible worthy abode for what the Guardian of the Zeus (or Jupiter) Initiation saw with the eye of the spirit. And it is the same with all the Art of Greece. The wisdom-treasures of the Initiates flowed by mysterious paths into the poets, artists and thinkers. In the cosmologies and philosophic edifices of the Greek thinkers we find again the secrets of the Initiates, in the form of concepts and ideas.

Manifold influences of the spiritual life — secrets of Asiatic and African places of Initiation — found their way into these peoples and their leaders. The great teachers of India, the associates of Zarathustra, the followers of Hermes, had all of them trained up disciples; and these disciples, or their successors, now founded places of Initiation in which the old wisdom-treasures came to life again in a new form. Such were the 'Mysteries' of antiquity. Here pupils were prepared, so as to be brought in due time into those states of consciousness where they could attain vision into the spiritual world. (Some details concerning these Mysteries of antiquity will be found in my book *Christianity as Mystical Fact*. More will also be said about them in later chapters of the present work.) From these centres of Initiation flowed treasures of wisdom to those who in Asia Minor, in Greece and in Italy guarded the spiritual secrets. Within the Grecian world important centres of Initiation arose in the Orphic and Eleusinian Mysteries. In the Pythagorean School of Wisdom the mighty wisdom-teachings and methods of primeval times worked on. Pythagoras himself had in course of his great journeys been initiated into the secrets of the most diverse Mysteries.

* * * * *

In post-Atlantean time the life of man between birth and death has had its influence also on the body-free condition after death. The more man turned his interest to the physical world, the greater was the possibility for Ahriman to find his way into the soul during earthly life, and then maintain his power over it after death. In the peoples of ancient India the danger was as yet very slight. During their life on Earth they had felt the world of the physical senses as an illusion; thereby they withdrew themselves after death from the power of Ahriman. The danger was correspondingly greater for the ancient Persian people, who in the time between birth and death had turned their gaze with interest upon the physical world. They would all too readily have fallen a prey to the snares of Ahriman, had not Zarathustra, with his teaching of the God of Light, impressed it so earnestly upon them that behind the world of the physical senses is the world of the Spirits of Light. According to the measure of what their souls received of the whole world-of-ideas which these teachings were capable of arousing, in such measure did they withdraw themselves from the clutches of Ahriman during earthly life and therewith also for their life after death, in which they would have to prepare themselves for a new life on Earth. In Earthly life the power of Ahriman misleads man into regarding the sense-perceptible, physical existence as the one and only reality, thus shutting himself off entirely from any kind of outlook into a spiritual world. In the spiritual world, Ahriman brings man to complete isolation, leading him to centre all his interest upon himself alone. Men who at death are in the power of Ahriman are born again as egoists.

In the spiritual science of our time, life between death and a new birth can be portrayed, such as it is when Ahriman's influence has to a certain extent been overcome. It has been so described by the present writer in other works, and in the first chapters of this book. And it is important that this should be done, so that man may be shown what he can indeed experience in yonder form of existence if he has gained the clarity of spiritual vision to behold what is actually present there. Whether a given individual experiences more or less, will depend upon how far he can overcome the Ahrimanic influence. Man is gradually approaching more nearly to what he can be in the spiritual world. How this, that he can be, is marred by other influences, must none the less be clearly envisaged when we are studying mankind's evolutionary course.

Among the Egyptian people Hermes saw to it that men should prepare themselves during earthly life for communion with the Spirit of Light. In that time, however, the interests of men between birth and death were already such that they were able only to a slight extent to look through the veil of the physical. Consequently, the spiritual vision of their souls was apt to remain clouded after death. Their perception of the World of Light was dim.

But the overclouding of the spiritual world after death came to a climax for the souls who passed into the body-free condition out of a body of the Graeco-Latin culture. In earthly life they had cultivated the physical life of the senses so that it blossomed forth under their hands. In so doing they had condemned themselves to a shadow-like existence after death. Hence the Greek felt life after death as an existence of the Shades. It is no empty phrase but a real feeling of the truth when the Hero of that time, devoted to the healthy life of the senses, exclaims: "Better to be a beggar upon Earth than a king in the realm of Shades." All this was still more marked in those of the Asiatic peoples who had in their very reverence and worship concentrated on the sensual images alone instead of on the spiritual archetypes. Such was indeed the situation of a great part of mankind during the Graeco-Latin epoch. The fact is here brought home to us that man's mission in post-Atlantean time — the conquest of the physical world — could not but lead to his estrangement from the spiritual world. Thus is greatness on the one hand necessarily bound up with decline upon the other.

Man's connection with the spiritual world was meantime nurtured in the Mysteries. There the Initiates were able in special states of soul to receive revelations from the spiritual world. In greater or less degree, they were successors to the Atlantean Guardians of the Oracles. To them was unveiled what had been veiled by the impulses of Lucifer and Ahriman. Lucifer concealed from man all that of the spiritual world which had, until the middle of the Atlantean time, been pouring into the human astral body without any participation on his part. If the life-body had not been partially separated from the physical, man could have experienced within him this region of the spiritual world as an inner revelation of the soul. Owing to the Luciferian intervention it was only in special states of soul that he could do so. A spiritual world then appeared to him in the garment of the astral. The Beings of this world revealed themselves in forms that possessed the members only of man's higher nature, and made manifest in these, in astrally visible pictures, their several spiritual virtues. Superhuman Beings revealed themselves to man in this way.

After the intervention of Ahriman another kind of Initiation was added. Ahriman had, since the middle of the Atlantean epoch, veiled all that of the spiritual world which would, but for his intervention, have appeared behind the perceptions of the physical senses. This was now unveiled to the Initiates, inasmuch as they practised in their souls all the faculties man had acquired since that time, *beyond* the measure needed for bringing about the clear impressions of the physical and sense-perceptible world. It was revealed to them that spiritual Powers underlay the forces of Nature. They could tell of spiritual Beings behind outer Nature. It was given them to behold the divine creative Powers underlying the forces that are at work in the realms of Nature beneath man. All that had worked on from Saturn, Sun and Moon, forming man's physical body, life-body and astral body, as well as the mineral, plant and animal kingdoms of Nature — all this made up the content of one kind of Mystery-secrets. These were the secrets over which Ahriman held his hand. What had led, on the other hand, to the sentient soul, intellectual soul and spiritual soul, was made manifest in a second kind of Mystery-secrets. But there was something of which the Mysteries could only tell prophetically, namely that in the fulness of time a human being would appear with an astral body such that, in spite of Lucifer, the Light-world of the Spirit of the Sun would come to consciousness in him through the life-body, apart from any special states of soul. And the physical body of this human being would be such that for him the realms of the spiritual world which Ahriman is able to conceal until physical death occurs would become manifest. Physical death can alter nothing in this human being's life, will have no power over it. In such a human being the I shines forth with so strong a radiance that even in his physical life the spiritual comes to full manifestation. Such a being is the bearer of the Spirit of Light, to whom the Initiates had two ways of ascent, in that they were led in special states of soul either to the spirit of the superhuman realm or to the very essence of the powers of external Nature. Inasmuch as they foretold that in course of time such a human being would appear, the Initiates in the Mysteries were prophets of the Christ.

One particular prophet in this sense arose within a nation who possessed by natural inheritance the qualities of the peoples of Western Asia, and by education the teachings also of the Egyptians. This was the nation of the Israelites, and the prophet to whom we refer was Moses. So abundantly had the influences of Initiation been received by Moses that in certain states of soul the Being revealed Himself to him who had undertaken, from the Moon, a long while ago in the normal course of Earth's evolution, the function of shaping human consciousness. In thunder and lightning Moses recognized not mere physical phenomena but the manifestations of this Spirit. And at the same time the other kind of Mysteries had also worked upon his soul. These enabled him to behold in astral visions the Superhuman, and perceive how it becomes the human through the I . Thus He who was to come revealed Himself to Moses from two sides, as the highest form of the I

With Christ there appeared in human form and figure what the high Being of the Sun had prepared as the great pattern for humanity on Earth. And with this Appearance, all the wisdom of the Mysteries had in a certain respect to assume a new form. Hitherto this wisdom had existed only to enable man to bring himself into a state of soul where he could behold the realm of the Sun Spirit beyond the confines of Earthly evolution. From now on, the wisdom-contents of the Mysteries had a different mission; they had to make man capable of recognizing Christ-become-Man, and then of learning to understand — from this centre of all wisdom — both the natural and the spiritual worlds.

In the moment of His life when His astral body had within it all that which is capable of being veiled by the Luciferian intervention, Christ Jesus began to come forward as a Teacher of mankind. From this moment on, the possibility was implanted in human evolution of receiving the wisdom whereby the physical goal of Earth can gradually be attained. And in the moment when the Mystery of Golgotha was fulfilled, another faculty was instilled into mankind — the faculty whereby the influence of Ahriman can be turned to good. Out of his life on Earth man can henceforth take with him through the Gate of Death that which will free him from isolation in the spiritual world. Not only for the physical evolution of mankind is the Event of Palestine the centre and focal point; the same is true for the other worlds to which man belongs. When the Mystery of Golgotha had been accomplished, when the Death on the Cross had been suffered, then did the Christ appear in the world where the souls of men sojourn after death, and set limits to the power of Ahriman. And from this moment on, the region which the Greeks had called the 'realm of Shades' was shot through by a spiritual lightning-flash announcing to its dwellers that Light was now returning to it again. What was achieved for the physical world through the Mystery of Golgotha shed its light also into the spiritual world.

Hitherto the post-Atlantean evolution of mankind had meant for the physical world an ascent — but at the same time a decline for the spiritual world. Everything that flowed into the world of the senses came from sources that had existed in the spiritual world from the most ancient times. Since the Event of Christ, human beings who lift themselves to the Christ Mystery can carry with them into the spiritual world what has been gained here in the world of the senses. And from the spiritual world it then flows back again, forasmuch as the human beings, when they reincarnate, bring with them what the Christ Impulse has become for them in the spiritual world between death and new birth.

All that was conferred upon human evolution through the coming of Christ, has been working in it like a seed. Only by degrees can the seed ripen. Up to the present, no more than the minutest part of the depths of the new wisdom has found its way into physical existence. We are but at the beginning of Christian evolution. In the successive epochs that have elapsed since His appearance, Christian evolution has been able to unveil only so much of its inner essence as men and nations were capable of receiving, capable also of assimilating to their power of understanding. The first form into which this recognition could be cast, may be described as an all-embracing ideal of life. As such it showed itself in striking contrast to the forms of life which had evolved in post-Atlantean humanity. We have described the conditions under which the evolution of mankind had been going forward since the re-population of the Earth in the Lemurian epoch. We saw how the human beings have to be traced back in their soul nature to diverse beings who, coming down from other worlds, incarnated in the bodily descendants of the old Lemurians. The varieties of race are a consequence of this. And when the souls reincarnated, all kinds of different interests arose in them, as an outcome of their Karma. While all this was working itself out, there could not exist for man the ideal of a 'universal humanity'. Mankind went forth from unity in the beginning, but Earth evolution hitherto had led to diversity. In the figure of Christ is given for the first time an ideal that can counteract all separation, for in the Man who bears the name of Christ live also the forces of the sublime Being of the Sun, and in these forces every human I will find its source and its foundation. Even the Israelites still felt themselves as a nation, with each man merely as a member of the nation. As man came to understand — to begin with, purely in thought — that in Christ Jesus lives the ideal Man, unaffected by any and every tendency to separation, Christianity became the ideal of universal brotherhood. Beyond all separate interests and kinships there arose the feeling that the inmost Self of man has in·every one the same origin. (Beside all earthly ancestors appears the common Father of all men. 'I and the Father are One.')

In the fourth, fifth and sixth centuries A.D. a new civilization-epoch was preparing in Europe. The actual beginning of it was in the fifteenth century, and we are still living in it now. Intended as it was by slow degrees to replace the fourth, the Graeco-Latin, this is the fifth post-Atlantean epoch. The peoples who after manifold wanderings and destinies came forward as the bearers of this epoch, were descended from those Atlanteans who had been least affected by what had taken place meanwhile in the four preceding epochs. They had not penetrated to the countries where the civilizations of these earlier epochs took root. They had instead transmitted the heritage of Atlantean civilizations in their own way. Among them were many who had preserved in large measure the heritage of the old dim clairvoyance — the intermediate state between waking and sleeping. Such men knew the spiritual world from their own experience and could tell their fellow-men of what goes on there. In this way there arose a world of stories about spiritual beings and events. The fairy-tales and sagas of the peoples came originally from these real experiences in the spirit; for in many human beings the dim clairvoyance lasted on into times by no means remote from the present. Others there were who, though they had lost the old clairvoy-ance, developed the new faculties in relation to the physical world with inner feelings and emotions that correspond to the experiences of clairvoyance. And beside all this, the Atlantean Oracles also had their successors here; centres of the Mysteries were to be found on every hand. The Initiation-secret chiefly developed in these centres was of the kind that leads to the revelation of that spiritual world which Ahriman keeps hidden. The spiritual Powers underlying the elemental forces of Nature were revealed. In the mythologies of the European peoples can be found traces of what the Initiates in the Mysteries were able to make known to men. Yet these mythologies also contain the other secret, though in a less perfect form than either the Southern or Eastern Mysteries. The superhuman Beings were known in Europe too; but they were seen in perpetual warfare with the associates of Lucifer. The God of Light was indeed proclaimed, but not in such form and figure as would enable one to say with assurance that He would conquer Lucifer.

Nevertheless these Mysteries too were irradiated by the figure of the Christ that was to come. Of Him it was prophesied that His Kingdom would replace the kingdom of that other God of Light. (The sagas that tell of the Twilight of the Gods, and kindred legends, originated in this knowledge of the European Mysteries.)

Influences such as these tended to produce in the man of the fifth civilization-epoch a duality of soul — a duality that has lasted on to this day and shows itself in many ways. From olden time these souls had preserved the leaning towards the spirit, yet not so strongly as to be able to maintain the inner link between the spiritual world and the world of the senses. They cherished the connection only in the devotion of the heart, in the life of feeling — not as an immediate beholding of the Supersensible. Meanwhile man's vision was increasingly directed to the world of the senses and to its conquest. And the forces of intellect awakened towards the close of the Atlantean epoch — all those forces in man, whose instrument is in the physical brain — were developed with this end in view: the understanding and the mastery of the world of the senses. Two worlds have been evolving, as it were, in the human breast.* The one is devoted to physical and sense-perceptible existence, the other is receptive to the revelations of the Spirit and though lacking direct vision, is ready to permeate the spiritual with feeling and emotion.

The inner tendencies to this duality of soul were already present when the Christ teaching found its way into the countries of Europe. The people received this new message of the Spirit into their hearts and drank it in with deep feeling, but could not build the bridge from it to what the intellect, directed to the senses, was discovering in outer physical existence. What we know to-day as the antagonism between external science and spiritual knowledge is nothing but a consequence of this fact. The Christian mysticism of Eckhart, Tauler and others is an outcome of the permeation of heart and feeling with Christianity. The science that is directed solely

* An allusion to the line in Goethe's *Faust* : 'Two souls, alas, reside within my breast.' (Note by Translators.)

220

to the outer world of sense and to the results that follow its application in life, is a consequence of the other tendency that lives in the soul. The achievements of our time in outer material civilization are unquestionably due to this division of tendency. Through being turned in a one-sided way towards the physical, those faculties of man whose instrument is in the brain could be so far enhanced as to make possible the science and technical civilization of to-day. And it was among the European peoples alone that this material civilization could originate. For they, among all the descendants of the Atlanteans, did not develop into actual faculties the inclination towards the physical world of sense until the inclination had reached maturity. Letting it slumber until then undisturbed, they lived on their inheritance of clairvoyance from Atlantis and on the communications of their Initiates. While outwardly their spiritual culture was devoted entirely to these influences, their aptitude for the material conquest of the world was all the time slowly ripening.

And now, at the present time, the dawn of the sixth post-Atlantean epoch is already making itself felt. For whatever is to emerge at a certain time in human evolution, will always be slowly maturing in the preceding time. One thing can even now begin to evolve in its initial stages, namely the finding of the thread which will unite the two spheres that claim man's devotion — the material civilization, and life in the spiritual world. To this end it is necessary on the one hand that the results of spiritual seership be received and understood, and on the other, that in man's observations and experiences of the sense-world the revelations of the Spirit be recognized. The sixth civilization-epoch will bring to full development the harmony between the two.

Herewith the studies in this book have reached a point where we may turn from the perspectives of the past to those of the future. But it will be better to precede the latter by a study of the Knowledge of Higher Worlds and of Initiation. Then, after this study and in connection with it, we shall be able to indicate in brief the outlook for the future, in so far as that can be done within the framework of this book.

CHAPTER V

KNOWLEDGE OF HIGHER WORLDS
(CONCERNING INITIATION)

AT THE present stage of evolution there are three possible conditions of soul in which man ordinarily lives his life between birth and death: waking, sleeping and, between the two, dreaming. The last-mentioned will be briefly dealt with in a later part of this book; for the moment we shall consider life simply as it alternates between its two main conditions — waking and sleeping. Before he can 'know' for himself in higher worlds, man has to add to these two a third condition of soul.

During waking life he is given up to the impressions of the senses, and to the thoughts and pictures that these evoke in him. During sleep the senses cease to make any impression, and the soul loses consciousness. The whole of the day's experience sinks down into the sea of unconsciousness. Let us now consider how it would be if man were able to become conscious during sleep, notwithstanding that all impressions of the senses were completely obliterated, as they are in deep sleep. Nor would any *memory* remain to him of what had happened while he was awake. Would he find himself in an empty nothingness? Would he now be unable to have any experience at all? An answer to this question is only possible if a condition resembling the description can actually be brought about in man, where his senses remain completely inactive and he has no memory of their activity in his waking hours, and is yet not asleep but awake to another world, a world of reality, even while in relation to the external world around him he is just as he is in sleep.

As a matter of fact, such a state of consciousness can be induced in man if he is prepared to evoke within him the kind of inner experience that spiritual science enables him to develop. And all that is here related about the worlds that lie beyond the world of the senses has been investigated in such a condition of consciousness. In the preceding chapters some information has been given concerning these higher worlds. The present chapter will tell — in so far as lies within the scope of this book — of the means whereby man may achieve the state of consciousness required for such research.

It is in this one aspect alone that the higher state of consciousness resembles sleep: the senses receive no impressions from without, and the thoughts too which have been evoked by sense-impressions are obliterated. Whereas however in sleep man is bereft of the power to have conscious experience, in this new state of consciousness he retains the power. A capacity for conscious experience is aroused in him, which in ordinary life requires to be stimulated by sense-impressions. The awakening of the soul to this higher state of consciousness may be termed *Initiation*.

The path that leads to Initiation takes man out of ordinary day-time consciousness and brings him into a new activity of soul where he makes use of spiritual organs of perception. These organs are present in man all the time, in a germinal condition; they require only to be developed.

Now it can happen that at some particular time in his life, without making any special preparation for it, a person discovers that higher organs of this nature have been developing within him. This will mean that a kind of involuntary self-awakening has taken place. He will find that he has through this become a completely changed man. His whole inner experience is now vastly enriched. And he will be fully persuaded that no knowledge of the physical world could ever afford him such bliss, such serene satisfaction, such inner warmth, as can the knowledge that opens up before him now that he has a faculty of cognition that is independent of physical impressions. Strength and confidence will stream into his will from a spiritual world.

Such instances of self-initiation do occur. They should however not lead one to imagine that the right thing to do is simply to wait for it and make no effort towards obtaining Initiation by means of a properly ordered training. We have no need to speak here any further of self-initiation, since it can come about without the person's following any rules or precepts. What we are concerned with is how the organs of perception that are latent in man's soul may be developed by spiritual training. If people do not feel any particular urge to take steps for their own inner development, it is easy for them to think that since the life of man goes forward under the guidance of spiritual Powers, he ought not to interfere in their leadership but should wait quietly for the moment when these Powers shall deem it right to open to him another world. They will feel that any desire to intermeddle in this way with the wisdom of spiritual guidance in quite unjustified, and bespeaks a kind of presumption. One who takes this view will only be persuaded to modify it when a certain line of thought begins to make a strong impression on him — namely when he is ready to say: 'The wise guidance of spiritual Powers has given me certain faculties. It has not bestowed these faculties on me for me to leave them unemployed, but rather that I may put them to use. The wisdom of the guidance is to be seen in the fact that seeds have been planted in me of a higher state of consciousness; and I fail to understand the guidance aright if I do not regard it as a duty to set before me the high ideal: that whatever can become manifest to man through the development of his spiritual powers shall become so manifest.' When such a thought has taken strong enough hold, then the mistrust that was felt of any training for the attainment of a higher state of consciousness will disappear.

Misgiving can however arise on another account. The development of inner faculties of the soul, someone might feel, implies an intrusion into man's most hidden holy of holies. It involves a change in his whole nature and character, and the method by which the change is to be wrought can obviously not be thought out by the person concerned. Only one who knows the path from actual experience can tell him how he is to reach a higher world; and in applying to such a person for help, he is permitting that person to exercise an influence over the innermost holy of holies of his soul. Nor will this scruple be met if the means whereby the higher state of consciousness is to be attained are set forth in a book. For it makes little difference whether one receives instruction by word of mouth or whether someone who has knowledge of these means has written them in a book and one reads them there. There are moreover among those who possess the requisite knowledge some who think it inadmissible ever to entrust the knowledge to a book. These persons will generally also regard with disapproval all communication to others of truths concerning the spiritual world. To hold such a view in the present epoch of mankind's evolution must, however, be described as out of date. Only up to a point, it is true, can the means to be employed for higher development be communicated. But if the pupil will apply himself diligently to what is given, he will be able to reach a stage in development whence he can find the way for himself. From all that he has gone through so far, he will obtain a right idea of his further path — and indeed he can do so in no other way.

On all these various grounds misgivings may arise in relation to the path of spiritual knowledge. They disappear, however, when one begins to grasp the true nature of the path of development which is set forth in the school of spiritual training appropriate to our age. Of this path we will now proceed to tell, hinting only briefly, as occasion arises, at other methods.

The training in question provides one who has the will to seek higher development with instructions that he can follow and so bring about the necessary changes in his soul. Anything like an unwarranted intrusion into the individuality of the pupil could only come into question if the teacher were himself to effect the change by methods of which the pupil was quite unconscious. But a training for spiritual development that is rightly adapted for our times will never employ such methods, turning the pupil into a blind instrument for his own development. It offers him instructions, and the pupil carries them out. As and when there is occasion to do so, it explains to him why this or that instruction is given. The acceptance of the instructions, and their observance, have no need to rest on blind faith. Blind faith should indeed be altogether excluded. If we have studied the nature of the human soul, in so far as it shows itself to ordinary self-observation unassisted by spiritual training, then on learning of the measures recommended we can ask ourselves: What effect will these have on the life of the soul? Before any training is begun, this question, if approached with a healthy and unbiased mind, can receive adequate answer. For it is perfectly possible, before setting out to follow the recommendations, to form a clear and true conception of how they work. Naturally, we cannot have actual *experience* of their working until we have embarked on the training. But there too we shall find we can accompany the experience all the time with understanding, provided only we are free from preconceived ideas and bring healthy good sense to bear on each step we take. And a genuine spiritual science will in these days recommend for development only such means as will stand that test. Whoever is prepared to enter upon such a training and will not allow himself to be led away by any mistaken prepossession into an attitude of mere blind credulity, will soon find that all misgivings disappear. Objections he may hear others raise against a systematic training for the attainment of a higher state of consciousness will not disturb him in the least.

Even for those who are endowed with the inner ripeness of soul which can lead them sooner or later to a self-awakening of the organs of spiritual perception — even for such, training is not superfluous; on the contrary, they have particular need for it. For there are few instances where such a person does not have to go down many a dubious by-path before he arrives at self-initiation. The training will spare him this. It will lead him straight forward on the right path. Where self-initiation occurs, it is due to the fact that the soul reached the necessary maturity in former lives. It may easily happen that the person has a dim feeling of his own ripeness, and this makes him disinclined to submit to training. The feeling may give rise to a kind of unconscious pride which hinders him from putting his trust even in a properly ordered school for spiritual training. Or it may be that the more advanced stage of soul may remain hidden in him until a certain age of life and only then begin to manifest. A training could in such an instance be the very means of bringing the ripeness to manifestation, and were the person to debar himself altogether from such training, it might well be that at the time when it should manifest, the faculty he possesses would still remain hidden and emerge again only in one of his later incarnations.

In this matter of spiritual training, it is important not to let certain fairly obvious misunderstandings gain ground. People may, for instance, have the idea that the training is going to make a great difference to a person's whole conduct and behaviour. But there is no question of giving the pupil general precepts on how to lead his life; he will be told of things he can do, *inwardly* in his soul, which, if he carries them out, will give him the possibility of beholding the supersensible. As for his other activities in life — activities that have nothing to do with observation of the supersensible — these are not *directly* influenced at all by what he undertakes in the course of training. What happens is simply that the pupil acquires, in addition to them, the gift of supersensible perception. This new activity is as different from the ordinary avocations of life as waking is from sleeping. The one cannot be allowed to disturb the other in the very least. Should anyone be inclined, for instance, to intersperse the ordinary course of his life with impressions that reached him from the supersensible, he would be like a sick person whose sleep was continually being interrupted by unwholesome periods of wakefulness. The trained observer will have it in his own control to evoke at will the state of consciousness wherein he can behold supersensible reality. *Indirectly*, the training is of course not unrelated to the general conduct and habit of life, inasmuch as anyone lacking in ethical stability and good feeling will either be unable to see into the supersensible, or if he can, it will do him harm. Very much therefore of the instruction that is given to lead the pupil to vision of the supersensible, contributes at the same time to the ennobling of his daily life. And besides this, through being able to see into the supersensible world, the pupil learns to recognize higher moral impulses that hold good also for the physical world. For there are ethical laws that can only be learned in higher worlds.

Another misunderstanding is possible. It might be imagined that some activity of the soul, intended to lead to supersensible cognition, were in some way connected with changes in the physical organism. As a matter of fact, such activities have nothing whatever to do with anything in man that belongs to the province of physiology, or to other aspects of natural science. They are processes purely of soul and spirit, as far removed from the physical as are ordinary healthy thinking and perceiving. The way in which they take place in the soul is no different from the way in which we think our thoughts or come to our decisions. As much or as little as healthy thinking has to do with the body, just so much and so little have the activities of a genuine training for supersensible knowledge. Any kind of training that affects man in a different way is no true spiritual training, but a caricature of it.

It may be assumed that the training now to be described fulfils the conditions we have seen to be necessary. It is only because supersensible knowledge is something that engages all man's faculties of soul that it might seem to demand overwhelming changes in him. Yet in reality it simply amounts to this: instructions are given which, if followed, will enable the pupil to have moments in his life when he can behold the supersensible.

*　　*　　*　　*　　*

The ascent to a supersensible state of consciousness has necessarily to take its start from ordinary waking consciousness. The pupil is living in this consciousness before he sets out on the ascent, and the school of spiritual training holds out to him means whereby he may be led forth from it. Among the first of the means put forward in the school which concerns us here, are activities that are already familiar to the pupil in his everyday consciousness. The most significant of them are in fact those that consist in still and silent activities of the soul.

The pupil has to give himself up entirely to certain thought-pictures. These are of such a kind as to have in them an awakening power; they awaken hidden faculties of the soul. They differ therefore from the thought-pictures that belong to everyday life, whose purpose it is to portray some external object. Indeed the more faithfully these do so, the truer they are; it belongs to their very nature to be true in this sense. The thought-pictures to which the soul has to devote itself for the purpose of spiritual training have no such part to play. Their function is not to depict an external object; they are formed in such a way as to have in themselves the property of awakening the soul. The best for the purpose are symbolic pictures. Others, however, can also be used. For the actual content is, in fact, of little importance, the main point being that the pupil shall direct the whole power of his soul upon the thought-picture and have nothing else whatever in his consciousness. Whereas in everyday life the soul's powers are distributed among many things, and thought-pictures are continually coming and going, in spiritual training everything depends on the entire concentration of the soul upon one idea or thought-picture, placed, by an act of will, in the very centre of consciousness. It is for this reason that symbolic thought-pictures do better than those that depict external objects or activities; for the latter have their point of support in the external world, so that the soul is not driven to rely upon itself alone, as is the case with the symbolic thought-pictures which have been built up by the soul's own exertions. The essential thing is, not what the picture represents, but that it is formed and imagined in such a way as to set the soul entirely free from dependence on the physical.

It will help us to form a clear conception of what this absorption in a thought-picture implies, if we call up before us the concept of *memory*. Say we have been looking at a tree and have then turned away so that we no longer see it. We can call up before our mind's eye the thought-picture or mental image of the tree. This thought-picture that we have when the tree is not in view is a *memory* of the tree. Suppose we hold on to this memory; we let our soul, as it were, come to rest in the memory-picture and try to shut out every other thought. Our soul is now immersed in the memory-picture of the tree. There you have an instance of absorption in a thought-picture — one that reproduces an outer object perceived by the senses. If we now do the same with a thought-picture we ourselves have placed into the field of consciousness, entirely of our own will, we shall in time become able to achieve the desired end.

In order to make this quite clear, let us take an example of absorption of the soul in a symbolic thought-picture. The first thing to be done is to build it up, and this we may do in the following way. We think of a plant, how it has its roots in the soil, how it sends out leaves one after another, and blossoms at length into flower. Now we imagine a man standing beside the plant. The thought lights up in our mind that the man has characteristics and capabilities which can truthfully be called more perfect than are those of the plant. He can move about at will, he can go this way or that way as he feels inclined; whereas the plant is rooted to the spot where it is growing. We may, however, then go on to think to ourselves: Yes, that is so, the human being is more perfect than the plant; but I also find qualities in him, the absence of which in the plant makes it appear to me more perfect in other respects than the human being. For he is filled with desires and passions, and these he sometimes follows in his behaviour, with the result that he goes astray, falls into error. When I look at the plant, I see how it follows the pure laws of growth from leaf to leaf, how it opens its blossom, calmly and tranquilly, to the chaste rays of the sun. I perceive therefore that whilst man is in some respects more perfect than the plant, he buys this comparative perfection at the price of letting impulses and desires and passions have their seat within him, instead of what appear to be the pure forces at work in the plant. Then we can go on to picture to ourselves how the green sap flows right through the plant, and how this green sap is the expression of the pure, unimpassioned laws of growth. And if we then think of the red blood as it flows through the veins and arteries of man, we find in this red blood the expression of impulses and desires and passions.

We then let this whole thought live in our soul. Carrying it a little farther, we call to mind how man is after all capable of development; he possesses higher faculties of soul, by means of which he can refine and purify his impulses and passions. We recognize that thereby the baser element in them is purged away, and they are re-born on a higher level. The blood can then be thought of as the expression of these purified and chastened impulses and passions. And now we turn our thought, let us say, to a rose. We look in spirit at the rose and say to ourselves: In the red sap of the rose, I see the green colour of the plant-sap changed to red; and the red rose follows still, no less than the green leaf, the pure, unimpassioned laws of growth. I can let the red of the rose be for me a symbol of a blood that is the expression of chastened impulses and passions which have thrown off their baser part and resemble in their purity the forces that are at work in the rose. And then we try, not merely to go on turning such thoughts over and over in our mind, but to let them come to life in our heart and feeling. A sensation of bliss can come over us as we contemplate the pure and dispassionate nature of the growing plant; and we feel obliged to admit that certain higher perfections have to be purchased by the acquisition at the same time of impulses and desires. This thought can change the bliss that we experienced before into a solemn feeling; and then a sense of liberation can come over us, a feeling of true happiness when we give ourselves up to the thought of the red blood that can become the bearer — even as the red sap in the rose — of experiences that are inwardly pure. In pursuing thus a train of thought that serves to build up such a symbolic picture, it is important to accompany the thought all the time with feeling. Then, having entered right into the experience of the thoughts and feelings, we can re-cast them in the following symbolic picture.

Imagine you see before you a black cross. Let this black cross be for you a symbol for the baser elements that have been cast out of man's impulses and passions; and at the point where the beams of the cross meet, picture to yourself seven resplendent bright red roses arranged in a circle. Let these roses symbolize for you a blood that is the expression of passions and impulses that have undergone purification.* Some such symbolic thought-picture shall the pupil of spiritual training call up before his soul, and he can do this in the same way as was explained above for a memory-picture. Devoting himself to it in deep, inner contemplation, he will find that the picture has power to call his soul awake. He must try to banish for the time being everything else from his mind. The symbol in question, and that alone, should now hover before him in spirit, as livingly as ever possible.

There is meaning in the fact that the symbolic picture has not simply been put forward as a picture that has in itself an awakening power, but that it was first built up by a sequence of thoughts concerning plant and man. What such a picture can do for the pupil depends on his having himself first put it together in the way described, before he uses it as an object of meditation. Were he to picture it without having gone through the construction of it in his own soul, it would remain cold and would have far less effect, for it is the preparation that endows it with power to enlighten the soul. The pupil should however not be recalling the preparatory steps while engaged in the meditation, but have then merely the symbolic picture hovering before him in spirit, quick with life — letting only the *feelings* that were aroused by the preparatory chain of thought echo on within him. In this way does the symbolic picture come to be a sign, appropriate to and accompanying the inner experience.

The efficacy of the experience depends upon how long the pupil is able to continue in it. The longer he can do so, without allowing any other idea to disturb the meditation, the greater its value for him. It is, however, also good if, apart from the

* It is of no consequence how far the above thoughts can be justified from the side of Natural Science, the whole point being to evolve thoughts in regard to plant and man which can be arrived at without reference to any theory, by simple and direct observation. Thoughts of this kind concerning objects in the world around us have their significance, alongside of the theoretical ideas of science which are, in their right place, no less significant. Here we are not putting forward thoughts for the purpose of presenting facts in scientific terms; what we want to do is to create a symbolic picture that shall prove capable of influencing the soul, irrespective of any criticisms that could be levelled at the composition of the picture.

times that he devotes to the meditation as such, he will frequently build up the picture all over again, letting the thoughts and feelings rise up in him in the way we have described, that the mood of the experience may not pale. The more ready the pupil is patiently to continue renewing the picture in this way, the greater significance will it have for his soul. (In my book *Knowledge of the Higher Worlds and its Attainment*, other subjects are suggested for meditation. Particularly fruitful in their results are the meditations on the coming-into-being and passing-away of a plant, on the forces of growth that lie dormant in the seed, on the forms of crystals, etc. In the present book, the intention has been merely to illustrate, by means of an example, the nature of meditation.)

A symbolic picture such as we have here described does not represent some external object that Nature has produced; and to this very fact it owes its power to awaken capabilities that belong entirely to the soul. Some persons may beg to differ! They may, for instance, say: Agreed, the symbolic picture as a whole is not to be found in Nature, but all its details are borrowed from Nature — the black colour, the roses, and so forth; these have every one of them been first perceived by the senses. If any reader be disturbed in his mind by such an objection, let him reflect that these component parts of the picture, which are undoubtedly derived from sense-perception, do not in themselves lead to the awakening of higher faculties in the soul; the awakening is brought about solely by the *way* in which the single details have been *put together* to form the picture. For that, no prototype is to be found in the outer world.

The endeavour has here been made, taking a particular symbolic picture as an example, to give a clear account of how meditation can take its course. For the purpose of spiritual training, a great variety of pictures of this kind can be used, and they can be built up in many different ways. Sentences, formulae, even single words, may also be given as subjects for meditation. In every instance the aim will be to wrest the soul free from sense-perception and rouse it to an activity for which the outer impressions of the physical senses are without significance, the whole import and aim of the activity being to unfold dormant faculties of the soul. Meditations that are directed wholly to certain feelings or emotions are also possible; they are indeed particularly valuable for the soul. Take the feeling of joy. In the ordinary course of life we can rejoice over something we see taking place. Suppose a man who has a healthily developed life of feeling observes someone performing an action that is inspired by real goodness of heart. He will be pleased, he will rejoice in the kind deed. And it may be, he will then go on to ponder over a deed of this nature in somewhat the following way. A deed that proceeded from kindness of heart, he may think to himself, is one in which the doer follows, not his own interests but the interests of his fellow-man; I may therefore call it a 'good' deed. But now he can go further. He can turn right away from the particular action that he observed and that gave him such pleasure, and create for himself the comprehensive idea of loving-kindness, 'goodness of heart'. He can picture to himself how it arises in the soul, namely through the person's absorbing, as it were, the interests of his fellow, making them his own. And he can rejoice in this moral conception of kindness. The joy that he now has is no longer over this or that event in the physical world, it is joy in an *idea* as such. If we try to let joy of this kind live on in our soul for a considerable time we shall actually be practising meditation upon a feeling. It is not the mere idea that will awaken the inner faculties, but the prolonged surrender of the soul to a feeling that is not just due to a particular external impression.

Supersensible cognition being able to penetrate more deeply into the real nature of things, feelings evoked by spiritual knowledge can be imparted and used for meditation. These will be all the more efficacious in unfolding the inner faculties of the soul. Necessary as this enhanced development will be for the higher stages of the pupil's training, he should nevertheless understand that meditations upon simple feelings and emotions such as the one concerning goodness of heart, if diligently carried out, can take him very far. Since people differ in nature and character, the means that prove most useful for individual pupils will naturally vary. As to the length of time that should be given to meditation, the thing of prime importance is that while engaged in it, the pupil shall remain calm and collected; its efficacy indeed depends on this. In the matter of time he should also be careful not to overshoot the mark. The exercises themselves will help him to acquire a certain inner tact which will teach him how far he may rightly go in this respect.

The pupil will as a rule have to carry out such exercises for quite a long while before he himself is able to notice any result. Patience and perseverance are absolute essentials in spiritual training. Unless the pupil evokes these qualities within him, going through his exercises so quietly and so regularly that patience and perseverance may be said to constitute the fundamental mood of his soul, he will make little progress.

It will be clear, from what has been said so far, that deep inner contemplation — meditation — is a means for the attainment of knowledge of higher worlds, and moreover that not just any thought-picture can be taken for meditation, but only one that has been built up in the way described.

The path that has been indicated leads in the first place to what may be called 'Imaginative cognition' — the first stage, that is, of higher cognition. The cognition that depends upon sense-perception and upon the elaboration of sense-perceptions by an intellect that is bound to the senses, may be called — from the point of view of spiritual science — 'objective cognition'. Above it are the various stages of higher cognition, the Imaginative being the first. The word Imagination may well raise distrust in the minds of those who take it to mean some idea that is engendered by mere fancy — some 'imaginary' idea or mental picture unrelated to reality. In spiritual science however, Imaginative cognition is to be understood as a cognition that results from the soul's having attained to a supersensible state of consciousness. What is perceived in this condition of consciousness are spiritual facts and spiritual beings whereto the senses have no access. Since this first supersensible consciousness is awakened in the pupil by his giving himself up in meditation to symbolic pictures or 'imaginations', it may be termed 'Imaginative consciousness' and the cognition connected with it 'Imaginative cognition' — meaning by this a cognition that is able to have knowledge of what is real in another sense than are the facts and objects perceived with the physical senses. The *content* of the thought-picture in the imaginative meditation is not the important thing; what is important is the faculty of soul that is thereby developed.

Another very understandable objection may be put forward to the employment of symbolic mental pictures. The building up of such pictures, it may be alleged, is carried out by a dreamlike thinking that makes use of arbitrary fancy, and the result can only be of questionable value. There is, however, no occasion to harbour any such misgiving in regard to the thought-pictures which form the basis of a right and sound spiritual training. Such thought-pictures are expressly chosen with this end in view — namely, that the relation they may have to external reality can be disregarded and their value sought purely in the power with which they work upon the soul when attention has been withdrawn from the outer world, when all sense-impressions and even all the thoughts the mind can entertain in response to sense-impressions have been eliminated.

If we want to form a clear and true picture of the process of meditation, we shall find it helpful to compare it with sleep. On the one hand it resembles sleep, whilst on the other hand it is the very opposite. For it is a sleep which in comparison with ordinary day-consciousness gives signs of a higher awakeness. The truth of the matter is that, having to concentrate upon one particular symbolic or other thought-picture, the soul is obliged to summon up from its depths much stronger forces than it is accustomed to employ in ordinary life or for the ordinary process of cognition. Its inner activity is enhanced thereby. The soul liberates itself from the body, even as it does in sleep. Only, instead of going over into unconsciousness, it now has living experience of a world it did not know before. Thus, the soul is in a condition which, although in its liberation from the body it may be likened to sleep, has nevertheless to be described as an *enhanced awakeness* in comparison with ordinary consciousness. The soul comes in this way to a living experience of itself in its inmost, true and independent being, whereas in ordinary waking life, when its forces are less strongly developed, it is only with the help of the body that the soul attains consciousness at all. It does not under these conditions have any conscious experience of itself, becoming conscious only in the picture which, like a reflection from a mirror, the body — or, one should rather say, the bodily processes conjure up before it.

The symbolic pictures that are built up in the way described cannot of course be said to have relation as yet to anything real in the spiritual world. Their purpose is to detach the soul from sense-perception, and from the instrument of the brain with which in ordinary life the intellect is bound up. This detachment cannot be effected until man feels: Now I am forming a thought-picture by the use of forces that need no assistance from the senses or from the brain. The very first experience that befalls the pupil on his path is this liberation from the physical organs. He can then say to himself: My consciousness is not extinguished when I abandon sense-perceptions and abandon also my ordinary intellectual thinking; I can lift myself right out of this thinking, and I then feel myself a living spiritual being, side by side with what I was before. Here then we have the first purely spiritual experience: the pupil becomes aware of himself as an I, an Ego, purely in the soul and spirit. A new self has arisen out of the self that is bound up with the physical senses and the physical intellect. Had the pupil freed himself from the world of the senses and the intellect without deep inner meditation, he would have fallen into the void of unconsciousness. Naturally, he already had in him this being of pure soul and spirit before he practised meditation, but it had then no instruments whereby it could observe in the spiritual world. It was not unlike a physical body that has no eyes to see with, no ears to hear with. The force that has been expended in achieving meditation has created organs of soul and spirit, has called them forth out of what was hitherto unorganized soul-and-spirit being.

What the pupil has in this way himself created, is also what he first perceives. Therefore his first experience is a kind of self-perception. It is in accord with the whole nature of spiritual training that, thanks to the self-education he has been undergoing, man is at this stage fully conscious that he is *perceiving himself* in the picture-worlds (Imaginations) which appear as a result of the exercises. These pictures seem to the pupil to be alive, and in a new world; yet he must recognize that, to begin with, they are nothing else than the reflection of his own being, strengthened as this now is by reason of the exercises he has carried out. Moreover not only has the pupil to come to a right conclusion on this point; he must in addition develop such a strong will that he is able at any moment to wipe out the pictures, to dismiss them altogether from consciousness. He must have it in his power to exercise authority over them in perfect freedom and confidence. And he will be able to do this, provided the training has been on sound lines. Otherwise, the pupil would be in the same plight in the realm of spiritual experience, as a man would be in the physical world if, when he turned to look at some object, his eye were to remain fettered to that object so that he was quite unable to look away from it. There is however one exception. One group of inner picture-experiences must *not* be blotted out at this stage of spiritual training. It is a group that relates to the heart and kernel of the pupil's own being; in the Imaginations of this group he is made acquainted with the very ground of his being, with that within him which passes through repeated earth lives. At this moment in his development he begins to feel — as a direct experience — the reality of repeated earth lives. In respect of everything else that he experiences in this realm there must be the freedom of which we spoke.

Only after the pupil has acquired the faculty of wiping out the Imaginations, does he approach the real external world of the spirit. In place of the pictures that have been wiped out, something else appears, and in this the pupil begins to attain knowledge of spiritual reality. His feeling of himself, from being dim and vague, reaches a clarity and definition hitherto unknown. And he has now to go further; he has to advance from this perception of himself to observation of the world of soul and spirit that surrounds him. This he will be able to do when he directs his inner experience in a way that will now be indicated.

To begin with, the soul is weak over against all that offers itself for perception in the world of soul and spirit. The pupil will already have had to expend considerable energy of soul in order to hold fast in meditation the symbolic or other pictures which he built up out of the data of the world of sense. But if he wants in addition to attain to actual observation in a higher world, he will have to do more than this. He must be able to abide in a condition wherein not only the stimuli of the external world no longer influence his soul, but even the Imaginative thought-pictures are completely obliterated from his consciousness. For the moment has now arrived when that which has been formed and fashioned within him by dint of deep inner concentration of soul can come to view. Everything now depends upon the pupil's having sufficient inner energy of soul to allow it to be actually *seen* by him spiritually; it must not escape his notice, as invariably happens when the forces of the soul are too little developed. The soul-and-spirit organism that has come to development within him and that the pupil has now to apprehend in self-perception is frail and evanescent. Many and serious are the disturbances that come from the outer world of sense and from memories of the same, and that persist in the mind even when the pupil does his utmost to shut them out. Nor is it only the disturbances of which we can be aware that come into question; still more serious are those of which we are totally unaware in ordinary life.

The very conditions however under which the life of man takes its course make possible here a transition stage. What the soul is unable to achieve when awake on account of these disturbances from the physical world, it can achieve in sleep. One who devotes himself to meditation will, if sufficiently attentive, begin to notice something new about his sleep. He will be aware that he is not always fully asleep the whole time, but that there are moments when his soul, although he is asleep, is nevertheless active in some way. At such times, the natural processes of sleep keep away the influences of the external world which he is not yet strong enough to keep away by his own efforts while awake. And now that the exercises in concentration and meditation have begun to take effect, the soul is released from complete unconsciousness during sleep and is able to feel the world of soul and spirit. This can come home to the pupil in either of two ways. He may be well aware during his sleep: 'I am now in another world', or he may have the memory when he wakes up: 'I have been in another world'. A greater inner energy is of course required for the first way than for the second, which will accordingly for a beginner be the more frequent of the two. And it may be that gradually the point is reached when the pupil, on awaking, has the impression: During the whole time that I have been asleep I have been in another world; I emerged from it only when I awoke. Moreover his memory of the beings and facts of this other world will grow more and more definite. This will mean that the pupil has attained in one or another form what may be called 'continuity of consciousness' (the persistence of consciousness during sleep). There is no implication that he will *always* retain consciousness during sleep. He will have made good progress in this direction if, while in general he sleeps as others do, there are times when during sleep he can be consciously gazing into a world of soul and spirit; or again if, when awake, he can look back upon short periods of such consciousness.

It must not be forgotten that this is only a transition state. It is good for his spiritual training that the pupil should go through this stage, but he must not imagine that it can afford him conclusive evidence in regard to the world of soul and spirit. He is, in this condition, still uncertain and cannot yet rely on his perceptions. Thanks however to experiences of this nature he does gradually gather power to attain the like result also in waking life — that is, to hold off the disturbing influences of the physical world upon his senses and upon his inner life, and so attain that 'observing' in soul and spirit where no impressions enter by way of the senses, where the brain-bound intellect is silent, and where even those thought-pictures are banished from consciousness, upon which he had been meditating in preparation for seeing in the spirit. (Things *published* in the name of spiritual science should invariably be the outcome of spiritual observations made in a fully wide-awake condition.)

There are two inner experiences, important in the course of spiritual training. The one enables the pupil to say to himself: If I now turn aside from every impression that can reach me from the surrounding physical world, I do not, when I look within, behold there a being that is totally inactive, but a being that is conscious of itself in a world of which I can know nothing as long as I only lay myself open to impressions that come to me through sense-perception and through everyday thinking. At this moment, the pupil can have the feeling that he has himself given birth to a new being that is there within him as the very heart and kernel of his soul, a being possessed moreover of entirely different qualities from those that have been his up to now.

The second experience is as follows. The pupil discovers that he can now have beside him the self he has been hitherto, as if it were another and distinct self. He is in a sense confronted by the being within which he has until now been confined. He feels he is temporarily outside what he has hitherto been accustomed to call his very own self, his I. It is as if he were living, with perfect calm and composure, in two selves. The first of them he knew before; the second self now confronts the first as a new-born entity. Moreover he feels the first becoming in a way self-subsistent, independent of the second, rather as man's body has an independent existence of its own apart from this first self. This is an experience of very great moment; for the pupil knows now what it means to live in that higher world which, with the help of his training, he has been endeavouring to reach.

The second, the new-born self, can now be brought to perceive in the spiritual world. Within it there can unfold for the spiritual world what the sense-organs are for the physical. When this development has reached the required stage, the pupil will be able to do more than feel himself as a new-born I. Just as he perceives the physical world by means of his senses, so will he now begin to perceive around him spiritual facts and spiritual beings. Here we have then a *third* significant experience. In order to pass through this stage successfully, the pupil will have to reckon with the fact that along with the strengthening of the soul's forces, self-love and self-conceit begin to assume proportions that are quite unknown in ordinary life. It would argue a complete lack of understanding, were we to imagine that this was no more than the ordinary kind of selfishness and self-love. Self-love grows so strong at this stage of the pupil's development, that it can actually seem to him like a force of Nature working within him, and a strenuous discipline of the will is required to get the better of this prodigious self-conceit. The latter does not come as a result of spiritual training. This self-conceit is always there in man, but only when the pupil comes to have real experience of the Spirit is it raised up into consciousness. Hand in hand therefore with spiritual training must always go the training of the will. The pupil is conscious of a tremendous urge to feel blissfully happy in the world which he has created within him. What he must now be able to do is to wipe out, as described above, the very thing he has taken such pains to achieve. Having reached the Imaginative world, he must there contrive to extinguish self. In opposition to this self-effacement are ranged within him the excessively strong impulses of self-opinion and self-conceit. It might easily be imagined that exercises for spiritual training were something quite apart and had nothing whatever to do with moral development. To this one can only reply that the moral force needed to overcome this self-conceit cannot possibly be acquired unless the whole ethical tone and disposition of the pupil be raised to a proportionate level. Progress in spiritual training is out of the question, unless progress be made at the same time in the ethical sphere. Lack of moral strength makes conquest of self-conceit impossible. The allegation that genuine spiritual training is not *ipso facto* moral training is entirely mistaken.

Only one who has no personal knowledge of such experience could here interpose the question: How are we to know, when we think we have spiritual perceptions, that we are facing realities and not the mere creations of our fancy — visions, hallucinations and the like? As a matter of fact, a pupil who has reached the above stage in proper spiritual training can distinguish between the figments of his own fancy and spiritual reality, just as a person of normal intelligence is able to distinguish between the mental picture of a hot iron and a real one he touches with his hand; he knows the difference by virtue of a sound and healthy experience of life. So too in the spiritual world, life itself provides the touchstone. In the world of the senses, we know that if we imagine a hot iron, then however hot we picture it, it will not burn our fingers; so does the pupil of the Spirit know whether he is only imagining that he confronts a spiritual fact or whether real facts and real beings are making their impression on the organs of spiritual perception that have been awakened in him. The instructions he will need to follow during his training to save him from falling a victim to illusion in this regard will be set forth in the following pages.

It is of the utmost importance that by the time the pupil becomes conscious of a new-born self within him, his whole character and morale shall have reached a high level. For it is like this. It belongs to man's I or Ego, to control his sensations and feelings and ideas, also his impulses, desires and passions. Perceptions, mental pictures and ideas cannot be simply let loose in the soul; they must be regulated by the exercise of a thoughtful discretion. The I, the self, administers the laws of thought, thereby bringing order into man's thinking and ideation. It is the same with his desires and impulses, his inclinations and passions. These are guided and controlled by his moral principles. Thus the self, by the exercise of ethically sound judgment and discretion, becomes man's guide in this domain. When now we have succeeded in drawing out of our ordinary self a higher self, the former will become to some extent independent. But it will at the same time be deprived of the energies now devoted to the higher self. Let us see what will happen if a pupil wants to give birth to his higher self, when he has not yet developed adequate ability or certainty in his application of the laws of thought nor in his powers of judgment and discretion. He cannot leave to his ordinary self any more ability in the field of thought than he has hitherto developed. Should this not suffice, then his everyday self, continuing on its own, will exhibit a thinking that is disordered, confused and fantastic. Since for such a person the new-born self can only be weak, the lower self, confused as it is, will gain control over his beholding in the supersensible, and he will fail to show discrimination in regard to what he observes there. Had he developed sufficiently his faculty for logical thinking, there would have been no difficulty in allowing his everyday self to assume independence.

The same applies in the realm of ethics. If a pupil has not acquired firmness in moral judgment, if he is not sufficiently master of his inclinations, his impulses and passions, he will be conferring independence on his everyday self when it is still in a condition of relative subjection to them. It can happen that such a person will not recognize in reference to his supersensible experience the same need to conform to a high standard of truth as he does in respect of what the outer physical world presents to his consciousness. Should he thus have a lax regard for truth, he could easily take for spiritual reality all manner of things that are nothing but figments of his own fancy. What is needed is that, before the higher self begins to be active in its quest for knowledge of the supersensible, the pupil's sense of truth be infused with a firmness of moral judgment and with a stability of character and of conscience, that have been developed in the self now left behind. This is not by any means said with intention to frighten people away from spiritual training; it is nevertheless a consideration that needs to be taken very seriously.

If the pupil is firmly resolved to leave nothing undone that will help to make his first self reliable in the strict performance of its functions, then he has no need to be afraid of this event that comes as a result of spiritual training — the liberation, that is, of a second self for the attainment of knowledge in the supersensible. He must however not forget that self-deception is apt to be particularly strong when one is deeming oneself 'ripe' for some new step. In the school of spiritual training we have here described, the pupil's life of thought undergoes a development which precludes the danger, so very often alleged, of being led astray. Thanks to the development of the life of thought, the pupil is able to undergo all necessary experiences of the inner life in such a way that there is no fear of their being accompanied by delusive and mischievous creations of the fancy. Where adequate development of the life of thought has been lacking, the experiences can well evoke serious uncertainty in the soul of the pupil. If the pupil is prepared in the way here recommended, he will acquire knowledge of the new experiences in much the same way as a man of healthy mind gets to know the objects he perceives in the physical world. Development of the life of thought tends rather to make him an *observer* of what he himself is experiencing, whereas without it he is absorbed in the experience — as it were, unreflective and unheeding.

In a proper school of spiritual training certain qualities are set forth that require to be cultivated by one who desires to find the path to the higher worlds. First and foremost, the pupil must have control over his thoughts (in their course and sequence), over his will, and over his feelings. The control has to be acquired by means of exercises, and these are planned with two ends in view. On the one hand, the soul has to become so firm, so secure and balanced that it will retain these qualities when a second self is born. And on the other hand, the pupil has to endow this second self, from the start, with strength and steadfastness.

The quality that thinking needs above all is objectivity. In the world of the physical senses life itself is our great teacher in this respect. Let a man fling his thoughts hither and thither in a purely arbitrary manner, he will find himself obliged to suffer life to correct him if he does not want to come into conflict with it. He must of necessity bring his thinking into correspondence with the facts. But when he turns his attention away from the physical world, this compulsory correction fails him; and if his thinking has not then the ability to be its own corrector, it will inevitably follow will-o'-the-wisps. The pupil of the spirit must therefore undertake exercises in thinking in order that his thinking may be able to mark out its own path and goal. Stability, and the capacity to adhere firmly to a once chosen subject, are what the pupil's thinking has to acquire. There is therefore no occasion for the exercises to deal with remote or complicated objects, much rather should they have reference to simple objects that are ready to hand. Whoever succeeds in directing his thought, for at least five minutes daily, and for months on end, to some quite commonplace object — say, for example, a needle or a pencil — and in shutting out during those five minutes all thoughts that have no connection with the object, will have made very good progress in this direction. (A fresh object may be chosen each day, or one may be continued for several days.) Even a person who considers himself a trained intellectual thinker should not be too proud to qualify for spiritual training by an exercise of this simple nature. For when we are riveting our thought for a considerable time upon something that is entirely familiar, we may be quite sure that our thinking is in accord with reality. If we ask ourselves: What is a lead pencil made of? How are the different materials prepared? How are they put together? When were lead pencils invented? and so on, we can be more sure of our thoughts being consistent with reality than if we were to ponder the question of the descent of man — or, let us say, of the meaning of life. Simple exercises in thinking are a far better preparation for forming commensurate conceptions of Saturn, Sun and Moon evolution than are complicated and learned ideas. As to our thinking, what is important at this stage is not the object or event to which it is directed, but that it should be strong and vigorous and to the point. If it has been educated to be so in reference to simple physical realities that lie open to view, it will acquire the tendency to be so even when it finds itself no longer under the control of the physical world and its laws. The pupil will find he gets rid in this way of any tendency he had before to loose and extravagant thinking.

As in the world of thought, so also in the sphere of the will, the self has to become master. Here too, as long as we remain in the world of the physical senses, life itself may be said to be our master. Some vital need asserts itself and the will feels impelled to satisfy the need. But one who undergoes a higher training has to acquire the habit of strict obedience to what he tells himself to do on his own initiative. In learning this he will be less and less inclined to cherish pointless desires. Dissatisfaction and instability in the life of will come from setting one's heart on some aim, of the realization of which one has formed no clear notion. Dissatisfaction of this kind can bring the whole inner life into disorder at the moment when a higher self is ready to come forth from the soul. A good exercise for the will is, every day for months on end, to give oneself the command: To-day you are to do *this*, at this particular hour. One will gradually manage to fix the hour and the nature of the task so as to render the command perfectly possible to carry out. In this way we rise above that deplorable state of mind which finds expression in words such as: I would like to do this, I wish I could do that — when all the time there is no real expectation of fulfilment. A great poet made a prophetess say: 'Him I love who craves for the impossible.'* And the same poet says in his own name: 'To live in the Idea is to treat the impossible as though it were possible.'† Such words should however not be quoted as refuting the above recommendation. For the demand that Goethe and his prophetess (Manto) are making can only be met by one who has first educated himself in the achievement of desires that *are* possible of fulfilment — in order then, by dint of his strengthened will, to be able to treat the 'impossible' in such a way as to change it by his will into the possible.

Passing on now to the world of feeling, the pupil must succeed in reaching a certain equanimity of soul. For this he will need to have under his control all outward expression of pleasure or pain, of joy or sorrow. Such advice will be certain to meet with prejudice. Surely, if he is not to rejoice over what is joyful, not to sorrow over what is sorrowful, the pupil will become utterly indifferent to the life that is going on around him! But this is not at all what is meant. The pupil shall by all means rejoice over what is joyful and sorrow over what is

* Goethe: *Faust*, Part II, Act II.
† Goethe: *Proverbs in Prose.*

sorrowful. It is the outward expression of joy and sorrow, of pleasure and pain that he must learn to control. If he honestly tries to attain this, he will soon discover that he does not grow less, but actually more sensitive than before to everything in his environment that can arouse emotions of joy or of pain. If the pupil is really to succeed in cultivating this control it will undoubtedly involve keeping close watch upon himself for a long time. He must not be slow to enter with fulness of feeling into pleasure and pain, but must be able to do so without losing self-control and giving involuntary expression to it. What he has to suppress is not the pain — *that* is justified — but the involuntary weeping; not the horror at a base action, but the outburst of blind fury; not the caution in face of danger, but the giving way to panic — which does no good whatever.

Only by the practice of an exercise of this kind can the pupil attain the inner poise and quiet that he will have need of when the time comes for the higher self to be born in the soul, and more especially when this higher self becomes active there. Otherwise the soul may lead an unhealthy life of its own alongside the higher self — like a kind of double. It is important not to fall a victim to self-deception in this matter. It may seem to many a pupil that he already possesses a good measure of equanimity in ordinary life and will not therefore need this exercise. In point of fact, such a one is doubly in need of it. A man may remain perfectly calm and composed in relation to the exigencies of everyday life, and then, when he rises into a higher world, exhibit a sad lack of poise — all the more so indeed, since the tendency to let himself go was there all the time, only suppressed. It must be clearly understood that what a pupil *appears* to have already of some attribute of the soul is of little account for spiritual training; what is far more important is that he should practise regularly and systematically the exercises he needs. Contradictory as such a statement may sound, it is true nevertheless. Say that life has endowed us with this or that virtue; for spiritual training it is the virtues *we ourselves have cultivated* that are of value. Are we by nature easily excitable, it is for us to rid ourselves of this excitability;

are we by nature calm and imperturbable, we must bestir ourselves to bring it about through our own self-education that the impressions we receive from without awake in us the right response. A man who cannot laugh has just as little control over his life as a man who without self-control is perpetually giving way to laughter.

It will be a further help to the education of his thinking and feeling, if the pupil acquire a virtue that I will call positiveness. A lovely legend is related of Christ Jesus. It tells how He is walking with a few other persons, and they pass by a dead dog. The others turn away from the revolting sight. Christ Jesus speaks admiringly of the beautiful teeth of the animal. One can train oneself to meet the world with the disposition of soul that this legend displays. The spurious, the bad and the ugly should not hinder us from finding, wherever they are present, the true, the good and the beautiful. Positiveness must not be confused with lack of discrimination, or with an arbitrary shutting of one's eyes to what is bad, or false, or 'good for nothing'. He who admires the 'beautiful teeth' of a dead animal sees also the decaying body. The unsightly corpse does not, however, prevent him from seeing the beautiful teeth. We cannot deem a bad thing good or an error true; but we can take care not to be put off by the bad from seeing the good, nor by the false from seeing the true.

The thinking, and together with it the willing, reaches a certain maturity if one tries never to let past experiences rob one of open-minded receptivity for new ones. To declare in the face of some new experience: 'I never heard of such a thing, I don't believe it!' should make no sense at all to a pupil of the Spirit. Rather let him make the deliberate resolve, during a certain period of time to let every thing or being he encounters tell him something new. A breath of wind, a leaf falling from a tree, the prattle of a little child, can all teach us something, are we but ready to adopt a point of view to which we have perhaps not hitherto been accustomed. One can, it is true, carry this too far. We must not, at whatever age we have reached, put right out of our minds everything we have experienced hitherto. We have most decidedly to base our judgment of what confronts us now upon past experience. That is on the one side of the balance, but on the other there is the need for the pupil of the Spirit to be ready all the time for entirely new experiences; above all, to admit to himself the possibility that the new may contradict the old.

These then are five qualities of soul the pupil has to acquire in the course of a right and proper training: control over the direction of his thoughts, control of his impulses of will, equanimity in the face of pleasure and pain, positiveness in his attitude to the world around him, readiness to meet life with an open mind. Lastly, when he has spent consecutive periods of time in training himself for the acquisition of these five qualities, the pupil will need to bring them into harmony in his soul. He will have to practise them in manifold combinations — two by two, three and one at a time, and so on, in order to establish harmony among them.*

These exercises have been assigned a place in spiritual training, because when thoroughly and effectually carried out they have not only their more immediate result in the cultivation of the desired qualities, but indirectly a great deal more will follow from them that is of no less importance for the pupil on his path to the spiritual worlds. Whoever gives sufficient time and care to their practice will, whilst he is doing them, come up against many blemishes and shortcomings in his soul, and will moreover find in the exercises themselves the means of strengthening and stabilising his thought life, as well as his life of feeling and indeed his whole character. He will undoubtedly need, many more exercises, adapted to his own individual faculties, to his particular character and temperament. These will emerge when the above have been practised in all thoroughness. One will indeed discover, as time goes on, that these six exercises give one indirectly more than at first appears to be contained in them. Suppose the pupil is lacking in self-confidence. He will after a time begin to notice that, thanks to the

* *Note by Translators.* In other writings and in lectures, Rudolf Steiner often referred to this harmonizing and uniting of the preceding five as a *sixth* exercise. Collectively they are then known as the six 'accessory exercises' (*Nebenübungen*).

exercises, he is gaining the self-confidence of which he stands in need. And it will be the same with other qualities of soul wherein he may be deficient. (Special exercises, described in more detail, will be found in my book *Knowledge of the Higher Worlds and its Attainment.*)

It is important that the pupil shall find it possible to go on developing the said six qualities in ever increasing measure. His control over his thoughts and sensations must become great enough to enable him to set aside times of complete inner quiet, when all the joys and sorrows, all the satisfactions and anxieties of everyday life — nay more, even all its tasks and demands are banished from mind and heart. In such times that alone which he himself wills to admit shall be allowed entry to his soul. Here again it is possible that some reader may feel misgiving. Will not the pupil become estranged from daily life and its tasks, if he withdraws from it in this way, banishing it from mind and heart for certain stated times during the day? In reality, however, this is far from being so. One who devotes himself in this way to periods of inner quiet, will find that he grows stronger in many respects for the tasks of daily life, and fulfils them, not only no less well, but decidedly better than before.

Such periods will have special value for the pupil if during them he refrains entirely from thinking of his own personal affairs and rises to the contemplation of the concerns of mankind at large. Should he be able at such times to fill his soul with communications that come from higher spiritual worlds, letting these take no less firm hold upon his interest than do his personal cares and concerns in ordinary life, he will be richly rewarded.

One who makes serious endeavour to gain this mastery over his life of soul will also find his way to a self-observation by means of which he will be able to regard his own concerns as coolly and quietly as if they had no connection with himself. To be able to look upon all experiences that come to one in life, all joys and sorrows, in the very same way as one looks upon those of others is a good preparation for spiritual training. The pupil will find he can gradually attain the necessary ability in this direction, if every evening when the day's work is done, he lets pass before his mind's eye pictures of the day's experiences, watching himself go through them. This will mean that he is looking at himself as he is in daily life — from without. To begin with, let him take small sections of the day. That will give him practice; and he will find that he grows more and more skilful in this 'looking backward' (*Rückschau*), until at last he is able to picture the whole day through in quite a short span of time. This beholding of our experiences in backward direction has a special value for spiritual training: it helps us disengage our thinking from its accustomed habit of holding on to the outer, material and sense-perceptible events. When we think backwards, we picture the events correctly, but we are no longer sustained by the obvious external sequence. The pupil needs this liberation if he is to make his way into the supersensible world. He will find too that by this freedom his thinking and ideation are strengthened, and in a thoroughly healthy manner. It is accordingly good also to review other things in backward order — a play, for example, a story, a melody, and so on.

A pupil of the Spirit will have it increasingly as his ideal to meet the events of life with inner quiet and confidence, forming his judgment on them, not as to how they accord with his own particular disposition but on the basis of their inherent meaning and inner value. By holding this ideal ever before him, he will be laying in his soul the foundation for that deep inner contemplation — of symbolic and other thoughts and also of feelings — of which we have been hearing.

It is essential for the pupil to fulfil the above conditions, for supersensible experience has to be built upon the ground on which he stands in ordinary life before he enters the supersensible world. His experience there is dependent in two ways on the point he reached before setting out. If he has not taken special care to see that an ability for sound judgment is at the very foundation of his spiritual training, he will develop supersensible faculties which perceive the spiritual world inaccurately and falsely. His organs of spiritual perception will evolve in a wrong way. As in the world of the senses we cannot see correctly with imperfect or diseased eyes, so in the spiritual world we cannot perceive correctly with organs lacking the foundation of sound judgment and discrimination.

Should it happen that a pupil sets out on the path with an immoral character, his power of vision, when he mounts up into the spiritual worlds, will be dim and clouded. He will be like a man in the world of the senses who gazes at it in a condition of stupor. With this difference, however: whereas the latter will have little of any consequence to tell, the observer in the spiritual world — even in his stupor — is more awake than man is in ordinary consciousness, and will accordingly give information of what he sees there. The information will however be erroneous.

*   *   *   *   *

The trustworthiness of the Imaginative stage of cognition can be assured if the pupil will lend support to his meditation by acquiring the habit of what may be called 'sense-free' thinking. When we form a thought, basing it on something we have observed in the physical world, the thought is dependent on the physical senses. This is, however, not the only kind of thought we are able to entertain. There is no need for our thinking to be empty of content when it is no longer being filled with the data of sense-observation. The surest way to attain sense-free thinking, the way too that lies nearest at hand for the pupil, is to let his thinking lay hold of the facts of the higher world, communicated in spiritual science. These facts cannot be observed with the physical senses. Yet the pupil will find that with sufficient patience and perseverance he can grasp them. It is impossible to undertake research in the higher world, impossible to observe there for oneself, without spiritual training; one can however without higher training understand what is communicated by those who have carried out such research. If someone asks: But how can I take on trust what spiritual researchers say, when I cannot see it for myself? — the question is in reality unjustified. For it is perfectly possible, by simple reflection, to arrive at the sure conviction that the communications are true. If anyone finds himself unable to do so, it is not because it is impossible to 'believe' something one does not see; it is due to the fact that the thought he has given to it has not been sufficiently free from prejudice, not comprehensive or deep enough. To be quite clear on this point, we must be ready to recognize that man's thinking can, if he applies it with energy and determination, grasp more than is generally supposed. For his thinking has within it an inner reality of being which has connection with the supersensible world. Man is, as a rule, unconscious of the connection, since he is accustomed to apply his thinking faculty to the sense-world alone; hence, when he hears of communications from the supersensible world, he sets them down as incomprehensible. They are however thoroughly comprehensible — and not alone to those whose thinking has been educated through spiritual training, but to *every* thinking person who is conscious of the full power of his thinking and ready to apply it.

By continuously apprising ourselves of what spiritual science tells, we grow accustomed to a thinking that does not take its start from outer observation by the senses. We learn how within our mind thought weaves on thought, thought seeks out thought, even when the connections have not been suggested by sensory observation. We make the significant discovery that the world of thought is inherently alive, and that when we are really and truly thinking we are already in the realm of a supersensible and living world. We say to ourselves: There is something in me that is developing a living organism of thought; moreover I myself am at one with it. As we continue to devote ourselves to sense-free thinking, we actually come to feel that there is something of real being — real inner substance — flowing into our inner life, even as when we observe with the senses there flow into us by way of our physical organs the properties of the things of sense.

Out there in space, says the observer of the sense-world, is a rose. I do not feel it in any way strange or remote, for it makes itself known to me by means of its colour and its scent. We need only be sufficiently free from preconceived ideas to be able also to say, when sense-free thinking is at work in us: Something quite real is making itself known to me, uniting thought with thought, forming within me a living body of thought. Yet there is an essential difference between the feeling we have towards the things we see in the external world of sense and on the other hand towards the reality of being that communicates itself to us in sense-free thinking. The observer of the external world of the senses will feel that he himself is *outside* the rose he is seeing with his eyes, whilst one who is devoting himself to sense-free thinking will feel *within* him the reality that is making itself known to him. He feels himself at one with it. And anyone who (whether quite consciously or less so) is only prepared to attribute reality to what confronts him as an external object, will naturally not entertain the idea that something inherently real can also become known to him through his being inwardly united and at one with it. There is an inner experience we need, to see the matter rightly. We have to learn to distinguish between the associations of thought which we ourselves produce more or less arbitrarily, and those we experience within us when we have silenced our own arbitrary will. In the latter instance we can say: I remain perfectly still, I myself bring about no association of thought with thought; I give myself up to that which 'thinks in me'. We are then perfectly justified in saying: Something real is at work in me — no less justified than when on seeing the rose colour and perceiving the scent, we say: A rose is there making an impression on me.

The fact that we receive the content of the thoughts from communications made by the researcher in the Spirit does not contradict this. True, the thoughts are already there; but it is not possible for us to *think* them without creating them anew every time in our soul. That is really the whole point. The researcher in the Spirit awakens in his hearers and readers thoughts that they have to evoke *out of themselves*, whereas one who is describing a 'real' object — real in the world of the senses — is calling attention to what his hearers and readers can observe in the external world.

(The path that leads to sense-free thinking by way of the communications of spiritual science is thoroughly reliable and sure. There is however another that is even more sure, and above all more exact; at the same time, it is for many people also more difficult. The path in question is set forth in my books *The Theory of Knowledge implicit in Goethe's World-Conception* and *The Philosophy of Spiritual Activity*. These books tell of what man's thinking can achieve when directed, not to impressions that come from the outer world of the physical senses, but solely upon itself. When this is so, we have within us no longer the kind of thinking that concerns itself merely with memories of the things of sense; we have instead *pure thinking* which is like a being that has life within itself. In the above-mentioned books you will find nothing at all that is derived from communications of spiritual science. They testify to the fact that pure thinking, working within itself alone, can throw light on the great questions of life — questions concerning the universe and man. The books thus occupy a significant intermediate position between knowledge of the sense-world and knowledge of the spiritual world. What they offer is what thinking can attain, when it rises above sense-observation, yet still holds back from entering upon spiritual, supersensible research. One who wholeheartedly pursues the train of thought indicated in these books is already in the spiritual world; only it makes itself known to him as a thought-world. Whoever feels ready to enter upon this intermediate path of development will be taking a safe and sure road, and it will leave with him a feeling in regard to the higher world that will bear rich fruit through all time to come.)

*   *   *   *   *

The end in view for which the pupil engages in meditation upon symbolic thought-pictures or upon certain feelings, is neither more nor less than the development, within the astral body, of higher organs of perception. These organs are created out of the substance of the astral body itself; they bring the pupil into contact with a new world, and in this new world he learns to know himself as a new I or Ego. They differ from the organs with which we observe the world of the physical senses in that they are active. Eye and ear remain passive, allowing light and sound to act upon them; of the organs of perception that belong to the soul and spirit it can truly be said that while they are perceiving they are in continual activity, and furthermore that they *comprehend*, quite consciously, the objects and facts that they perceive. This gives us the feeling that when we 'know' with our soul and spirit, the very knowing is at the same time a blending with the facts we come to know; we feel we are living within them.

The several organs of soul and spirit that develop in this manner may be called, by way of comparison, lotus-flowers; the name accords with the form in which supersensible consciousness has to picture them — picture them, that is, Imaginatively. (It need hardly be said that such a designation has no more direct relation to reality than has the expression '*Flügel*' or 'wing' in the word 'Lungenflügel', meaning 'lobe of the lung'.) Specific kinds of meditation work upon the astral body in such a way as to lead to the development of one or other of these 'lotus-flowers'. After all that has been given in this book, it should be quite unnecessary to stress the fact that we have not to think of these organs of perception as though the symbolic picture of them which the name suggests were a direct imprint of their real nature. They are supersensible and consist in a definite activity of the soul; indeed they only exist in so far and for so long as the activity continues. We could as little speak, in connection with them, of anything observable by the senses, as we could of seeing a mist or cloud around a man when he is thinking! Those who insist on picturing the supersensible in sensual terms will inevitably be involved in misunderstandings. Superfluous as this remark should be, I let it stand, since one is constantly meeting with people who believe in the supersensible and yet want to picture it in far too sensual a way; also there are opponents of supersensible knowledge who imagine that when the scientist of the Spirit speaks of 'lotus flowers' he thinks of them as tangible objects howsoever refined — objects perceptible to the outer senses.

Every meditation undertaken for the attainment of Imaginative cognition has its influence, if rightly carried out, upon one or other of these organs. (In my book *Knowledge of the Higher Worlds and its Attainment* meditations and exercises are given

257

that take effect on this or that particular organ.) A proper spiritual training will arrange the several exercises in such order as to enable these organs of the soul to develop singly, together, or in due succession, as the case may be. This development asks for great patience and perseverance on the part of the pupil. The degree of patience a man gains in the ordinary course of life will not suffice. For it will be a long time — in many instances a very long time indeed — before the organs are so far developed that the pupil can make use of them for perceiving in the higher world. The moment he does become able to do this, he enters upon the stage of *Enlightenment*, so-called in contradistinction to the stage of *Preparation*, *Probation* or *Purification*, where the pupil is engaged upon the exercises that are given for the development of the organs. (The word 'Purification' is used, because by means of the exercises he undergoes, the pupil 'cleanses' a certain region of his inner life, casting out from it everything that has its source in the external world of the senses.) It may well happen that even before he reaches the stage of Enlightenment, a man will frequently experience sudden flashes that come from a higher world. These he should receive with thankfulness. The fact that he has them enables him already to bear witness to the spiritual world. He must however not weaken in his resolve if no such moments come during the time of Preparation — which may perhaps seem to him to be lasting all too long. Anyone who allows himself to grow impatient because he can still 'see nothing' has not yet succeeded in finding his right relation to a higher world. He alone has done so who can look upon the exercises he undertakes in his training as an end in themselves. With these he is in very truth doing work upon something in him that is of the nature of soul and spirit, namely, upon his astral body. And even when as yet he 'sees nothing', he can *feel*: I am really working and functioning in soul and spirit. If however he has made up his mind beforehand as to what he is going to 'see', he will not have this feeling. He will in that case be disregarding what is in truth of incalculable significance. He should on the contrary be paying careful attention to all that he experiences while doing the exercises. For this is radically different from anything he meets with in the world of sense. Already at this stage he will remark that in working upon his astral body he is not working into some indifferent substance, but that in his astral body lives a world of quite another kind — a world of which his life amid the outer senses tells him nothing. Even as the external world of the senses works upon the physical body, so are the higher Beings working upon the astral body. The pupil will 'impinge' upon the higher life in his own astral body, provided he himself does not stand in the way. If he is continually saying to himself: 'I can perceive nothing at all', it will generally mean that he has formed his own idea of what the spiritual percept has to look like, and since he does not see it in the form he has imagined, he says: 'I see nothing at all'.

The pupil who has the right attitude to his exercises will find increasingly that the very doing of them is something he can love for its own sake. He knows moreover that the doing of them places him already in a world of soul and spirit, and he waits with patience and above all with devotion for what is to come. This mood in the pupil can be best lifted into consciousness in the following words: 'I am resolved to carry out whatever exercises are right for me, and I know that I shall meantime be receiving as much as is important for me to receive. I do not demand it, I am not impatient; I simply hold myself ready all the time to receive it.' It is quite wrong to contend: 'So then the pupil is to grope his way on in the dark, perhaps for an incredibly long time, with no means of knowing that he is on the right path until success prove it to him!' For it is simply not true that the pupil has to wait for the exercises to achieve their end before he can be assured of their validity. If he undertakes them in the right spirit he need not wait for their eventual outcome; the satisfaction that he has in doing them will of itself make it clear to him that he is on the true path. Proper practice of exercises belonging to a path of spiritual training brings with it a sense of satisfaction that is no mere satisfaction but certain knowledge. The pupil knows: I am engaging in an activity which I can see is taking me forward in the right direction. Every pupil of the Spirit can have this certainty at every moment, if only he observes his experiences with sensitive discernment. If he is crudely inattentive, he is letting them go past him like a person out walking who is so deeply absorbed in his own reflections that he does not see the trees on either side of his path — although he could quite well be seeing them if he would only turn his eyes in their direction.

It is indeed undesirable that any other result than this one, which always attends the doing of the exercises, should be induced before the time is due. For it may well be that a seemingly successful result is no more than the smallest fraction of what should ensue in right and proper course. In spiritual development a partial success will often lead to a prolonged postponement of complete success. Moving familiarly among such forms of spiritual life as disclose themselves at an imperfect stage renders one insusceptible to influences that lead to higher levels of development. The seeming boon — namely the fact that one has after all had sight of the spiritual world — is not really a boon at all; this kind of 'beholding' cannot impart objective truth but only delusive pictures.

*   *   *   *   *

The organs of soul and spirit, the lotus-flowers, that are in course of development in one who is undergoing training, reveal themselves to supersensible consciousness in the neighbourhood, as it were, of particular bodily organs. From amongst the number of these organs of the soul, mention will here be made of the following. There is, first, the organ that is perceived as though about midway between the eyebrows (the so-called two-petalled lotus-flower); then, the organ in the region of the larynx (the sixteen-petalled lotus-flower); thirdly, the organ in the region of the heart (the twelve-petalled lotus-flower); and then a fourth in the neighbourhood of the pit of the stomach. Others come to view near other parts of the physical body. (The appellation two- or sixteen-petalled is not inappropriate, for the organs in question are in appearance comparable to flowers with these numbers of petals.)

The lotus-flowers become manifest to the consciousness of

the pupil in his astral body. As soon as he has developed one or other of them, he knows that he has it. He feels he can make use of it and that in doing so he does actually enter a higher world. The impressions he receives there still resemble in many respects those of the physical world. One who has attained Imaginative cognition will thus be able, in speaking of this new higher world, to describe his impressions by reference to sensations, for example, of warmth or of cold; or he may compare them to hearing music or speech, or to the effect upon him of light or colour. For this is the kind of feeling he has of them. He is however conscious that perceptions acquired in the Imaginative world tell of something altogether different from those acquired in the world of sense. He knows that what gives rise to them is not physical or material, but of the nature of soul and spirit. Suppose he receives an impression resembling the sensation of warmth. He will not ascribe it, for example, to a piece of hot iron, but will consider it as emanating from some soul situation or event of a kind that he has hitherto been aware of only in his inner life of soul. He knows that his Imaginative perceptions are due to things and happenings of the nature of pure soul and spirit, even as his physical perceptions are due to facts and entities of a material, physical nature.

Along with this resemblance of the Imaginative to the physical world there is at the same time a significant difference between them. One ever-present feature of the physical world shows itself in the Imaginative world in a totally different way. In the physical world we can observe a continual coming into being and passing away again, a constant alternation of birth with death. In the Imaginative world we find instead perpetual *transformation* taking place — one thing *changing* into another. For instance, in the physical world we see a plant droop and die. In the Imaginative world, as the plant fades away, another form — invisible to the physical senses — is all the time seen to be arising, into which the dying plant gradually changes. When the plant has quite disappeared, before us in its place is this new form, fully developed. Birth and death are conceptions which lose their meaning in the Imaginative world. In their place we have the concept of transformation or metamorphosis — *one thing changing into another.*

This is how it is that the truths concerning the being of man which have been communicated in the chapter on 'The Nature of Humanity' become accessible to Imaginative cognition. With the physical senses, only the processes of the physical body can be perceived, and these take place in the 'realm of birth and death'. The other members of man's nature — the life-body, the sentient body and the I — are subject to the law of transformation; Imaginative cognition is therefore able to perceive them. One who has progressed to this stage can see how at death something as it were releases itself from the physical body and lives on further in a different kind of existence.

But spiritual development does not come to an end in the Imaginative world. If we wanted to remain in that world and go no farther, we would be unable to give any explanation for the changes that were taking place; we could not find our bearings in the world to which we had gained access. The Imaginative world is a restless place. Everywhere in it there is movement, nothing but movement and change; nowhere does it come to rest. Only when we develop beyond the stage of Imaginative cognition and reach what may be called 'cognition through Inspiration' do we find a resting-place.

It is not essential that one who sets out to attain knowledge of the supersensible world shall first acquire Imaginative knowledge in full measure and only then proceed to Inspiration. A pupil's training may be so regulated that exercises leading to Imagination are continued side by side with exercises for the development of Inspiration. He will then, in due time, come into a higher world where he does not merely perceive but can also orientate himself — a world in which he can begin to see meaning. In point of fact, it will indeed generally happen that as the pupil progresses, glimpses of the Imaginative world are first of all vouchsafed him, and that then, after a time, he has the feeling: Now I am beginning also to find my bearings.

Yet it must also be realized that the world of Inspiration is something different and new, compared to that of Imagination. With Imaginative cognition we perceive events and processes in mutual transformation. With Inspiration we come to know the inner qualities of the *beings* who are undergoing transformation. With Imagination we see the manifestation of these beings in the realm of soul. With Inspiration we penetrate to their inner spiritual nature; above all, we come to know a multiplicity of beings and learn of the connections between them. In the physical world we also have to do with a multiplicity of beings or entities of various kinds, but in the world of Inspiration this multiplicity is of quite another character. There each single being has its distinctive connections with other beings, connections that are determined, not as in the physical world by some outward impressions that the beings make upon one another, but by their inner character and spiritual nature. When we perceive a being in the world of Inspiration, we are not looking at some external influence that the being is exerting upon another being, comparable with the influence exerted by one physical being upon another; what confronts us there is a relationship between two beings that comes about solely through the inner character both of the one and of the other. There is in the physical world one kind of relationship to which this may bear comparison — such a relationship as obtains between the several sounds or letters of a word. Say we have before us the word 'bold'. The word comes about through the sounding together of the sounds b–o–l–d. The sounds b and o, for example, do not collide or react on one another in some external way; they act together and each fulfils its part within the whole by virtue of its inner character. The activity of 'observing' in the world of Inspiration can therefore be compared with *reading*. The beings in that world present themselves to the observer like letters that he must first learn and that will then be revealed to him in their several relationships, forming as it were a spiritual script or supersensible writing. Spiritual science may therefore avail itself of this comparison and call the knowledge acquired through Inspiration: the Reading of the Hidden Script.

How the Reading of the Hidden Script is done, and how what is read may be communicated shall now be explained with reference to the earlier chapters of the present book. A description was given in the first place of the being of man, telling of how it is built up of several members. Then it was shown how the world in which man is evolving has itself passed through various stages of evolution — the Saturn condition, then the Sun, the Moon and now the Earth condition. Imaginative cognition brings within our reach perceptions that make us acquainted, on the one hand with the members of man's being, on the other hand with the successive conditions of our Earth and the changes it has undergone up to the present time. We then had to go further and learn of the relationship that exists between the Saturn condition of our Earth and the physical body of man, between the Sun condition and his ether-body and so on. We were shown how the seed for the physical body came into being as long ago as the Saturn condition, and has continued developing throughout Sun, Moon and Earth conditions right up to its present form. It became necessary also to show, for example, what changes came about in the being of man owing to the separation of the Sun from the Earth, and again what further changes were wrought in him by the parallel event in respect of the Moon; and then what kind of co-operation was needed to bring about those still later changes in mankind that found expression during the Atlantean time and the epochs that followed it — the Indian, Persian, Egyptian and so on. The picture that was given of these connections was derived not from Imaginative perception, but from knowledge attained through Inspiration, from Reading in the Hidden Script. In relation to this 'reading' the perceptions of Imagination are like the individual letters or sounds. Nor is it only explanations of this kind for which the reading is required. The course of man's life could not be understood if we were to study it with the help of Imaginative knowledge alone. We would, it is true, perceive how at death the soul-and-spirit members disengage themselves from what remains behind in the physical world; but we would not under-stand how the events that happen to man after death are related to past and future conditions, unless we already knew our way about the world we perceived Imaginatively. Without the knowledge acquired through Inspiration, the Imaginative world is like a script at which we merely stare, without being able to read it.

When the pupil of the Spirit goes forward from Imagination to Inspiration, he very quickly realizes what a mistake it would be to neglect to cultivate an understanding for the great events and phenomena of the Universe and to want to restrict his attention to the facts that bear upon his more immediate human interests. It can easily happen that one who has not been initiated into these matters will say: 'The one thing of importance for me is to learn about the destiny of the soul of man after death. If I can receive information upon that, then I am satisfied. Why does spiritual science set before me such remote matters as the Saturn and Sun conditions of our Earth, the separation of the Sun — and later of the Moon — from the Earth, and so on?' Whoever has been introduced in the right way to the whole subject of higher knowledge will come to see that he cannot attain authentic information about man's destiny after death, until he has first learned about those greater themes that might have seemed unnecessary. A picture of the condition into which man is brought after death will remain for him quite unintelligible and therefore worthless, if he cannot bring it together with conceptions that have grown out of these more remote themes. The very simplest observation that can be made by means of supersensible cognition requires him to be acquainted with them. When, for instance, a plant passes from the flowering stage and begins to bear fruit, then if we are watching it with supersensible powers of observation, we see a change taking place in an astral entity which in the flowering time has been enveloping the plant from above like a cloud. But for the 'fertilization' as it is called (leading from flower to fruit), this astral entity would have passed on into an altogether different form from the one it has assumed in consequence of fertilization. And we can only comprehend the whole process when seen with supersensible perception if we have prepared our understanding by studying the great cosmic event which the Earth and all her inhabitants experienced at the time of the separation of the Sun. Before fertilization the plant is in a similar condition to that of the whole Earth before the Sun went out from her. After fertilization, the flower of the plant is like the Earth was when the Sun had left and the Moon forces were still within her. If we have mastered the conceptions that can be acquired by studying the separation of the Sun from the Earth, then the significance of the 'fertilization' of a flowering plant will present itself to us in a way we can express by saying that before it the plant is in a Sunlike, and after it in a Moonlike condition. It is not too much to say that the smallest event in the world can only be rightly comprehended when we recognize in it an image of the great cosmic events. Without this recognition we are as far from understanding its real nature as we would be from understanding a Raphael Madonna that was all covered over except for one little patch of blue.

Everything that happens to man is in this way an image, having its prototype amid those great events of cosmic evolution with which his existence is bound up. If we would understand what supersensible consciousness perceives in human life — whether in the life between birth and death, or in the life between death and a new birth — we shall find we are able to do so if we take to our help the sublime conceptions that can be gained from dwelling on the great events of cosmic evolution. These will furnish us with the key to an understanding of the life of man. From the point of view of spiritual science, study of Saturn, Sun and Moon evolution is thus at the same time study of man.

Through Inspiration we learn how the Beings of the higher world are related to one another. A still further stage of knowledge opens up the possibility of coming to know these Beings in their innermost nature. This stage may be given the name of Intuitive cognition. (The words 'intuitive' and 'intuition' are sometimes used for a kind of vague insight or sudden notion that may or may not quite accord with truth. What is here meant by 'Intuition' is altogether different. It means a kind of cognition that is of the utmost light-filled clarity, a cognition that carries with it absolute assurance of its validity.) To have knowledge of an object perceived by the senses is to be *outside* the object and judge it in accordance with the impression it makes upon us from without. To know a Spirit-Being through Intuition is to become one with that Being, to be inwardly united with him. Stage by stage the pupil of the Spirit rises to a knowledge of this kind. With Imagination, he is already beyond feeling that his perceptions reveal the mere external characteristics of the Beings he perceives. Imagination leads him to recognize, in his perceptions, emanations of a living reality of soul and spirit. Inspiration takes him a step further into the inner essence of the spiritual Beings: he learns to understand what they are to one another. In Intuition, he penetrates right into their inner being.

Once again we can refer to the account of evolution that has been given in this book, in order to demonstrate the significance of Intuition. The foregoing chapters do not only relate how Saturn, Sun and Moon evolution took their course, they also tell of Beings who took part in this progress in many different ways. Allusion was made to the Thrones or Spirits of Will, to the Spirits of Wisdom, Spirits of Movement and so forth. And in connection with Earth evolution itself, the Spirits of Lucifer and of Ahriman were mentioned. The whole edifice of the Universe was traced back to Beings who all had their share in bringing it into existence. What can be learned concerning these Beings is acquired by Intuitive cognition. And the Intuitive cognition is likewise needed if we want to understand the course of human life. What is released from the physical body after death passes through various stages, as time goes on. The situation in which man finds himself immediately after death is, up to a point, capable of description by the exercise of Imaginative cognition. What happens later, however, when man is further on in the time between death and a new birth, would have to remain totally incomprehensible if Inspiration did not supervene. Inspiration is required to discover what can be said about the life of man in Spirit-land when the time of purification is over. Then comes a stage where even Inspiration no longer suffices, where it loses the

way and fails to understand. In the course of man's development between death and a new birth, he enters upon a time
where Intuition alone can follow him. The part of man that
undergoes this experience is however *always* in him, and if we
would understand it in its true inwardness, then we must look
for it also — again by means of Intuition — during the time
between birth and death. Whoever is content with a knowledge
of man acquired by Imagination and Inspiration will find
himself without means of access to what goes on in man's very
innermost being from one incarnation to the next. It is therefore only with Intuitive cognition that adequate research can
be made into repeated lives on Earth and into the workings of
Karma. Everything that claims to be true information concerning these must be derived from research that is made by
means of Intuitive cognition. And if man desires knowledge
of himself in his inmost being, this too he can attain only
through Intuition. By means of Intuition he perceives that
within him which goes forward from one Earth-life to another.

* * * * *

The faculties of cognition that belong to Inspiration and
Intuition — these too can only be attained by means of
exercises in the realm of soul and spirit. The exercises are akin
to those given for the attainment of Imagination, described
above as deep inner contemplation (meditation). Whereas
however the exercises leading to Imagination are still associated
with sense-impressions, in those that lead to Inspiration all
such association must be increasingly eliminated. In order to
make quite clear what has now to happen, let us return once
more to the symbol of the Rose Cross. When we meditate upon
the Rose Cross we have before us a picture, the component
parts of which are derived from the sense-world — the black
colour of the cross, the roses, and so forth. But the assembling
of the parts to form the Rose Cross is a deed the origin of which
is no longer in the sense-world. If now the pupil of the Spirit
will try to let the black cross and also the red roses — pictures,
both of them, of objects real in the world of the senses — disappear completely from his consciousness, retaining there

nothing but the spiritual activity which brought the parts together, in this activity he has the substance of the kind of meditation that can lead him, in course of time, to Inspiration. He should look into his own soul and ask himself: What was I doing when I brought cross and roses together to form a symbolic picture? What I was doing — the process I was bringing about in my soul — *that* will I now hold fast; the picture itself I will let disappear from consciousness. And now, without letting the picture rise up before me, I will *feel* what my soul was doing to produce the picture. I will for the time being live a completely inward life, living solely in my own activity that created the picture. I will enter, that is, into deep contemplation, not of any picture, but of my own picture-creating activity.

Meditation of this kind has to be undertaken by the pupil in connection with many different thought-pictures. It will in time lead him to knowledge through Inspiration. To take another example. We meditate the thought-picture of a sprouting, and then again of a dying, plant. First, we let the picture rise up in our mind of a plant that is gradually coming into being; we see it sprouting from the seed, we see how it unfolds leaf after leaf and finally brings forth blossom and fruit. Then we see it begin gradually to wither, until at last it dies right away. Meditating upon such a picture, we begin to acquire a feeling of the process as such — the process of coming-into-being and dying-away-again — of which the plant merely gave us a picture. And from this feeling, if we persevere in the exercise, there can arise the Imagination of that spiritual transformation which underlies the physical coming-into-being and dying-away. If we want to go further and reach the corresponding Inspiration, we shall have to do the exercise in another way. We shall have to concentrate our attention on the activity of soul that we ourselves engaged in, in order from the picture of the plant to arrive at the idea of the coming-into-being and dying-away. The plant has now to disappear entirely from consciousness, and we then left meditating upon what we have been doing in our own soul. Only by means of such exercises is the ascent to Inspiration possible.

To begin with, the pupil will not find it altogether easy to be quite clear in his mind as to how he is to set about an exercise of this nature. If he has been accustomed to let his inner life be determined by external impressions, then, when he wants to develop in his soul an inner life that has broken loose from all connection with external impressions, he will be at a loss how to proceed. Hence on the path to Inspiration it will be still more essential than before to accompany the given exercises with all those precautionary measures that were recommended to him when setting out to attain Imagination — measures for ensuring stability and confidence, alike in his powers of discrimination, in his life of feeling and in his conduct and character. If he succeeds with these, the pupil will find they have a twofold effect upon him. He will not run the risk of losing his balance when he attains to vision of the supersensible; and he will also become capable of fulfilling quite exactly and faithfully the demands made upon him by the new exercises. The pupil will need to develop here a specific mood and disposition of soul, with the feelings that rightly belong to it; till he has done so, he may well find the exercises difficult. If however he will patiently and perseveringly cultivate within him the qualities of soul that are favourable to the birth of supersensible cognition, it will not be long before he finds himself able to understand the exercises and also to carry them out. Let him make a habit of communing often with his own soul — but not with a view to musing upon himself! Rather should he set out before his mind's eye the successive experiences he has met with in life and consider them quietly. The effort will be well rewarded. He will find that his thought and ideas, and also his feelings, are enriched by bringing these experiences into relation with one another. He will come to realize how true it is that we gain new experience not only by having new impressions or undergoing new events in life, but also by letting the old work on within us. The pupil who really succeeds in letting his experiences — yes, and even the opinions he has gained — play upon one another, as though he himself, with his sympathies and antipathies, his personal interests and feelings, were in no way concerned, will be preparing within

270

him particularly good ground for the growth of the faculty of supersensible cognition. He will 'in very truth develop what one may call a *rich inner life.*

What is throughout of the very first importance is that balance and harmony should reign among the various qualities and inclinations of the soul. When man devotes himself to some particular activity of soul, he tends all too easily to become one-sided. Having realized how beneficial is the habit of inner reflection, of sojourning now and again in the world of one's own thoughts, he may grow so fond of doing this that he tends increasingly to shut himself off from the impressions of the world around him. Such a habit could only lead to a bare and arid inner life. He will advance farthest who retains, along with the ability to withdraw into his own soul, an open-minded receptiveness for all that the external world offers for his perception. And here we should not have in mind merely such objects and events as are commonly considered important; everyone — be his situation in life never so mean and never so circumscribed — can find experience enough within its walls, provided he foster in mind and heart a sensitiveness to all that goes on around him. He has no occasion to go out in search of experiences; they are around him on every hand.

Emphasis has also to be laid on the *way* in which we receive and reflect upon our experiences. You may, for instance, happen to discover one day that a person whom you revere has some feature in his character which you cannot but regard as a blemish. As you think it over, the discovery may affect you in either of two ways. You may simply say to yourself: Knowing what I now know, I can no longer revere him as I did. Or, you may ask yourself the question: How can it have come about that this person, for whom I have such veneration, has to labour under a defect of this kind? Ought I not perhaps to look upon the fault, not just *as* a fault, but as a result of the life he has led, perhaps even consequent upon his qualities of greatness? Having seriously faced this question, you may perhaps find that your reverence for him is, after all, undiminished by the discovery of a flaw in his character. Every such experience will have taught you something: your understanding of life will be the truer for it. You would of course be making a bad mistake if you let your appreciation of this way of meeting life mislead you into excusing anything and everything in people or in things to whom or to which you are partial; or if you allowed yourself to drift into a habit of shutting your eyes to whatever is blameworthy, imagining that you were thereby furthering your own inner development. For this you will certainly *not* be doing, if it is to satisfy your own inclinations that you refrain from blaming faults and try instead to understand and condone them. It will be helpful only if this attitude is called for by the nature of the case, irrespective of whether you yourself are to gain or lose by its adoption. It is undoubtedly true that one can never *learn* by passing judgment on a fault but only by coming to understand it. Anyone however who in his desire to understand the fault proceeds to banish from his mind all sense of displeasure at it, will be making little headway in his development. So here we have again an instance where what is required is not onesidedness in one or other direction, but balance and harmony between the several virtues of the soul.

This is true in quite a special degree of one property of the soul that is of outstanding significance for higher development — I mean, the feeling of reverent devotion. One who cultivates this feeling or who has always possessed it as a kind of gift of Nature, has a good foundation upon which to build the faculties of supersensible cognition. Has he been able in childhood to look up with devotion and admiration to persons who stood for him as lofty ideals, then his soul will provide good ground whereon new powers of cognition can grow and flourish. And whoever in later life, in years of riper judgment, gazes up at the starry heavens, filled with wonder and boundless devotion at the revelation he there divines of sublime spiritual powers, will be well on the way to grow ripe for knowledge of supersensible worlds. The same holds true of one who is able to feel wonder and admiration at the powers that are active in the life of man. And of no less significance is also that reverence which a person of maturer years may continue to cherish in full measure for other human beings whose worth he divines or recognizes. Indeed only where such reverence is present, is it possible to come within sight of the higher worlds. A man who is incapable of reverence will not progress very far on the path of knowledge. To one for whom there is nothing in all the world that he deems worthy of his esteem, the real nature of things will ever remain a closed book.

Should anyone on the other hand allow himself to be misled by feelings of reverence and devotion to the complete annulment of his own healthy self-assertion and self-confidence, he too will be sinning against the law of harmony and balance. The pupil of the Spirit will work continuously at his development, that he may grow ever more and more mature; and if he is doing this, then it is only right that he should have confidence in himself and feel assured that his powers are growing all the time. Would he see the whole matter in its true light, let him say to himself: Hidden within me are spiritual powers, and I can call them forth out of my inner life. Hence when I see something that commands my respect because it is higher than I, not only should I feel reverence for it, but I may be confident that I myself shall in time come to the stage of development where I am like it.

The more a man is able to be *attentive* to happenings or situations in his life which in the ordinary course are unfamiliar to him and would elude his judgment, the greater ability will he have to lay the foundation for right development on the path into the spiritual worlds. An example can help make this clear. A person comes into a situation where it is open to him to carry out some particular action — or to leave it undone. His judgment says to him: Do it! But he has in his soul an unaccountable feeling that draws him back. It may happen that he pays no heed to this feeling but simply goes ahead in accordance with the verdict of his judgment. Or again, it may happen that he yields to this inexplicable urge within him, and refrains. If then he follows up the matter to see what happens later, it may turn out that had he obeyed his judgment, harm would have come of it, but that good has resulted from his leaving the action undone. Such an experience can set going in the pupil a train of thought that may run as follows. Within me, he may say to himself, lives something which guides me better than can my faculty of judgment at its present stage of development. I must keep an open mind for this 'something' which is on a much higher level than I can reach with my present powers. If we pay careful heed to situations of this kind as we meet them in life, we shall receive considerable benefit from doing so. We shall begin to sense (and this itself is already a sign of health in our inner life) that there is more in man than comes within the range of his ordinary judgment. The very recognition of such a fact widens the soul. Here again, however, we might be led into highly questionable byways. Should we acquire the habit of constantly shutting down our faculty of judgment because some dim feeling impels us to take another course, we might well become the plaything of all manner of undefined motives. And from such a habit the way leads all too quickly into weak-mindedness and superstition.

Fatal for the pupil of the Spirit is superstition of every sort. He can only hope ever to find the right and true path to the realm of Spirit-life by carefully guarding himself from superstition, from flights of fancy, and from all day-dreaming. A person who feels glad when he is brought up against something in life which is 'beyond human understanding' will not be the one to enter the spiritual world in the right way. Fondness for the 'inexplicable' is emphatically not a qualification for discipleship of the Spirit. Indeed the pupil should utterly discard the notion that a true mystic is one who is always ready to surmise the presence of what cannot be explained or explored. The right way is to be prepared to recognize on all hands hidden forces and hidden beings, yet at the same time to assume that what is 'unexplored' to-day will be able to be explored when the requisite ability has been developed.

There is a certain mood of soul which it is important for the pupil to maintain at every stage of his development. He should not let his urge for higher knowledge lead him to keep on aiming to get answers to particular questions. Rather should he continually be asking: How am I to develop the needed faculties within myself? For when by dint of patient inner work some faculty develops in him, he will receive the answer to some of his questions. Genuine pupils of the Spirit will always take pains to cultivate this attitude of soul. They will thereby be encouraged to work upon themselves, that they may become ever more and more mature in spirit, and they will abjure the desire to extort answers to particular questions. They will *wait* until such time as the answers come.

Here again, however, there is the possibility of a one-sidedness, which may prevent the pupil from going forward in the way he should. For at some moment he may quite rightly feel that — according to the measure of his powers — he can answer for himself even questions of the highest order. Thus at every turn moderation and balance play an essential part in the life of the soul.

Many more qualities of soul could be cited that may with advantage be fostered and developed, if the pupil is seriously wanting to work through a training for Inspiration; and in connection with every one of them we should find that emphasis is laid on the supreme importance of moderation and balance. These attributes of soul help the pupil to understand the exercises that are given for the attainment of Inspiration, and also make him capable of carrying them out.

The exercises for Intuition demand from the pupil that he let disappear from consciousness not only the pictures to which he gave himself up in contemplation in order to arrive at Imaginative cognition, but also that meditating upon his own activity of soul, which he practised for the attainment of Inspiration. This means that he is now to have in his soul literally nothing of what he has experienced hitherto, whether outwardly or inwardly. If, after discarding all outward and inward experience, nothing whatever is left in his consciousness — that is to say, if consciousness simply slips away from him and he sinks into unconsciousness — then that will tell him that he is not yet ripe to undertake the exercises for Intuition and must continue working with those for Imagination and Inspiration. A time will come however when, after all experiences, inner and outer, have been banished from it, consciousness is not left empty, but something remains in it to which the pupil can now give himself up in deep contemplation even as he formerly gave himself up to what came to him from outer or inner impressions. This 'something' is of a very special nature. In relation to all that the pupil has hitherto experienced and learned it is entirely new. When he feels it there in his consciousness, he knows: This is something of which up to now I have had no knowledge at all. It is a clear perception, and I perceive it, just as I should perceive a note of music that my ear was hearing; yet it can only enter my consciousness through Intuition, even as the music can only enter there by way of the ear. In Intuition the impressions man receives are stripped bare of the last remnant of connection with the physical senses. The spiritual world now begins to lie open for his cognition in a form that has nothing in common with the properties of the sense-world.

* * * * *

Imaginative cognition is attained when the lotus-flowers unfold from the astral body. As a result of the exercises undertaken for the attainment of Inspiration and Intuition, movements and currents make their appearance in man's ether- or life-body, which were not there before. These movements are the organs that enable man to add to his faculties the 'Reading of the Hidden Script' and yet further powers that lie beyond. The changes that are wrought in his ether-body when a pupil has attained Inspiration and Intuition, reveal themselves to supersensible cognition in the following way. Somewhere as if in the neighbourhood of the physical heart one becomes conscious of a new centre in the ether-body, which forms itself into an etheric organ. From this centre all manner of movings and streamings run out to the various parts of the physical body. The most important of these go to the lotus-flowers, flow right through them and through their several petals, then turn outwards and pour themselves into outer space like rays of light. The more highly developed a pupil is, the larger is the circle around him in which these currents are perceptible. Under a properly regulated training this centre in the neighbourhood of the heart does not however develop right at the beginning.

Preparation has to be made for it. A preliminary centre appears first in the head, is then transplanted into the region of the larynx and finally comes to rest in the neighbourhood of the physical heart. If development is irregular, it may be that this organ is formed in the region of the heart from the outset. There will then be a danger that instead of attaining calm and objective supersensible perception, the pupil might develop into a fantastic dreamer.

As he progresses further, the pupil comes to the point where he can release these currents and memberings of his ether-body from dependence on the physical body, and make use of them directly, without reference to the physical body. The lotus-flowers serve him then as instruments by means of which he moves his ether-body. Before this can happen, certain special streams and rays must have been forming in the whole circumference of the ether-body, enclosing it as though with a fine network, rendering it a distinct, self-contained entity. Then there is nothing to hinder the movements and streamings that are going on in the ether-body from making contact with the external world of soul and spirit and from uniting with it, so that what is happening without and what is happening within — that is to say, within the human ether-body — are able to flow into one another. That will mean that the moment has come when the human being can perceive consciously the world of Inspiration. This kind of cognition shows itself from the first to be of quite a different character from the cognition that relates to the physical world. Here, we receive impressions through our senses and then proceed to entertain ideas and concepts about these impressions. The acquisition of knowledge by means of Inspiration is not like that. The 'knowing' is achieved in one single act; there is no thought-process following the perception. What in the act of cognition by means of the physical senses is acquired only subsequently in the concept, is in the Inspirational cognition given simultaneously with the percept. This being so, the pupil would flow right into the surrounding world of soul and spirit, would merge with it and be unable to distinguish himself from it, had he not formed before in his ether-body the network that has just been described.

The exercises that are given for Intuition influence not only the ether-body; they also leave their mark on the supersensible forces that are at work in the physical body. This must not be taken to mean that changes are effected there, perceptible to ordinary sense-observation. Supersensible cognition alone can form any true idea of them; they are right outside the scope of a cognition that is concerned with externals. The changes come about as a result of the pupil's consciousness being so far matured that, notwithstanding his having banished from it all that he has experienced in the past, whether outwardly or inwardly, he is nevertheless able to have conscious experience in Intuition.

Yet the experiences that come with Intuition are intimate, are tender and delicate. Man's physical body, at its present stage, is quite coarse in comparison; consequently, it offers stubborn resistance to these results of the exercises for Intuition. If however the exercises are persevered in with energy and patience, and with the necessary inner quiet, they will at length overcome the formidable hindrances that the physical body presents. The pupil will begin to notice that he is gradually bringing under his control certain activities of his physical body that formerly took their course without his being in the least conscious of them. He will become aware also of a change of another kind. He may observe that for a short while he feels a need so to order his breathing — or some other bodily process — as to bring it into harmony with what his soul is doing in the exercises or whatever else he is undertaking in inner, meditative life. The ultimate ideal is that no exercises of any kind should be done with the physical body as such, not even breathing exercises; so that whatever happens in the physical will occur simply and solely as an *outcome* of the exercises for Intuition.

* * * * *

When the pupil is making his way upwards on the path that leads to higher worlds, he will remark at a certain stage that the interconnection of the activities of his personality is beginning to assume a new form. In the world of the physical senses the I sees to it that the various faculties of the soul co-operate in an orderly manner. In the affairs of everyday life these faculties — we refer here especially to Thinking, Feeling and Willing — always stand in a certain recognized relation to one another. Let us say we are looking at some object. It pleases us, or perhaps we dislike it. That is to say, a feeling associates itself, almost inevitably, with our mental picture, our idea of the object. Very possibly we may also wish we could possess it or we may feel impelled to alter it in this or that particular. That is to say, desire and will unite themselves with the thought and the feeling. That this association comes about is due to the fact that the I unites ideation (thinking), feeling and willing into a harmonious whole, thus bringing order into the forces of our personality. This healthy harmony would be broken if the I were to show itself powerless in the matter — if desire, for example, were to branch off in another direction than feeling or thinking. If someone thought that a particular course was right, and yet his will were set on following another course — one that did not commend itself to him — his soul would certainly not be in a healthy condition. The same could be said of a person who was bent on having, not what he liked, but rather what he disliked.

The pupil will, however, find that on the way to the attainment of higher powers of cognition, thinking, feeling and willing do definitely separate one from another, each of them assuming a kind of independent existence. A thought, for instance, will not now of its own accord stir up a particular feeling and evoke a particular volition. The situation will be that whilst in our thinking we can perceive a thing objectively and truly, yet before we can have any feeling about it or come to any resolve in the matter, we shall need to develop within us a distinct and independent impulse. While engaged in supersensible observation, our thinking, feeling and willing do not continue to be simply three powers of the soul raying out, as it were, from the I, as the single centre of our personality; they become independent beings. It is as though they were three separate personalities. The implication is that our I or

279

Ego needs to be made all the stronger, for it has no longer merely to ensure that order reigns among three faculties of soul; it has to guide and lead three beings. This partition into three distinct beings must, however, only be allowed to subsist during the time of supersensible observation. Here again we see how important it is to include among the exercises for more advanced training those that give stability and firmness to the faculty of thoughtful judgment, to the feeling life and to the life of will. For if we fail to bring with us into the higher world the necessary stability and firmness of soul, then we shall very soon find how weak the I will prove itself to be — no fit guide for the thinking, feeling and willing! Should such weakness manifest in the I, it will be as though the soul were being pulled in different ways by distinct personalities; its inner integrity will inevitably be destroyed. If, however, development has taken its right course, the change will signify a genuine advance. The Ego does not lose control but remains in command even of the independent beings that now constitute the soul.

As development proceeds, a further step is taken. The thinking that has become independent evokes a fourth being of soul and spirit, a being that may be described as a direct inpouring of spiritual streams that are of the nature of Thought. The whole Universe now confronts the human being as a mighty edifice of Thought even as the plant or animal world confronts him in the realm of the physical senses; he beholds it before him like a mighty edifice built of thought. The Feeling too and the Will, that have become independent, evoke powers in the soul which become active there as independent beings. And there appears in addition yet a seventh power, a seventh entity which bears resemblance to one's own I — to the I as such.

With this whole experience another is united. Before reaching the supersensible world man was familiar with thinking, feeling and willing purely as inner experiences of the soul. No sooner has he entered the supersensible world than he begins to perceive things that are the expression, not of anything physical, but of soul and spirit. Underlying what he is able to perceive in the new world are beings of soul and spirit. These beings present themselves to him as an external spiritual world, just as stones and plants and animals present themselves to the senses in the physical world. The pupil can however perceive a significant difference between the world of soul and spirit that is now unfolding before him and the world he has been accustomed to observe with the help of the physical senses. A plant in the latter remains as it is, whatever man may feel or think about it. It is not so with the pictures of the soul-and-spirit world. These change according as man has this or that thought or feeling towards them. Man himself stamps them in this way with a character that is derived from his own being. Suppose a certain picture appears before him in the Imaginative world. To begin with, he may perhaps be quite indifferent to it; in that case, it will manifest in a certain form. But the moment he begins to feel pleased with it or to take a dislike to it, it will change its form. This is what is so striking about the pictures of the supersensible world: they are not only the expression of something outside man and independent of him, they also reflect what the man is himself. They are, in fact, thoroughly permeated with his being. His being overlays them as with a veil. And what man sees when he is faced with a real spiritual being, is not that being at all, but something he himself has produced. He may thus have before him something true in itself, yet what he sees may still be false. Nor is it only what he is aware of in himself that works in this way; there is nothing in him that does not leave its mark on the Imaginative world. Someone may, for instance, have deeply hidden inclinations, held in check by dint of education or force of character; they will nevertheless be making their impression on the world of soul and spirit. That world receives its colouring according to the entire being of the man, irrespective of how much or how little he himself may know of his own nature and character.

If the pupil is to be capable of going forward from this stage of development, he must learn to make a clear distinction between himself and the surrounding spiritual world. To this end he has to learn to put a stop to any kind of influence that he himself might exert upon the world of soul and spirit that is around him. The only way to ensure this is to be fully cognizant of what it is that he is taking with him into the new world. In other words, it is a matter of acquiring, first and foremost, genuine and searching self-knowledge. Once he has that, he will be able to see with clear, unclouded vision the world of soul and spirit by which he is surrounded. Now thanks to certain facts in the whole development of man, self-knowledge of this kind cannot but arise — as it were, quite naturally — when a man enters the higher world. In the everyday physical world man develops, as we know, his I or Ego, his consciousness of self; and this his I acts as a centre of attraction for his whole personality. All his inclinations, his sympathies and antipathies, his passions and propensities, his views and opinions group themselves around his Ego. A man's Ego too is the centre of attraction for what we call his Karma. If we were able to see this our Ego naked and undisguised, we would at the same time be perceiving that we have yet to undergo such and such strokes of destiny in our present and future incarnations, owing to the way we lived and the tendencies we acquired in past incarnations. Therefore this Ego, with all its encumbrances, must necessarily be the first picture that confronts the human soul on ascending into the world of soul and spirit. According to a certain law of the spiritual world, this — the man's 'Double' — is bound to be the very first impression man receives on entering the spiritual world. We can well understand the law when we reflect how in his life on the physical plane man perceives himself only in so far as he experiences himself in thinking, feeling and willing. In other words, he perceives himself only from within; his 'self' does not confront him from without, as do the stones and plants and animals. Moreover, the knowledge he thus gains of himself is very partial and incomplete.

For there is that in human nature which hinders him from attaining deeper self-knowledge. It is the urge, wherever dawning self-knowledge compels him to admit some imperfection in his character, and he *does not want to deceive himself about it* — the urge to set to work to alter the unpleasant trait.

If he is not obedient to the urge, but turns his attention away from himself and remains as he is, then it need hardly be said that he robs himself of the possibility of attaining self-knowledge in that direction. If on the other hand he examines himself intently and, refusing to give way to self-deception, boldly faces the trait he has observed in his own character, then either he will find he can improve it, or it may be that — such as he is at present — he is unable to do so. In the latter instance, a feeling will steal over him that one can only call a kind of shame. This is, in fact, how healthy human nature works: self-knowledge gives rise to a sense of shame — a feeling that may show itself in many ways. Now as we know, in everyday life the sense of shame has a particular effect upon us. A man of healthy feeling will take care that those aspects of his character which make him feel ashamed shall not take effect in the world at large — shall not find expression in his deeds. Shame is thus a power that impels man to shut something up inside him and not allow it to be seen.

Thinking this over carefully, we shall have little difficulty in understanding that spiritual science ascribes even more far-reaching effects to an experience of the soul that is very nearly akin to the familiar one of a sense of shame. Spiritual research discovers in the depths of the human soul a kind of hidden *sense of shame* of which in physical life man is unconscious. This hidden feeling is none the less active in the soul. It works there in much the same way as does the sense of shame of which a man is normally conscious. It prevents his having before him in a clearly perceptible picture his real and inmost being. If this feeling were not there, man would see displayed before him what he is in very truth. He would no longer experience his thoughts and ideas, his feelings and his will in a merely inward way, but would perceive them even as he perceives the stones and animals and plants. Thus does a hidden sense of shame conceal man from himself. Nor is that all; it hides from him at the same time the entire soul-and-spirit world. For since his own inner being is hidden from him, he cannot get sight of that domain within him where he should now be endeavouring to develop the organs that will enable him to attain knowledge of the world of soul and spirit. He misses the opportunity of so transforming his inner being that it may acquire organs of spiritual perception.

When however in the pursuit of a right spiritual training man labours to promote the development within him of these organs of perception, the very first impression that confronts him is his own self. He perceives what he truly is, he perceives his Double. This perception of oneself is inseparable from perception of the world of soul and spirit. In ordinary life in the physical world, the hidden sense of shame is continually shutting for man the door into the world of soul and spirit. Is he about to take one step into that world, at once an unconscious sense of shame comes in the way and hides from him that corner of the soul-and-spirit world which was on the point of coming into view. The exercises, however, that have been described open the way to yonder world. In effect, the sense of shame which he bears hidden within him is a great benefactor to man. For the measure of intelligent discrimination and of right feeling and strength of character we can acquire in ordinary life without special training will not suffice us when we have to face our very inmost being in its true form. We would not be able to endure it; we would lose our self-confidence, we would even lose all consciousness of self. That this may not happen, we have yet again to have recourse to those precautionary measures that need to be taken alongside of the exercises for the attainment of higher powers of cognition — namely the special exercises for the cultivation of sound judgment, good feeling and strength of character. In the course of a right and healthy spiritual training, the pupil learns incidentally enough of the truths of spiritual science and also of the measures he requires to take in order to attain self-knowledge and self-observation, for him to be able to face his own Double with courage and with strength. What it will mean for him then is simply that he sees in another form, as a picture belonging to the world of Imagination, what he has already made acquaintance with here in the physical world. If in the physical world we have grasped the law of Karma with our understanding, we shall have no occasion to be horror-struck when we behold the seeds of our future destiny visibly before us in the picture of our Double. If we have made an intelligent study of the evolution of the world and of man, and have learned how at a particular moment in this evolution the forces of Lucifer penetrated into the human soul, we shall not be unduly disturbed when we become conscious of the presence, in the picture of our own being, of the Luciferic beings and their activities.

We can however see from this how necessary it is that man should not demand entry into the spiritual world until he has learned and understood certain essential truths of that world by the simple exercise of his everyday intelligence, developed in the physical world. If spiritual development follows the right and normal path, then before he aspires to enter the supersensible world the pupil will already have mastered with his ordinary intelligence the whole of the earlier contents of this book.

In a training where care is not taken to develop in the pupil certainty and stability in his powers of judgment and discrimination as well as in his emotions and his moral character, it may happen that the higher world presents itself to him before he has the inner faculties with which to face it. The encounter with his Double will in that event cause him great distress and lead him astray. If on the other hand — as would also be possible — he were completely to elude the meeting with the Double, he would still be just as incapable of coming to any true knowledge of the higher world. For he would then be unable to distinguish between what the things around him really are and what he himself is seeing into them. To be able to do this, he must first have seen the distinct picture of his own being; then he can separate and distinguish from his environment whatever has flowed over into it from his own inner life.

As far as his life in the physical world is concerned, the moment man begins to draw near to the world of soul and spirit, the Double immediately makes himself invisible, and therewith also conceals from him the whole soul-and-spirit world. The Double stands in front of it like a Guardian, forbidding entrance to those who are not yet competent to enter.

285

He may therefore rightly be called 'The Guardian of the Threshold of the World of Soul and Spirit'.

Besides meeting with him when approaching the supersensible world by the method that has been described, man also meets this Guardian of the Threshold when he passes through physical death. And in the course of the time between death and a new birth, while man's soul and spirit are undergoing development, the Guardian progressively reveals himself to him. There, however, the encounter cannot disquiet man unduly, since he now has knowledge of the higher worlds which between birth and death were not within his ken.

Were man to enter the world of soul and spirit without encountering the Guardian of the Threshold, he would be liable to succumb to one delusion after another. For he would never be able to distinguish between what he himself brings into that world and what rightly belongs to it. A sound and proper training, however, should lead the pupil only into the realm of truth, never into the realm of illusion. The training itself should ensure that the meeting with the Guardian will follow as a necessary consequence. For this meeting with his Double is one of the testing experiences that are indispensable to the pupil aspiring to conscious perception in supersensible worlds, and that protect him from the possibility of illusion or false fantasy.

It is of urgent importance that every pupil of the Spirit should take himself in hand and see to it that he does not become a visionary and a dreamer, for then he would all too easily fall a victim to delusion and self-deception (suggestion and auto-suggestion). Where the instructions for training are faithfully carried out, the very sources of delusion are destroyed in the process. It is naturally not possible to enter here in detail into all the steps that have to be taken by the pupil in this connection. We can only indicate wherein their main import lies.

There are two chief sources for delusions of this kind. They may, in the first place, be due to the fact that reality receives a colouring from the nature and disposition of the pupil himself. In ordinary life in the physical world there is comparatively little danger of delusion arising from such a source; the external world impresses its true form upon the observer in all distinctness, however much he would like to colour it in conformity with his own wishes and interests. No sooner, however, does he enter the world of Imagination than its pictures change under the influence of these desires and interests of his, and he has then before him, giving every appearance of reality, what are in effect merely his own creations, or forms that he has at least helped to create. But in meeting the Guardian of the Threshold the pupil learns to know what he has within him; thus he knows well what he may be bringing with him into the world of soul and spirit, and so this first source of delusion is eliminated. Thanks to the preparation he undergoes before entering the world of soul and spirit, the pupil has already grown accustomed to eliminate self in his observation of the physical world and to let its objects and events speak to him purely by virtue of their own inherent nature. If the preparation has been sufficiently thorough, he can await unperturbed the meeting with the Guardian. This meeting will put him to the final test as to whether, when he confronts the world of soul and spirit, he will be able there too to eliminate himself.

Besides this, there is another source of delusion. It shows itself when we interpret incorrectly some impression we receive. A simple example of this in everyday life is the illusion we fall into when we are sitting in a train and think that the trees are moving in the opposite direction to that of the train, whereas it is really we ourselves who are moving with the train. There are of course countless instances where an illusion of this nature is more difficult to dispel than in the simple example of the moving train; nevertheless it will easily be seen that in the physical world ways and means can always be found of correcting such illusions, if with sound judgment we avail ourselves of every circumstance that can serve to make the matter clear. No sooner, however, have we penetrated into supersensible realms than we find a different state of affairs. In the world of the senses the facts are not altered by our misconception of them; thus the way is left open for unprejudiced observation to correct the delusion by reference to the facts.

In the supersensible world this cannot so easily be done. Suppose we are wanting to observe some supersensible fact, and as we approach it we come to a wrong conclusion about its nature. The incorrect conception we have formed, this we now carry into the fact itself, and it becomes so closely interwoven with the latter that the one cannot readily be distinguished from the other. What we then have is not the mistake within ourselves, and the true fact in the object observed; the mistake has been incorporated in the outer fact — has become part of it. It is therefore no longer possible simply to correct the illusion by looking at the fact again with open mind.

We have here been describing an all too frequent source of deception and false fantasy for one who approaches the supersensible world without due preparation.

Yet even as the pupil becomes able to rid himself of delusions that arise from the phenomena of the supersensible world being coloured by his own character and inclinations, so must he now also find the way to render powerless this second source of delusion. He is able to obliterate what comes from himself if he has first made acquaintance with his own Double; he will be able to get rid of this second source of delusion when he has learned to recognize from its very nature and character whether a fact of the supersensible world is reality or mere delusion. If delusions looked exactly like realities, there would naturally be no possibility of distinguishing them. But it is not so. In the supersensible world delusions have properties peculiar to themselves by which they can be distinguished from realities. And it is important for the pupil to know what are the properties by which he may recognize realities. One who is unacquainted with spiritual training will very naturally doubt the possibility of ever being safe from delusion, when the sources of it are so numerous. How, he will say, is any pupil of the Spirit ever to be sure that all the higher knowledge he imagines himself to have gained does not rest on delusion and self-delusion? The one who argues in this way has failed to observe that in every genuine spiritual training the sources of delusion are dispelled — dried up as it were, through the whole way the training proceeds.

In the first place, the genuine pupil of the Spirit will in the course of his preparation have learned a great deal about all the things that can give rise to illusion and self-deception, and will thus be on his guard against them. In this respect he has far more opportunity than his fellow-men of learning to lead his life with calm detachment and sound judgment. All that he learns and experiences is calculated to save him from having anything to do with vague premonitions and uncontrolled fancies. His training makes him very careful. Moreover, every right and true training introduces the pupil from the start to grand and sublime conceptions, teaching him of events in the great Universe; he has to put forth his best powers of discernment to grasp the great cosmic facts, and will find these his powers growing ever finer and keener in the process. Only one who shrinks from venturing into realms so remote, preferring to cling to 'revelations' that are nearer home, will be in danger of missing that sharpening of his mental faculties which can ensure for him the ability to distinguish clearly between deception and reality.

With all this, however, we have not yet touched on the most important factor of all — namely, what is latent in the exercises themselves. The exercises that belong to a right and proper spiritual training have necessarily to be so regulated and arranged that the pupil, while engaged in meditation, is fully conscious of all that is taking place in his soul. As he sets out on the road to Imagination, he forms, to begin with, a symbolic picture. In this picture are still contained mental images that owe their origin to what he has perceived in the outer world. He is not the sole creator of the picture; something besides himself has shared in the creation of its content. This means that he may still be under an illusion as to how the content of the picture has come about; he may ascribe it to a mistaken source. When the pupil progresses further and embarks on exercises for Inspiration, he banishes this content from consciousness and gives himself up entirely to the contemplation of his own activity of soul, which formed the picture. Here again, error may still creep in. For the particular character of his soul's activity he is indebted to his education — in the widest sense of the word. It is impossible for him to be fully informed of its origin. But now there comes the time when even the pupil's own activity of soul has to be expelled from consciousness. If there is still anything left, this remaining content is fully exposed to view. Nothing can intrude here that cannot be perceived and appraised in all its parts and aspects. The pupil has in his Intuition something that reveals to him the essential character of pure reality in the world of soul and spirit. From now onward, in everything that enters his field of observation he can look for what he has learned to recognize as the characteristic marks of soul-and-spirit reality, and will thus be able to discern between what is real and what is only apparent. And he can be assured that in applying this test he will be just as safe from the risk of delusion in the supersensible world as in the physical world — where it would be quite impossible for him to mistake an imaginary bar of hot iron for one that could really burn him.

It will of course be understood that the pupil can have this relation only to facts of the supersensible worlds that he has seen for himself — that have thus become for him a matter of actual experience — and not to those communicated by others, which he comprehends with his ordinary powers of understanding, aided by a natural and healthy feeling for the truth. He will indeed be at pains to draw a sharp dividing line between the spiritual knowledge he has acquired in the one and in the other way. He will be ready and willing to receive communications about the higher worlds and will summon up his best powers of judgment to comprehend them. On the other hand, when he describes something as the fruit of his own experience and spiritual observation, he will always first have tested whether it showed itself to him with the qualities he has learned to recognize in a genuine Intuition.

* * * * *

The pupil of the Spirit having now undergone the meeting with the Guardian of the Threshold, further experiences await him as he ascends into supersensible worlds. In the first place, he will notice that there is an inner connection between this

Guardian of the Threshold and what was described above as a seventh power in the soul, which took on the form of an independent being. In truth, this seventh being is, from a certain point of view, none other than the Double, than the Guardian himself, whose presence sets the pupil a specific task. He has to place what he is in his ordinary self — which he has now before him in picture — under the leadership and guidance of his new-born Self. A kind of struggle will ensue, the Double striving continually to gain the upper hand. If the pupil can succeed in establishing a right relation to the Double, not allowing him to do anything that is not inspired by the new-born I , he will find that his true human powers gain in strength and in stability.

In the matter of self-knowledge the situation is somewhat different in the higher world from what it is in the physical. In the physical world self-knowledge is a purely inward experience, whereas in the higher world from the very outset the new-born Self manifests as an external phenomenon of soul. The pupil sees it there before him as a distinct being. He is not however able to have a complete perception of this new-born Self. For no matter how many stages he may have reached on the path into supersensible worlds, there are always higher stages ahead; and at every one of them the pupil will perceive more of his Higher Self. At any particular stage, it can be only partially revealed to him. When the pupil first begins to be aware of the Higher Self, he is strongly tempted, as it were, to regard it from the vantage-point he has gained in the physical world. Indeed it is good that he should feel thus tempted; it is even necessary if his development is to proceed in the right way. For he has to contemplate what appears to him as his Double, the 'Guardian of the Threshold', he has to see all this in face of the Higher Self, and so perceive the vast disparity between what he is now and what he is meant to become. Once the pupil enters upon this comparison, the Guardian of the Threshold begins to assume another form, presenting himself as a picture of all the hindrances that stand in the way of the development of the Higher Self. The pupil now sees what a burden he is dragging about with him all the time in the ordinary self. And should the preparation he has undergone have failed to give him the strength to say at this point: I am not going to stand still, but shall make ceaseless effort to carry my development ever on and on in the direction of the Higher Self — should he not be strong enough to say this, he will falter and shrink from what is yet in store for him. He will indeed have entered into the world of soul and spirit, but as one who has relinquished all idea of making further efforts for his development. He then becomes a prisoner of the form that stands before him in the Guardian of the Threshold. The significant thing, however, is that he does not feel himself a prisoner; he imagines he is passing through an entirely different experience. The form that is evoked by the Guardian of the Threshold may even give rise in his soul to the impression that in the pictures he beholds at this stage of his development he already has a complete survey of all possible Worlds; that he has arrived at the very summit of knowledge and has no need to exert himself any further. Far indeed from seeing himself as a prisoner, he feels he is now the possessor of inexhaustible riches, even of all the secrets of the Universe. That such an experience — the complete reversal of the true state of affairs — should be possible will not astonish us, when we remember that the man undergoing it is in the world of soul and spirit, a world where things are apt to show themselves in their opposites. Attention was called to this characteristic of the soul-and-spirit world in an earlier chapter, when studying the life after death.

In the figure that the pupil is perceiving at this stage of his development, there is more than in the form in which the Guardian of the Threshold first presented himself to him. At that time he could perceive in the Double all the qualities that the ordinary self possesses in consequence of the influence of the Luciferic powers. In the course of evolution, however, owing to the influence of Lucifer, another power has found its way into the human soul; we called it in earlier sections of this book the power of Ahriman. This is the power that hinders man, so long as he is living in physical existence, from having sight of the soul-and-spirit Beings who underlie what the senses perceive at the surface of the outer world. What the soul has become under the influence of this power, the pupil now beholds — as in a picture — in the figure that confronts him in the experience we are now describing. If he is duly prepared for this experience, he will assign to it its true meaning; and then, quite soon, yet another figure will be revealed to him. It is the 'Greater Guardian of the Threshold', so called to distinguish Him from the 'Lesser Guardian', hitherto described. The Greater Guardian tells the pupil that he must not remain at this stage but must press forward with untiring energy. He calls upon him to realize that the world into which he has won his way can only become truth for him if he perseveres in his efforts. Otherwise it will change for him into illusion. Were a pupil to submit himself to a wrong kind of training and come to this experience unprepared, he would, on approaching the 'Greater Guardian of the Threshold', find himself completely overwhelmed — overwhelmed with a feeling that can only be compared with boundless fear and terror.

The meeting with the Lesser Guardian of the Threshold afforded the pupil the opportunity of testing whether he is proof against the delusions that may arise through carrying his own being into the supersensible world; and the experiences that lead him at long last to the Greater Guardian of the Threshold will now enable him to discover whether he can stand up to the delusions that spring from the second source above mentioned. If he is proof against the captivating delusion which makes the picture-world he has attained seem to him like a rich possession — when all the time he is but a prisoner thereof — he will be protected from taking appearance for reality in the further course of his spiritual evolution.

The 'Guardian of the Threshold' will to some extent assume an individual and different form for every single person. For the meeting with him is the very experience by means of which the personal character of supersensible perceptions is eventually overcome and the way opened into a region of experience that is free from all personal colouring — a region universally valid, to which every human being has equal access.

*   *   *   *   *

Having come thus far in his experience, the aspirant is now able to make distinction in the surrounding world of soul and spirit between what is himself and what is outside him. He will now be in a position to appreciate how necessary it was to study the evolution of the world as described in this book, in order to arrive at a true understanding of man and of his life. For we can only understand man's physical body if we know how it has been built up right through the Saturn, Sun, Moon and Earth evolutions. So too for the other members of man's being. To understand the ether-body, we need to follow its development through Sun, Moon and Earth evolutions. And if we are to understand all that has to do with the Earth's own evolution at the present time, we shall need to know how it has gradually unfolded, stage by stage. One who has undergone spiritual training will be in a position to recognize the relationship between what is contained in man and the corresponding facts and beings of the world around him. For it is so indeed: there is no member or part of man that does not stand in some relation to the rest of the world — the world in its entirety. In this book it has hardly been possible to do more than give indications in barest outline of this universal correspondence. But we must not forget that the physical body, for example, was, during Saturn evolution, only in its very first beginnings. Its organs — heart, lung, brain and so on — developed out of these first beginnings, during the Sun, Moon, and Earth periods. They therefore are connected with Sun, Moon and Earth evolution. The like must be said of man's other members — the ether-body, the sentient body, the sentient soul and so on. The whole of the immediately surrounding world has gone to the forming of man; no single part or feature of him that has not its corresponding process or being in the world without. And when he has reached the above-described stage in his development, the pupil of the Spirit learns to recognize this relationship of his own being to the great world. Such is the characteristic experience at this stage: he becomes conscious of the correspondence that exists between the 'little world', the Microcosm — the world, that is, of man himself — and the 'great world', the Macrocosm.

When the pupil has worked his way through to this perception, a new experience awaits him. He begins to feel as though he had grown together with the whole vast structure of the Universe, retaining, however, at the same time the consciousness of himself as a fully independent being. A feeling nevertheless comes over him, as if he were being merged into the whole vast Universe, were becoming one with it — yet without losing his individuality. This stage of development may be described as the 'becoming one with the Macrocosm'. It is essential not to think of it as though implying that separate consciousness should cease and the human individuality be poured out into the All. Such an idea could arise only from an inexact and untrained way of thinking.

We may now set down in order the stages on the way to higher powers of cognition, attained in the training for Initiation that has here been described:

1. Study of spiritual science. To begin with, the pupil applies himself to this study with the powers of thought and sound judgment acquired in the physical world.
2. Attainment of Imaginative Cognition.
3. Reading of the Hidden Script. (This stage is equivalent to Inspiration.)
4. Living one's way into the Spiritual World that is around one (equivalent to Intuition).
5. Knowledge of the relationships between Microcosm and Macrocosm.
6. Becoming one with the Macrocosm.
7. A fundamental mood of soul determined by the simultaneous and integral experience of the foregoing stages.

The reader is not however to imagine that the seven stages necessarily follow one another in precise order. Much will depend on the individual character of the pupil. It can be that an earlier stage has only partially been reached when a pupil begins to undertake exercises belonging to the next. For example, it may be perfectly right, when he has had but a few genuine Imaginations, for him already to be doing exercises designed to bring Inspiration or Intuition, or even knowledge of the relationship of Microcosm to Macrocosm, within the reach of his own personal experience.

*   *   *   *   *

When the pupil has got so far as to have an experience of Intuition, then in addition to having knowledge of the pictures that belong to the world of soul and spirit, and being able to read from the Hidden Script how these pictures are inter-related, he also comes to know the Beings through whose co-operation the world to which man belongs has been called into existence. Then too he learns to know himself in his own archetypal form as a soul-and-spirit being in the world of soul and spirit. He has wrestled his way through to a perception of his Higher Self, and now sees clearly what he has still to achieve in order to gain control over his Double, the 'Guardian of the Threshold'. And he has furthermore had the meeting with the 'Greater Guardian of the Threshold' who stands there before him, continually calling upon him to work on further at his development. This 'Greater Guardian of the Threshold' now becomes for him the Ideal, the Example that he will do his utmost to follow. Having once come to this resolve, the pupil will be enabled to recognize who it is that is there before him as the 'Greater Guardian of the Threshold'. For now this Greater Guardian changes for the eyes of the pupil into the figure of the Christ, whose nature and whose part in the evolution of the Earth have been explained in the earlier chapters of this book. Through this experience the pupil is initiated into the sublime Mystery that is connected with the name of Christ. Christ shows Himself to him as the great human Prototype and Example, united with the Earth's true evolution.

Having thus come through Intuition to a knowledge of Christ in the spiritual world, the aspirant will find that he is able also to understand what took place historically on Earth in the fourth post-Atlantean period — the time of the Greek and Roman civilization. How the great Sun Being, even the Christ, intervened in Earth evolution, and how He is still working in it now and on into the future, the pupil of the

Spirit knows henceforth from his own experience. This then is what he attains through Intuition: the very meaning and significance of Earth evolution are communicated to him.

The path to knowledge of the supersensible worlds that has here been described is one that everyone can tread, no matter what his situation or circumstances in life. When speaking of such a path, we must not forget that the goal of knowledge and truth has been and is the same throughout all epochs of Earth evolution, but that the starting-point has been different in different epochs. Man cannot set out to-day from the same starting-point as did, for example, the candidate for Initiation in ancient Egypt. Neither can the exercises that were given to a pupil in ancient Egypt be simply taken over by a man of the present age. Since that epoch men's souls have **been** through sundry incarnations, and this moving on from incarnation to incarnation is not without meaning and purpose. The capabilities and qualities of the soul change from one incarnation to the next. Even a superficial study of history will convince us that since the twelfth and thirteenth centuries of our era the conditions of life have been very different from what they were before; men's opinions and feelings, even their capacities, have quite altered from what they were in earlier times. The path to higher knowledge that has here been described is one that is adapted for souls who are incarnated in the immediate present. It takes for its starting-point the situation of a human being of to-day, living under any of the typical conditions of the present age. As evolution progresses, the outer forms of man's life on Earth undergo change; so too in the paths of higher development every succeeding epoch calls for new ways and new methods. It is of vital importance that at every stage harmony should reign between man's life in the world at large and the Way of Initiation.

CHAPTER VI

PRESENT AND FUTURE EVOLUTION OF THE
WORLD AND OF MANKIND

IN SPIRITUAL SCIENCE, it is impossible to know the future evolution of the world and man without first coming to an understanding of the past. For when the scientist of the spirit observes the hidden facts of the past, what he perceives also contains, latent within it, all that is knowable to him of the present and the future. We have described Saturn, Sun, Moon and Earth evolutions. To understand the Earth itself in the light of spiritual science, we had to study the preceding stages. What man encounters in this Earth-world here and now may indeed be said to contain within it the facts of Moon, Sun, and Saturn evolutions. The Beings and entities that partook in Moon evolution underwent further development, and from them all that constitutes our present Earth came into being. Physical consciousness cannot however fully perceive all that evolved from Moon to Earth. Part of it remains invisible to the outer senses; it is seen only at a certain stage of super-sensible awareness. When this stage has been reached, our earthly world is seen to be united with a world supersensible, containing within it the portion of Old Moon-existence which has not condensed to physical perceptibility. It contains it however as it is *at present*, not as it was during Old Moon evolution. Yet in the course of supersensible research a picture of that earlier condition can be reached. For upon further contemplation the perception of the present state gradually divides of its own accord into two distinct pictures. The one picture manifests the form the Earth was actually in during Old Moon evolution, whilst in the other we soon recognize that it contains a form still in its germinal beginnings — one

298

which will only in the cosmic future become real in the way the Earth is real to-day. And as we persevere in spiritual observation, we see that something is perpetually streaming into this future form, wherein we recognize the outcome of what is happening on Earth. We are therefore beholding what our Earth is destined to become. The effects of Earth-existence will unite with what is taking place in the supersensible world to which we here refer, and from their union there will arise the new cosmic entity into which Earth will be metamorphosed, even as Old Moon was metamorphosed into Earth.

This future evolutionary form may be named the 'Jupiter' condition. One who is able supersensibly to observe it will see quite clearly that in the cosmic future certain things are bound to happen. For in the supersensible part of the Earth-world deriving from Old Moon, beings and entities are present which will assume certain predestined forms when the appropriate events have taken place upon the physical, sense-perceptible Earth. Jupiter therefore will contain what is already pre-determined by Old Moon evolution, and in addition some-thing new, making its entry into the evolutionary process only in consequence of what has meanwhile been enacted upon Earth. Supersensible consciousness can thus attain some know-ledge of the events and processes of Jupiter evolution. Yet the beings and events seen in this field are not of a kind to be perceived by outer senses; they cannot even be described as thin and unsubstantial forms of air, such as might still give rise to anything like sense-perceptible effects. All we receive from them are the impressions of purely spiritual sound, spiritual light and spiritual warmth. They do not find expres-sion in material embodiment. Only the supersensible consci-ousness can apprehend them. And yet these beings can be said to have a kind of body. Within their soul-nature — the soul which manifests their present being — they bear a store of *concentrated memories*. This is their 'body'. For we are able to distinguish in these beings what they are undergoing in the present and what they lived through in the cosmic past and can remember. This cosmic memory they bear within them as a kind of body. They experience it in the same way as man on Earth his body.

To a stage of seership higher than is needed for gaining knowledge of Old Moon and of the future Jupiter, beings and entities become perceptible which are the further-developed forms of what was present during Old Sun evolution. They are now at such a lofty level of existence as to elude a power of perception whose range is limited to the Old Moon and to the forms deriving from it. Also the spiritual picture of this higher world divides on further contemplation into two. The one part leads to a knowledge of the past Sun evolution; the other manifests a future cosmic form of the Earth, namely the form into which it will have changed when the results of all that has taken place on Earth and on Jupiter have flowed into the forms of yonder world — the forms deriving from the past Sun-condition. In the language of spiritual science, the future universe a higher stage of consciousness is thus enabled to perceive may be designated as the Venus state. Lastly a super-sensible consciousness even more highly developed perceives an evolutionary state of the more distant future to which the name of Vulcan may be given. Vulcan is in like relation to Saturn evolution as Venus to Sun and Jupiter to Moon. Thus in considering the past, the present and the future of Earth evolution we have to name its successive stages: Saturn, Sun, Moon, Earth, Jupiter, Venus and Vulcan.

Now even as these vast evolutionary stages of the Earth become accessible to spiritual consciousness, so do the facts of a less distant future. But at this point we have to utter an essential warning — one which cannot be over-emphasized. To gain true knowledge of these things, one must completely rid oneself of the idea that ordinary philosophical reflection, trained as it is to begin with in contemplation of sense-perceptible realities, can be of any help at all. These things cannot be — nor are they meant to be — discovered by dint of reasoning and reflection. If anyone imagines that having learned from spiritual science of Old Moon, he can by dint of thought — setting to work, let us say, to combine the known facts of the present Earth with those of the Old Moon — make out for himself what Jupiter will look like, he will soon become involved in illusion. These things are only meant to be discovered by the developed consciousness reaching up to their direct perception. Only when thus discovered and properly communicated, then alone — and then indeed — can they be understood even without supersensible consciousness of one's own.

The scientist of the spirit is however in a different situation when communicating future things than when telling of the past. For to begin with it is impossible for man to contemplate future events with the same candour and detachment as those that have already taken place. What is about to happen in the future cannot but stir up his feeling and his will; the past is bearable in quite another way. Everyone who has observed the life of man will know how true this is even in day-to-day existence. But to have any notion of the immensely heightened degree to which it applies when dealing with occult facts, or of the many subtle ways in which it shows itself, one needs to have some knowledge of supersensible worlds and of their latent difficulties. This branch of spiritual science is hence confined within determined limits, which have to be respected.

Even as we can trace the great sequences of cosmic evolution from Saturn to Vulcan, so too we can the shorter periods — the periods, for example, of Earth evolution proper. Since the tremendous upheaval that brought the life of old Atlantis to an end, there have been the successive stages in man's development described in this book as the ancient Indian, the ancient Persian, the Egypto-Chaldean and the Graeco-Latin epochs. The fifth is the present — the epoch man is going through to-day. In preparation ever since the fourth or fifth century A.D., it began gradually about the twelfth, thirteenth and fourteenth centuries, to emerge fully in the fifteenth. The preceding epoch — the Graeco-Latin — began about the eighth century B.C., the Christ-Event taking place when the first third of it was over. With the transition from the Egypto-Chaldean into the Graeco-Latin epoch, the whole mode and disposition of man's soul and all his faculties had undergone an essential change. The kind of logical thinking and intellectual comprehension of the world with which we are now familiar did not exist in Egypto-Chaldean times. Knowledge, which man to-day acquires by the deliberate exercise of his intelligence, he then received directly; it was given to him as an intuitive and inner — in some respects, supersensible — knowledge. Such was the form of cognition proper to that age. Man saw the objects around him, and in the very act of looking at them, the concept — the picture of them his soul needed — arose of its own accord within him. Now when cognition is of this nature, pictures not only of the sense-perceptible world make their appearance in man's soul, but from the depths of the inner life there dawns a knowledge, howsoever limited, of facts and beings imperceptible to the outer senses. This was a remnant of the dim and pristine supersensible awareness, once the common property of all mankind.

In the Graeco-Latin epoch an ever growing number of people were born in whom such faculties were lacking. Men now began to think about things with purely intellectual reflection. They drifted farther and farther away from the direct though dreamlike perception of the world of soul and spirit. Instead, they had to form an intellectual picture of it for themselves — intellectual, though aided by the life of feeling. Broadly speaking, man may be said to have been in this condition throughout the fourth post-Atlantean epoch. Those alone, who — as an heirloom from the past — retained the earlier faculties of soul, were able still to receive the spiritual world into their consciousness directly. But they were the belated remnants of a bygone age; their manner of cognition was no longer suited to the time. For by the very laws of evolution, an older faculty of soul loses its full significance when new faculties develop. The life of man becomes adapted to the new and has no further use for the old. There were however individuals who began to supplement the newly acquired faculties of intellect and feeling with the fully conscious development of higher powers of cognition, whereby they could penetrate once more into the world of soul and spirit. They had to set about it in a different way from the disciples of the old Initiates, who had not yet had to reckon with the new faculties of mind and soul due to the fourth post-Atlantean epoch. Thus the fourth epoch witnessed the first beginnings of the modern form of spiritual training, described in the present work. But this was in its infancy; it could only come to full development in the fifth epoch (from the twelfth and thirteenth and more especially the fifteenth century onward). Those who contrived to reach up into the supersensible worlds in this new way were able by their own Imagination, Inspiration and Intuition to gain knowledge of the higher regions of existence. Those on the other hand who did not get beyond the recently developed powers of intelligence and feeling, could only learn of what the old clairvoyance had still known from the traditions which were handed down through the generations, whether by word of mouth or in writing.

This was also true of the Christ-Event. If they themselves could not reach up into the supersensible worlds, men who were born after its time could only learn of the real essence and mystery of this Event from tradition. It should be added however that there were some Initiates of another kind — Initiates who still retained natural faculties of supersensible perception, by the development of which they could ascend into higher worlds, even while disregarding the new powers of intellect and feeling. They helped in the transition from the old way of Initiation to the new. Also throughout the later centuries individuals of this kind were still living. Yet the distinguishing mark of the fourth epoch was the shutting-off of the human soul from direct intercourse with worlds of soul and spirit, for by this very fact the human faculties of understanding and good feeling became deepened and enhanced. Souls who in their incarnations in the fourth epoch evolved these faculties to a high degree would bring the fruits of this development into their incarnations in the fifth. Shut out though they were in those days and left to their own resources, to compensate for this there were the sublime traditions of the ancient wisdom and above all of the Christ-Event, which by the very power of their content gave them the confident assurance of a higher world.

Yet all the time, as we said before, there were also those who in addition to the faculties of intellect and feeling developed higher powers of cognition. It fell to them to experience the facts of the higher worlds and more especially the mystery of the Christ-Event by direct supersensible cognition. From them there always flowed into the souls of other men as much as they could understand and beneficially receive.

The spread of Christianity began therefore at the very time when faculties of supersensible cognition were undeveloped in a large proportion of mankind. This was intended. It was in harmony with the whole trend of mankind's evolution upon Earth, and it accounts for the overwhelming influence of tradition at that time. The strongest influence was needed to give men faith and trust in the supersensible world when they themselves had not the faculty of spiritual sight. With the exception of a brief interval in the thirteenth century, there were however nearly always present upon Earth some individuals, able to lift themselves into the higher worlds by Imagination, Inspiration and Intuition. These were the true successors in the Christian era of the Initiates who in pre-Christian times had guided and partaken in the old Mystery-wisdom. It was their task to regain by their own human faculties the knowledge reached and entertained in bygone ages by the methods of the ancient Mysteries. To this they had to add the knowledge of the Christ-Event and of its deeper meaning.

Thus there arose among the new Initiates a power of cognition which could reach out to all that had been the theme and content of the old Initiation, while in the focus of it radiated the higher knowledge of the Mysteries of the Christ-Event. Only to a very small extent could this Initiate-knowledge find its way into the wider life of mankind during the fourth epoch, the task of which was still to strengthen and make firm in human souls the faculties of reasoned thought and feeling. Throughout this epoch it was accordingly a very 'hidden knowledge'. Then came the dawning of the present epoch, known as the fifth, the character of which may be described as follows. In the first place the powers of man's intellect go on developing and will continue doing so to an unprecedented extent both now and in the future. After the gradual preparation for this, beginning slowly in the twelfth and thirteenth centuries A.D., from the sixteenth century onward the pace has been and still is rapidly accelerating. Thus the fifth epoch has become a period of human evolution ever more given up to the cultivation of intellectual powers, while the traditional knowledge from the past — the knowledge entertained in simple trust and faith — loses its hold upon the human soul. But there has also been a steadily increasing inflow of the higher knowledge, arrived at by the modern forms of supersensible consciousness and cognition. Imperceptibly at first, the 'hidden knowledge' has been seeping into men's thoughts and ways of thought. That intellect as such should hitherto have tended and still be tending to reject this knowledge, is natural enough and was to be expected. But though it be rejected for a time, what is predestined will be fulfilled.

The hidden knowledge which is gradually taking hold of mankind, and will increasingly be doing so, may in the language of a well-known symbol be called the Knowledge of the Grail. We read of the Holy Grail in old-time narratives and legends, and as we learn to understand its deeper meaning we discover that it most significantly pictures the heart and essence of the new Initiation-knowledge, centering in the Mystery of Christ. The Initiates of the new age may therefore be described as the 'Initiates of the Grail'. The pathway into spiritual worlds, the first stages of which were set forth in the preceding chapter, culminates in the 'Science of the Grail'. It is a characteristic of this new Initiation-knowledge that while its facts can only be investigated with higher faculties of cognition (the methods of attaining which have been described), once investigated and discovered they are well able to be comprehended precisely by the faculties of mind and soul which the fifth epoch has developed. These faculties will more and more find satisfaction and fulfilment in the higher knowledge. It will be evident increasingly as time goes on. We are now living at a time when the higher knowledge needs to be far more widely received into the general consciousness of mankind than hitherto; it is with this in view that the present work has been written. And as the cultural evolution of mankind absorbs the knowledge of the Grail, in the same measure will the spiritual impulse of the Christ-Event become effective; its true significance will be revealed and it will grow from strength to strength. The more external development of Christianity as hitherto will increasingly be supplemented by the inner, esoteric aspect. What man can come to know by dint of Imagination, Inspiration and Intuition of the higher worlds in unison with the Mystery of Christ, will permeate men's thinking, their feeling and their willing — ever increasingly as time goes on. The 'hidden knowledge of the Grail' will become manifest and grow to be a power in man's life, entering ever more fully into all the ways and walks of man.

Throughout the fifth epoch the knowledge of supersensible worlds will thus continue to flow into the consciousness of men, and by the time the sixth begins it will be possible for mankind to have regained on a higher level the knowledge they possessed in pristine ages by virtue of the dim and dreamlike supersensible vision of those ancient days. But the renewed possession will be of quite another form than the old. What the soul knew of higher worlds in olden time was not yet permeated with her own human powers of intelligence and feeling. It came of its own accord — was 'given' as a kind of spiritual inspiration. In future, man will not only be receiving 'inspirations' of this kind, but will understand them through and through, feeling them as his very own, the true expression of his inmost being. When spiritual knowledge comes to him concerning beings or events, his own intelligence will find it true and sound and thus confirm the knowledge. Or if in spiritual knowledge some moral precept or principle of human conduct dawns upon him, he will say to himself: My feeling about it is only vindicated if I put into practice the implications of this knowledge. By the sixth epoch this mood and disposition of the soul should be achieved in a sufficiently large number of human beings.

The fifth epoch brings a kind of repetition of what the third — the Egypto-Chaldean — contributed to mankind's evolution. In the third epoch the human soul was still able to perceive some at least of the realities of supersensible worlds, though the perception was dwindling. The intellectual faculties which were to shut man off from higher worlds for a time, although not yet developed, were impending. In the fifth epoch the

supersensible facts, seen in the third in a dim state of consciousness, will become manifest once more, but taken hold of now
by man's own intelligence, realised with individual feeling, and
permeated too with what the soul has gained by knowledge of
the Mystery of Christ. Hence in the fifth epoch they take on an
altogether different form. When man received impressions
from supersensible worlds in olden time, they felt like forces
influencing and impelling him from an external spiritual world
— a world in which he himself was not. Evolution, leading on
into the new era, will have wrought a change. Man will now
feel these impressions as emanating from a world into which he
himself is growing — a world in which he too will have his
place, ever more as time goes on. We have not to picture the
repetition as though the human soul were simply to re-absorb
what lived in the Egyptian and Chaldean culture and has been
handed down traditionally. The Christ Impulse, truly understood and received into the soul of man, enables him to feel
himself a member of a spiritual world, outside of which he was
till now. Not only does he feel it thus; he knows it in full
consciousness and bears himself accordingly.

Even as the third epoch comes to life again in the fifth,
permeated in the souls of men with the new gifts and values
acquired in the fourth, so will the sixth epoch be related to the
second, and the seventh to the first — the ancient Indian. Thus
in the seventh epoch the possibility will be given for all the
marvellous wisdom proclaimed by the great Teachers of ancient
India to be living once again in human souls. And it will now
be their very own — the truth they live by.

The things and creatures of the Earth apart from man are
also undergoing change — changes related to the evolution of
mankind. When the seventh epoch has run its course, another
great convulsion will overwhelm the Earth, comparable to the
catastrophe between the end of Atlantean and the beginning
of post-Atlantean time. Under the altered conditions following
upon this event the life of man will once again evolve through
a succession of seven epochs. The souls who will then be incarnated will experience in an enhanced degree the community
with spiritual worlds enjoyed by the Atlanteans on a lower

level. But among human beings not everyone will without more ado prove equal to the new conditions then prevailing. It will only be those in whom souls are incarnated who have duly benefited by the influences of the Graeco-Latin and the succeeding fifth, sixth and seventh post-Atlantean epochs. Their inner life will be in harmony with what the Earth will have become. The others will perforce remain behind, whilst formerly they had been free to choose whether they were making themselves fit to go forward with the world's progressive evolution or were neglecting to do so. For the conditions that will prevail after the coming cataclysm, those above all will be well fitted who, in their incarnations between the fifth post-Atlantean epoch and the sixth, succeed in integrating the supersensible wisdom with their own human powers of intelligence and feeling. The fifth and sixth are the decisive epochs. In the seventh, the souls who have reached the evolutionary goal of the sixth will go on evolving. For those who have not, even the surrounding world will be too greatly altered; they will find little opportunity to recover their lost ground, and must await a more distant future when the conditions will again be favourable.

Thus evolution moves on from epoch to epoch. The future changes recognized by supersensible cognition involve however not the Earth alone, but the surrounding heavenly bodies in their relation to the Earth. Thus there will come a time when the Beings and forces who during old Lemuria were obliged to leave the Earth will be able to be reunited with her. In the Lemurian epoch they had to be detached to enable the inhabitants of Earth to go on evolving. Now the progressive evolution of the Earth and of mankind will have made it possible for them to join again. The Moon will reunite with the Earth, for by that time a sufficient number of human souls will have strength enough to make a fruitful use of the re-integrated Lunar forces for their further evolution. Yet that will also be a cosmic time when, side by side with human souls who have attained this high level of development, others will be living who have turned into a path leading towards evil. These backward souls will have burdened their Karma with so much of error, ugliness and ill-doing as to constitute a special group on their own, subject to aberration and evil and bitterly opposed to the progressive community among mankind.

By virtue of their spiritual development the good humanity will then be able to make use of the Moon forces and with their help transmute the bad, enabling them too to partake in the further evolution of the Earth, albeit as a distinct kingdom. And through this labour of the good humanity, the Earth — united now with the Moon — will in due evolutionary time also become able to reunite with the Sun, and with the other planets.

After a cosmic interval — a sojourn in a higher world — the Earth will then be transmuted into the Jupiter condition. In Jupiter what we now call the mineral kingdom will exist no longer; the forces of this kingdom will have been changed into plant-like forces. Thus upon Jupiter the vegetable kingdom, though in a very different form, will be the lowest. Above it will be the animal kingdom, likewise considerably altered, and then a human kingdom, recognizable as the spiritual descendants of the bad humanity originating upon Earth. Lastly, the descendants of the good humanity will constitute a human kingdom on a higher level. This is the human kingdom proper, and a great part of its work will be to influence and ennoble the souls who have fallen into the other group, so that they may yet gain entrance to it.

In the Venus stage of evolution the plant kingdom too will have disappeared. The lowest will then be the animal kingdom, metamorphosed a second time. Above it will be three human kingdoms, differing in degrees of perfection. During the Venus stage the Earth will remain united with the Sun. In Jupiter evolution on the other hand there will come a time when the Sun will separate again and Jupiter will be receiving the Solar influences from without. Then, after Sun and Jupiter have again become united, the transition to the Venus state will gradually be accomplished. From Venus, at a certain stage, a separate celestial body becomes detached. This — as it were, an 'irreclaimable Moon' — includes all the beings who have persisted in withstanding the true course of evolution. It enters now upon a line of development such as no words can portray, so utterly unlike is it to anything within the range of man's experience on Earth. The evolved humanity on the other hand, in a form of existence utterly spiritualized, goes forward into Vulcan evolution, any description of which would be beyond the compass of this book.

We see then that the 'Knowledge of the Grail' culminates in the highest imaginable ideal of human evolution — the ideal of spiritualization, brought about by man's own efforts. This is the ultimate outcome of the harmony achieved in the fifth and sixth epochs of the present age — the harmony between the powers of intelligence and feeling man has by now acquired, and the true knowledge of the spiritual worlds. What man is thus achieving in his own inner life is destined ultimately to become an outer world. Great and sublime are the impressions he receives from his surrounding world, and in the aspiration of his mind and spirit, as he goes out to meet them, he at first divines and at last clearly recognizes spiritual Beings of whom these impressions are the outer garment. His heart responds to the infinite majesty and sublimity of it all. Moreover he begins to know that the experiences and achievements of his own inner life — in intellect, in feeling, in character and strength of purpose — are seeds of a future spiritual world, a world in process of becoming.

It may be asked if human freedom is not incompatible with all this foreknowledge, this predetermination of the cosmic future. But a man's freedom of action in the Earth's future will not depend on the predestined cosmic plan any more than will his freedom in a year's time be impaired by his present resolve that he will then be moving into the house, the plan of which he is now deciding. Living incidentally in the house he has had built, he will be as free as his character allows. So too on Jupiter and Venus — once more, within the conditions there prevailing — man will be free according to the scope and measure of his own inner being. Freedom will depend, not on what is pre-determined by the cosmic past, but on what the soul has become by her own efforts.

* * * * *

Earth evolution bears within it the outcome of Saturn, Sun and Moon evolutions. In all the processes of Nature going on around him, man upon Earth finds Wisdom. Wisdom is in them as the fruit of what was done in the preceding epochs. Earth is the cosmic descendant of Old Moon, which — as related in a former chapter — evolved with all its creatures into a 'Cosmos of Wisdom'. With Earth herself an evolution is beginning whereby a new virtue, a new force, is being added to — instilled into — this Wisdom. As a result of Earthly evolution man comes to feel himself an independent member of a spiritual world. He owes it to the fact that upon Earth the I or Ego is engendered in him by the Spirits of Form, even as was his physical body by the Spirits of Will on Saturn, his life-body by the Spirits of Wisdom on the Sun, his astral body by the Spirits of Movement on Old Moon. All that now manifests as Wisdom has come into being by the working-together of the Spirits of Will, Wisdom and Movement. That the beings and processes of Earth can harmonize in Wisdom with the other beings of their surrounding world, is due to the work of these three Hierarchies of Spirits. Now, from the Spirits of Form, man receives his independent I, his Ego. And in the future the I of man will harmonize with the beings of Earth, Jupiter, Venus and Vulcan by virtue of the new force which Earthly evolution is implanting in the pristine Wisdom. It is the power of Love. In man on Earth it has to have its beginning.

The Cosmos of Wisdom is thus evolving into a Cosmos of Love. All that the I of man brings to development within him will grow into Love. It is the sublime Sun Being, of whom we had to tell when describing the evolution of the Christ-Event, who at His revelation stands forth as the all-embracing proto-type of Love. Into the innermost depth of man's being the seed of Love is thereby planted. Thence it shall grow and spread until it fills the whole of cosmic evolution. Even as the pristine Wisdom now reveals its presence in all the forces of Nature, in all the sense-perceptible outer world upon Earth, so in the future will Love be revealed — Love as a new force of Nature, living in all the phenomena which man will have around him. This is the secret of all future evolution. The knowledge man acquires, and also every deed man does with true understanding, is like the sowing of the seed that will eventually ripen into Love. Only inasmuch as Love arises in mankind, is true creative work being done for the cosmic future. For it is Love itself which will grow into the potent forces leading mankind on towards the final goal — the goal of spiritualization.

To the extent that spiritual knowledge flows into the evolution of mankind and of the Earth, there will be viable and fertile seeds for the cosmic future. For it is of the very nature of true spiritual knowledge to be transmuted into Love. The whole course of history we have been tracing, from the Graeco-Latin through the present time and on into the future, shows how this transmutation is to come about and reveals the future evolutionary trend of which this is the beginning.

The Wisdom that was prepared all through the Saturn, Sun and Moon evolutions lives in the physical, etheric, and astral bodies of man. It manifests as Wisdom of the World. Then, in the I of man, it is turned inward. From Earth evolution onward, the Wisdom of the outer world becomes inner Wisdom — Wisdom in man himself. And when thus resurrected in the inner life, in the I of man, it grows into the seed of Love. Wisdom is the premiss, the forerunner of Love; Love is the outcome of Wisdom re-born in the I of man.

Should anyone be prone to think that this account of cosmic evolution implies a fatalistic picture, he will have misunderstood it. To think that by this evolution a fated number of human beings will be condemned to belong to the 'bad humanity' argues a mistaken notion of how the two realms — the external and sense-perceptible, and that of soul and spirit — are related. They represent, within certain limits, two distinct evolutionary streams. It is from forces inherent in the former stream — in the external, material and sense-perceptible — that the forms of the 'bad humanity' arise. A human soul — a human individual — will only be under necessity of incarnating in such a form if he himself has given rise to the conditions for it. When the time comes it might even happen that among human souls who have been through the earlier evolutionary times there were none left to ensoul these forms. They might, without exception, be too good for bodies of that kind. In that event, the forms would have to be ensouled out of the Universe in some other way than by human souls who had lived through the preceding epochs. They will only be ensouled by human souls if the latter have themselves incurred this kind of incarnation. Supersensible cognition can only tell what it sees. It sees that in the cosmic future there will be two human kingdoms — 'good' and 'bad'. It has not to start reasoning and to conclude, from the condition of human souls to-day, what their condition will have to be in the cosmic future, as though by some necessity or law of Nature. The evolution of human forms and the evolution of the destinies of human souls have to be looked for along two distinct paths of spiritual research. A tendency to confuse the two would be an unavowed survival of materialism, impairing the clear outlook of supersensible science.

CHAPTER VII

DETAILS FROM THE DOMAIN OF
SPIRITUAL SCIENCE

The Ether-Body of Man

WHEN HIGHER members of man's nature are observed by supersensible perception, the perception is never exactly similar to one that is given by the outer senses. When by the touch of an object we have a sensation of heat or warmth, a distinction must surely be made between what comes from the object — streaming from it, so to speak — and what our soul experiences. The inner experience of the sensation of heat is not the same thing as the heat emitted by the object. Now think of this actual experience in the soul, without the object; think of the soul's experience of the sensation of warmth without any outer physical object being there to cause it. If such an experience arose without any cause, it would be mere fancy. The student of spiritual science has such inner perceptions for which there is no physical cause, above all no cause attributable to his own body. But at a certain stage of development, from the way in which these perceptions appear, he can know by the very nature of the experience (as was explained in an earlier chapter) that the inner perception is no mere fancy but is due to a being of soul and spirit belonging to a supersensible outer world, just as the ordinary sensation of heat, for example, is due to some physical object.

It is the same with a perception of colour. A distinction must be made between the colour of the object and the soul's inner experience of the colour. Now think of what the soul experiences when perceiving a red object in the physical world. Let us picture to ourselves that we retain a vivid memory of the impression but look away from the object. The memory-picture of the colour is an inner experience; we can distinguish between the inner experience evoked by the colour and the external colour as such. These inner experiences are substantially different from the immediate outer sense-impressions. They bear much more the stamp of feelings of pain or joy than do our normal and immediate sensations. We have to picture an inner experience of this kind arising in the soul without being caused either by an outer, physical object, or by the memory of such an object. Such an experience may come to someone who is on the way to attaining supersensible knowledge. Moreover he will be able to know in a given case that it is no mere figment of the mind, but that a real being of soul and spirit finds expression in it. And if evoking the same impression as a red object of the physical world, the being may be said to be 'red'. With a physical object however, the outer impression will always come first and be followed by the inner experience. In true supersensible vision, for a human being of the present epoch, the process must be the reverse: first the inner experience — shadowy, like a mere memory of colour — and then a living picture, growing ever more vivid. Unless it is realized that such must be the sequence, it will be hard to distinguish between genuine spiritual perception and the delusions of fancy (hallucinations, and the like).

Whether, in a spiritual perception of this kind, the picture becomes truly vivid and alive — whether it remains shadowy, like a dim inkling, or its effect grows as intensely real as that of an outer object — depends upon the stage of development which the aspirant has reached.

The general impression which the seer has of the ether-body of man may now be described as follows. If the aspirant for supersensible knowledge has developed such strength of will that even when a physical man is standing in front of him he can turn his attention right away from what is seen by the physical eyes, he will be able to look with supersensible consciousness into the space occupied by the physical man. Naturally, will-power must be greatly enhanced before it is possible to divert attention not only from what is in one's own mind but from something with which one is actually confronted, so that the physical impression is entirely obliterated. But such enhancement of the will is possible and is achieved by means of the exercises for the attainment of supersensible cognition. It is then possible for the student to have, to begin with, a general impression of the ether-body. There arises in his soul the same inner experience which he has at the sight, let us say, of the colour of a peach-blossom; this experience then becomes vividly alive, and he can say: the ether-body has a 'peach-blossom' colour. Then he perceives the several organs and currents of the ether-body. But the ether-body can also be described in terms of other experiences of the soul — experiences which correspond to sensations of warmth, impressions of sound, and so on, for it is not only a colour-phenomenon. Moreover the astral body and other members of man's being can be described in like manner. Bearing in mind what has here been said, it will be realized how the descriptions of spiritual science are to be understood. (Compare Chapter II.)

The Astral World

As long as the physical world alone is being observed, the Earth — man's dwelling place — appears as a separate heavenly body. When supersensible cognition rises to other spheres, there is no longer this separation. Hence it was possible to say that together with the Earth, Imaginative consciousness perceives the Old Moon condition, such as it has become up to the present time. The world thus entered is one to which not only the supersensible nature of the Earth belongs; other heavenly bodies, physically separated from the Earth, are part of it as well. In that realm the knower of supersensible worlds observes the supersensible nature not only of the Earth but of other heavenly bodies too. (It is, once more, the *supersensible* nature of other heavenly bodies which he observes to begin with. This should be borne in mind by those who feel impelled to ask why the seer does not tell us what it looks like on Mars, and so on. In putting questions of this kind they think of physical and sense-perceptible conditions.) Hence in the course of this book it was also possible to speak of relationships obtaining between the evolution taking place on Earth and simultaneous evolutions on Saturn, Jupiter, Mars, and so on. When man's astral body is drawn away in sleep it belongs not only to the Earth and earthly conditions, but to worlds in which other cosmic realms — stellar worlds — participate. Moreover, these worlds penetrate into man's astral body even in the waking state. Therefore the term 'astral body' appears justified.

Man's Life after Death

Reference has been made in the course of this book to the period of time during which the astral body remains united with the ether-body after a man's death. A gradually fading memory of the whole of the life just ended is present throughout this time (see Chapter III). It varies in duration with different individuals, depending upon the tenacity with which the astral body holds the ether-body to itself — in other words, the power which the astral body has over the etheric. Supersensible cognition can get an impression of this power by observing a human being who, by the state of his soul and body, ought really to be sleeping but keeps himself awake by sheer inner strength. It becomes evident that different people can, if need be, remain awake without being overcome by sleep for different periods of time. The memory of the life just ended — which means that the connection with the etheric body is still maintained — lasts for about as long after death as the extreme length of time for which, if compelled to do so, the individual would have been able to stay awake.

*　　*　　*　　*　　*

When the ether-body is detached from the human being after death (see Chapter III), something that may be described as a kind of extract or quintessence of it remains for the whole of his future evolution. This extract contains the fruits of the past life. It is the bearer of the 'seed' of his coming life — the seed which is developing throughout man's spiritual evolution between death and a new birth.

*　　*　　*　　*　　*

The length of time between death and a new birth is determined by the fact that as a rule the I of man returns into the physical world only when this world has been so transformed as to give opportunity for new experiences. While the Ego is in the spiritual worlds, man's earthly dwelling-place is changing. In one respect this change is connected with the changes that are taking place in the great Universe — changes, for example, in the relative position of the Earth to the Sun. Periodic changes involving cosmic repetitions are connected with the development of new conditions on the Earth. They find expression, for example, in the fact that the region of the heavens where the Sun rises at the vernal equinox makes an entire circuit in about 26,000 years. Throughout this period the vernal point has therefore been moving from one region of the heavens to another, and in a twelfth of this period of time — that is to say, in about 2,100 years — conditions on the Earth will have altered sufficiently for the soul to be able to have essentially new experiences upon Earth. Moreover as these experiences differ according to whether one is incarnating as a woman or as a man, two incarnations will *as a rule* take place during this time — one as a man, one as a woman. However, these things also depend upon the forces gathered during earthly life — forces the individual takes with him through the gate of death. Therefore all such indications as have been given here are only valid in the most general sense; there will be many and manifold individual variations.

Thus it is only in one respect that the length of the human Ego's sojourn in the spiritual world between death and new birth depends upon the above-mentioned cosmic data. In another respect it will depend upon the stages of the evolution through which the human being passes in the spiritual world. After a time this very evolution brings the I of man into a spiritual condition where he no longer finds sufficiency in the inner experiences of the Spirit. He begins to long for that altered consciousness which is reflected in physical experience and derives satisfaction from this reflection. The re-entry of the human being into earthly life is an outcome of these two factors: the inner thirst of the soul for incarnation, and the cosmically given possibility of finding a suitable bodily nature. Two factors therefore have to work in conjunction. Hence in one instance incarnation may result even before the 'thirst' has reached its full intensity, a well-adapted incarnation being within reach; while in another it may have to wait till the thirst has outlived its normal culmination, since at the proper time no opportunity to incarnate was given. In so far as it is due to the whole character and quality of his bodily constitution, a man's prevailing mood and attunement to life will also be the outcome of these conditions.

The Stages of Man's Life

Fully to understand the life of man and its successive stages between birth and death, it is not enough to consider only the physical body as seen by the outer senses. It is essential also to take into account the changes undergone by the supersensible members of man's nature. They are as follows. At physical birth man is released from the physical integument of the maternal womb. Forces hitherto shared by the human embryo with the mother's body must from now on be functioning independently in the body of the little child. Now the fact is that for supersensible perception other events of this kind are undergone in the further course of life — supersensible events, analogous to that of physical birth as seen by the outer senses. For his etheric body man is enveloped by an ethereal sheath — an etheric integument — until about the change of teeth, the sixth or seventh year, when the etheric integument falls away. This event represents the 'birth' of the etheric body. After it man is still enveloped by an astral sheath, which falls away at the age of puberty — between the 12th and 16th year. The astral body in its turn is 'born'. Then at an even later point of time the I is born. (The very helpful educational points of view arising from these supersensible realities are set forth in my booklet *The Education of the Child in the Light of Spiritual Science*, where the facts briefly indicated here are described in greater detail.) With the birth of the I, man's adult life begins. With the three members of the soul (Sentient Soul, Intellectual or Mind-

319

Soul, and Spiritual Soul) progressively awakened and activated by the I , he finds his proper place in life amid the prevailing world-conditions, to which he makes his own active contribution. At length however there comes a time when the etheric body begins to decline, reversing the development it enjoyed from the seventh year onward. There is a change in the functioning of the astral body. To start with it unfolded the potentialities brought with it from the spiritual world at birth. After the birth of the Ego it was enriched by all the experiences coming to it from the outer world. But now the moment comes when in a spiritual sense the astral body begins to feed on its own etheric body. It draws on the etheric body and consumes it. And in the further course of life the etheric body in its turn begins to draw upon the physical body and consume it. These facts are closely related to the physical body's degeneration in old age.

The life of man is thereby naturally divided into three epochs. First is the time during which the physical and etheric bodies grow and develop. In the middle period the astral body and the I come into their own. The third and last is the period of bodily decline, when the youthful development of the etheric and physical bodies is in a sense reversed. Now in all these events — from birth until death — the astral body is concerned. Moreover inasmuch as it is not spiritually born until the 12th to 16th year, and in the final epoch is obliged to draw upon the forces of the etheric and physical bodies, what the astral body has to achieve by virtue of its own faculties and forces unfolds at a slower rate than it would do if it were not inhabiting a physical and etheric body. Hence after death (as explained in Chapter III), when the physical and etheric bodies have been cast off, the evolution of the astral body through the 'time of purification' takes about a third as long as the past life between birth and death.

Higher Regions of the Spiritual World

Through Imagination, Inspiration and Intuition super-sensible cognition gradually reaches up into the regions of the

spiritual world where it can apprehend the Beings who participate in the evolution of the World and Man. There too it can
perceive and, in perceiving, find intelligible the life of man
between death and a new birth. Now there are even higher
regions of existence, though we can do no more than briefly
allude to them here.

Having once risen to the stage of Intuition, supersensible
cognition lives and moves amid a world of spiritual Beings.
But the spiritual Beings too are evolving. The concerns of
present-day mankind reach up, as it were, into the spiritual
realm accessible to Intuition. True, in the course of his development between death and a new birth man receives influences
from yet higher worlds, but he does not experience them
directly; the Beings of the spiritual world convey them to him.
In the Intuitive contemplation of these Beings we perceive all
that they are doing in and on behalf of man. Their own concerns however — what they require for themselves to enable
them to guide human evolution — can only be apprehended
by forms of cognition higher than Intuition.

In saying this we refer to worlds among whose lower functions are the highest that are known to us on Earth. Reasoned
resolves for example are among the highest things on Earth;
the actions and reactions of the mineral kingdom among the
lowest. For the sublime worlds to which we are now referring,
reasoned resolves have approximately the same value as have
the mineral reactions on Earth. Beyond the realm of Intuition
is the region where the great cosmic plan is being woven out
of purely spiritual causes.

The Members of Man's Being

Towards the end of Chapter II it was described how the I
or Ego works upon the members of man's being to transform
them — the astral body into Spirit-Self, the etheric body into
Life-Spirit, the physical body into Spirit-Man. This was in
reference to the working of the Ego on man's nature by virtue
of the highest faculties — faculties, the development of which
has only been beginning during the successive stages of Earthly

321

evolution. Now there is also a preliminary transformation on a lower level, whereby the Sentient Soul, the Intellectual or Mind-Soul and the Spiritual Soul are developed. As in the course of man's evolution the Sentient Soul comes into being, far-reaching changes are going on in the astral body. So too the development of the Intellectual Soul and of the Spiritual Soul involves a transmutation of the ether-body and of the physical body respectively. Much of this was incidentally described in the chapter on the evolution of the Earth.

Thus in a sense it is true to say that the Sentient Soul is due to a transmuted astral body, the Intellectual Soul to a transmuted ether-body and the Spiritual Soul to a transmuted physical body. But it may equally well be said that all three members of the soul are part and parcel of the astral body. The Spiritual Soul, for example, can only come into being as an astral entity in an appropriate physical body. It lives an astral life in a physical body moulded and worked upon to be its proper habitation.

The State of Consciousness in Dreaming

In some respects the dream has been described in the third chapter of this book. Dream-consciousness is on the one hand a relic of the picture-consciousness which man enjoyed on the Old Moon, and — for a long time too — in former periods of Earth evolution. Earlier conditions generally go on working even while evolution is advancing to fresh stages. Dreaming is thus a relic of the normal state of consciousness of former times. And yet the dream-condition of today differs essentially from the old picture-consciousness, for the Ego, which has since developed, influences what goes on in the astral body during sleep whilst we are dreaming. It is therefore a picture-consciousness transmuted by the presence of the Ego. Yet inasmuch as the Ego's influence on the dreaming astral body is unconscious, nothing deriving from the dream-life can be a direct source of spiritual-scientific knowledge of higher worlds. The same applies to what is often spoken of as visions, premonitions, and second sight. In all of these the Ego is more or less eliminated, in consequence of which, relics of earlier states of consciousness can supervene. They have no direct spiritual-scientific application; what man perceives in such conditions cannot be included among the valid researches of true spiritual science.

The Way to Supersensible Cognition

The way to the attainment of knowledge of higher worlds, of which a fairly detailed account has been given in this book, may be described as the 'direct path' of knowledge. There is also another way, known as 'the path of feeling.' Not that the former way leaves feeling undeveloped; quite on the contrary, it leads to an immeasurable deepening of the life of feeling. But the other path — the 'path of feeling' — appeals to the feeling-life directly, seeking to rise from thence to detailed spiritual knowledge. The fact is that a feeling to which a man unreservedly devotes his inner life for a sufficient length of time becomes transformed of its own accord into cognition — into Imaginative vision. If, for example, the soul is deliberately steeped for weeks and months or even longer in feelings of humility, the feeling-content is transformed into spiritual perception. A gradual ascent through this and other feelings of this kind can thus become a pathway into the supersensible. But it is very difficult to carry out in ordinary present-day surroundings. Seclusion — withdrawal from the prevailing conditions especially of modern life — is well-nigh indispensable for this spiritual pathway. For above all in the initial stages, the impressions one is constantly receiving from every-day life in our time disturb and interfere with what the soul would otherwise achieve by dwelling on deliberately chosen feelings. The path of knowledge here described is different; it can be carried through no matter what one's situation is amid the typical conditions of our time.

The Observation of Particular Events and Beings

It may be asked whether by meditation, contemplation and kindred methods of attaining supersensible cognition described in this book, we arrive only at the general realities — say, of the life between death and rebirth, and other spiritual facts — or whether we are also enabled to perceive particular events and beings, for example an individual human soul after death. The answer is that one who has thus acquired the ability to see into the spiritual world also becomes able to perceive in detail what is going on there. He does indeed become capable of communication with individuals living in the spiritual world between death and new birth. But in accordance with true spiritual science it can only be done after a regular and proper training has been undergone, for this alone makes it possible to distinguish truth from illusion as to the several beings and events. Those who would claim to recognize the spiritual details without having undergone a proper training are liable to countless illusions. Even the most elementary requirement, namely the true interpretation of the impressions one receives, presupposes spiritual training — training the more advanced where the impressions relate to detailed facts and individual beings.

Thus the same training which enables one to see the facts of higher worlds described in this work on Occult Science, also enables one to perceive an individual human soul during his life after death, or severally to observe and understand the diverse spiritual beings who influence the manifest from hidden worlds. Yet the reliable observation of the particular is only possible against the background of a more universal knowledge — namely a spiritual knowledge of the great facts of the Universe and Man, facts which relate to all mankind in common. Craving the former without the latter, one will go astray. In observation of the spiritual world it is an unavoidable experience. Into the very regions for which a man is most apt to long, entry is only granted when he has gone along the stern and exacting path of knowledge, where interest is focused upon universal questions and he gains insight into the deeper meaning of all life.

When he has walked along these paths in the sincere and unselfish quest of knowledge, then and then only is a man fit to observe the details, the premature exploration of which would but have satisfied in him a hidden egoism. For in the longing to see into the spiritual world it is only too easy to persuade oneself that one is actuated by pure love — such as the love of an individual friend who has died. Unalloyed insight into the single facts and beings is only possible for those whose sincere interest in the universal truths of spiritual science enables them to receive the detailed revelations too in a scientific spirit and without selfish longing.

SUPPLEMENTARY NOTES

(Page 45-6) Such explanations as have here been given about memory are all too easily misunderstood. For when one only looks at the external aspect one is apt to miss the essential difference. When something seemingly like memory occurs in animals, even in plants, it is by no means the same as the genuine memory experienced by man, the essential character of which we have delineated. When an animal performs the same action for the third or fourth time and then again and again, externally it may appear as though due to memory and the consequent ability to learn. Some of our scientists and their philosophic followers extend the concept even farther. The chicken only just emerged from the shell begins to peck at the grains of corn, moving its head and body from the outset with the requisite precision. It cannot possibly have learned to do this while inside the egg; therefore it must have learned it through the many thousands of generations from which it is descended (thus Hering among others). Admittedly the phenomenon can be described so as to look like a kind of memory. Yet for a genuine understanding of man's being we have to focus on the essential feature, namely *the conscious perception of an earlier experience at a later point of time*. This is a very different thing from the mere fact that subsequent are influenced by earlier conditions. It is this faculty to perceive the past which is called memory in the present work, and not the mere recurrence — however modified — of earlier in later conditions. If we insisted on using the word memory for these and related phenomena in the animal and plant kingdoms, we should need another term for human memory. The explanations given here are not concerned with the mere word, but with the unequivocal recognition of an essential difference — essential above all to an understanding of man's being. The same applies to the seemingly high degree of intelligence which animals are often seen to manifest in skill of action and behaviour. It cannot truly be attributed to memory as here defined.

(Page 54) No hard and fast dividing line can be drawn between the changes wrought by the Ego in the astral and in the etheric body. They merge into one another. When a man learns, thereby enlarging his mind, extending his range of judgment, a change has taken place in his astral body. When the widening of outlook has influenced the whole mood and tenor of his soul — when his habitual feeling towards the subject he has learned about is different from what it was before — it will be evidence of a change in his etheric body. Everything we really make our own, till it comes naturally to us to recall it, argues a change in the etheric body. Whatever seeps into our inner life to be indelibly remembered, shows that the working of the Ego on the astral body has reached down to the etheric.

(Page 63) The relation between sleep and fatigue is generally not regarded in a realistic way. Sleep is supposed to follow in consequence of fatigue. But this is far too simple an idea; a man need not be tired in the least to fall asleep, say, in a lecture he finds uninteresting. The obvious rejoinder, that in the human being boredom of this kind must therefore also be a cause of fatigue, is surely not quite serious or scientific. In the last resort, unbiased observation leads us to discern in waking and sleeping two distinct relations of the soul to the body — relations which in the normal course of life must, like the swing of a pendulum, alternate in rhythmic sequence. To be filled for a time with the impressions of the outer world arouses in the soul the craving to go over from this into another state, in which the soul is surrendered to the processes of her own bodily nature. There is this alternation: the state of being given up to the impressions of the outer world, and that of being given up to one's own body. During the former state, the craving for the latter is unconsciously engendered, and this in turn then takes its course entirely in the unconscious. It is the longing to be devoted to one's own bodily nature which manifests as fatigue. In truth we ought rather to say that we feel tired because we want to fall asleep, not that we want to fall asleep because we feel tired. Now habit often makes it possible for the human soul deliberately to evoke conditions which in normal life would of necessity ensue in their due time. Therefore when one is wilfully obtuse to some impressions, it is not difficult to induce the longing to be given up to one's own body. The soul then goes to sleep, even though by the man's natural condition there is no cause to do so.

(Page 93) It would be easy to misunderstand the contention that if a man's individual talents depended on mere heredity they would have to manifest at the beginning of a line of descent and not at the end. Surely, it might be answered, the talents cannot yet emerge at the beginning; they must have time to develop. But the objection is invalid. To prove that a later thing is inherited from an earlier, we have to show that it was there in the earlier generation and is found again in the later. If it were shown that something was present at the beginning of a genealogical tree and reappeared in its further course, it would be logical to speak of heredity, but it is obviously not so when there occurs at the end what was not there before. The turning of the proposition into its converse was only to show up the fallacy.

(Page 110) In the fourth and sixth chapters of this book it was described how the World to which Man belongs, and Man himself, evolve through the successive states called 'Saturn, Sun, Moon, Earth, Jupiter, Venus and Vulcan.' Some indication was also given of how human evolution is related to the existing heavenly bodies other than the Earth — Saturn, Jupiter and Mars, for example. They too are of course evolving, and in their present stage of evolution the physical part of them is perceptible to our senses in the forms known to physical Astronomy as 'Saturn', 'Jupiter', 'Mars' and the rest.

Seen in the light of spiritual science, the present Saturn is a kind of reincarnation of Old Saturn. It came into existence because, before the Sun had separated from the Earth, Beings were there who would not have been able to leave with the Sun. They were so much imbued with Saturnian character-istics that they could not live where Solar properties above all were to be developed. So too the present Jupiter arose because Beings were there with characteristics which cosmic evolution as a whole will be unfolding in the future Jupiter and not till then. Mars on the other hand is a heavenly body inhabited by Beings whose evolution on Old Moon was such that they could not have benefited from any further progress upon Earth. Mars is a reincarnation of Old Moon on a higher level. The present Mercury is a dwelling-place for Beings who are ahead of earthly evolution in that they have developed certain earthly qualities in a higher form than is possible upon the Earth herself. Likewise the present Venus is a prophetic anticipation of the future Venus state.

Such are the reasons for naming the past and future stages of World-evolution after the heavenly bodies — their present representatives, as it were, in the Cosmos. The kind of intel-lectual and scientific judgment trained in the observation of external Nature will scarcely fail to object to this nomenclature, with its implied relation of the physical heavenly bodies of to-day to cosmic evolutionary stages — Saturn, Sun and so on — supersensibly perceived. Yet even as with mathematical think-ing the solar system can be seen in the mind's eye — a clear, intelligible picture of cosmic happenings in space and time — with supersensible cognition it is possible to imbue the mathem-atical picture with an inner life of soul. Then the implied relation proves to be valid. In point of fact this ensoulment of the cosmic picture is in the straightforward line of development of strictly natural-scientific thought and study. Science, it is true, is still only prepared to look for the relation between the Solar System and the Earth in terms of mathematical and mechanical concepts. Yet in the very act of doing this, the Natural Science of the future will be led further. It will be led, even in its own domain, to concepts supplementing and enlarging the mechanical with the aspect of soul and spirit. Even in the light of current scientific concepts, this enlargement

329

is already due, nay overdue. It would be possible to show this, though it would need the writing of another book. Here we can only indicate the fact, though it be at the risk of fresh misunderstandings.

The discrepancies between Spiritual Science and Natural Science are often only apparent. The reason for them lies in the continued reluctance of the latter to evolve ideas which are in fact being called for not only by supersensible cognition, but also by the kind of knowledge which adheres to outer, sense-perceptible data. In the findings of modern science an open mind can perceive on every hand the indication of new fields of observation and discovery — discovery, once more, by purely natural-scientific methods — discovery of sense-perceptible facts. These facts will show that our research into outer Nature fully confirms what is known to spiritual sight. In so far as the cosmic happenings revealed to supersensible cognition have any counterpart in sense-perceptible Nature, it will prove to be so.

TRANSLATORS' NOTE

IN EARLIER English editions of this and other standard works by Rudolf Steiner the technical terms of anthroposophical spiritual science have been variously rendered. The following notes will therefore be helpful.

For the three soul-members Rudolf Steiner's terms and the English equivalents approved — or in some instances suggested — by him are as follows.

Empfindungsseele.	Sentient soul.
Verstandes-oder Gemütsseele.	Intellectual or Mind-soul.
Bewusstseinsseele.	Spiritual soul.

In earlier translations *Bewusstseinsseele* had been rendered more literally: 'Consciousness-soul'. Dr. Steiner subsequently gave 'Spiritual soul' as the true equivalent. This we have used throughout, though in some contexts — it is generally agreed — 'Consciousness-soul' can still be a helpful alternative.

'Mind-soul' for *Gemütsseele* was also approved, indeed suggested, by Dr. Steiner. To understand it rightly one should recall that 'mind' had at one time a less one-sidedly intellectual, less cold significance than it generally has to-day. In the mental processes of thought the heart — the entire man — not only the head was felt to be concerned. This should be borne in mind when the fourth post-Atlantean or Graeco-Latin epoch (8th century B.C. to 15th A.D.) is spoken of as the age of the Intellectual or Mind-soul. The fuller meaning is still implied in the verbal use of 'to mind' in the sense of tending and caring for; or again, in old-fashioned and colloquial usage, sharing the memory of a past experience — memory always with a touch of feeling. This is intended when the otherwise untranslatable word *Gemüt* is rendered 'mind'. The difficulty is evident in earlier efforts to translate *Gemütsseele*, as in the first English edition of Rudolf Steiner's *Theosophy*, where it is rendered 'Soul of the higher feelings'.

Dr. Steiner's names for the three members of the human spirit — equivalent to the eastern Manas, Budhi, Atma — present no special problems. *Geistselbst, Lebensgeist* and *Geistmensch* become in English: Spirit-self, Life-spirit and Spirit-man.

Of the three bodily members, Dr. Steiner sometimes refers to the Astral body as *Seelenleib* — 'Soul-body' — or again as *Empfindungsleib* — 'Sentient body'. For the Etheric — *Aetherleib, aetherischer Leib* — we have the corresponding alternatives, 'Ether-body' and 'Etheric body'. In the adjectival form, 'Ethereal body' would in our view be preferable and indeed more natural. Till it was introduced in theosophical writings of the late 19th century, the form 'etheric' rarely, if ever, occurs. 'Ethereal' on the other hand is a well-established word, reaching back through the centuries to a time when the experience of the cosmic Ether was not yet lost to Western man. In this respect it answers exactly to the German *aetherisch*. From its descriptive use and literary associations, it evokes an immediate feeling of the peripheral and expansive quality of those entities and forces which constitute the Ether-body of man and other living creatures. This quality — the inner connection of the Ether-body with the vast expanse of the Heavens — was frequently insisted on by Dr. Steiner in his later books and lectures (at a time when he was also giving to it the alternative designation *Bildekräfteleib* — 'Body of Formative Forces'). But when a certain form has for so long become familiar to students, one is reluctant to impose a sudden change; hence for the present edition we have adhered to the term 'Etheric body'.

For the nine ranks of Beings of the Spiritual Hierarchies (often referred to in groups of three as the First, Second and Third Hierarchy) there are the two or three alternative sets of names — those of the Christian esoteric tradition in their Greek or Hebrew forms; then in some instances the traditional translation of these names into English or other European language; lastly, the modern spiritual-scientific names coined by Rudolf Steiner. They are as follows.

First Hierarchy:

Seraphim	Spirits of Love
Cherubim	Spirits of the Harmonies*
Thrones	Spirits of Will

Second Hierarchy:

Kyriotetes	Dominions	Spirits of Wisdom
Dynamis	Mights, or Virtues	Spirits of Movement
Exusiai	Powers	Spirits of Form

Third Hierarchy

Archai	Principalities	Spirits of Personality
Archangels		Fire-Spirits
Angels		Sons of Life or of Twilight

For the Archai — the Greek word literally means 'Beginnings' — Rudolf Steiner gives as the German equivalent *Urbeginne:* Ur-beginnings, First Beginnings, Primal Beginnings. They are the Beings who attained the human stage at the beginning of our evolutionary cycle, on Old Saturn. In Dr. Steiner's well-known lectures on the Apocalypse of St. John, they are described as the eldest of the 'Elders' of mankind. In *Genesis* and other lecture-cycles, the 'Elohim' are identified as of the hierarchical rank of the Exusiai, Spirits of Form.

Other alternative names, notably for the Archai and the Thrones, will be found in Rudolf Steiner's 'Chapters from the Akashic Records' — *Aus der Akasha-Chronik*, entitled *Cosmic Memory* in the 1959 American edition. These had been published seriatim in the periodical *Lucifer-Gnosis*, a year or two *before* the first edition of *Occult Science*.

Concerning the Hierarchies more will be found in Dr. Steiner's lecture-cycles, now available in book form. We refer especially to those entitled *Spiritual Hierarchies* (Düsseldorf, 1909) and then again *Spiritual Beings in the Heavenly Bodies and in the Kingdoms of Nature* (Helsingfors, 1912). Stages of world-

---

* *Geister der Harmonien,* hitherto translated 'Spirits of Harmony'. *Harmonien* is however the plural form. 'Spirits of the cosmic Harmonies' would perhaps convey most truly the feeling of the original.

creation and evolution are dealt with in the *Genesis* lectures above-mentioned, in the (Dornach, 1923) lectures *Man as Symphony of the Creative Word*, and above all in the lecture-cycle *Inner Realities of Evolution* (Berlin, 1913). The last-named is an invaluable supplement to the Evolution chapter of *Occult Science*. One other lecture-cycle, frequently recommended for study by Rudolf Steiner, may here be mentioned; it bears especially on Chapter III. It is entitled *Life between Death and Rebirth in relation to the Cosmic Conditions* (Berlin, 1912–13).

The term *das Ich* for the middle and essential member of Man's being is here translated alternatively as 'the I' or 'the Ego'. To use only the Latin form 'Ego' with its rather hardening suggestion of egoism and self-assertion would, we believe, convey a wrong impression. Through the very sound and character of the word *ich*, as Rudolf Steiner pointed out, the German language is particularly fortunate in this respect. In older theosophical literature the real being of the I is often referred to as the true Self of Man.

An unavoidable difficulty is presented by the word *Vorstellung* and the kindred verb and verbal noun, *das Vorstellen*. In the first English edition of *The Philosophy of Spiritual Activity* Prof. Hoernlé translated *Vorstellung* 'idea'. To this there are obvious objections, yet in our everyday usage — for which there is also a very respectable philosophical background — the English *idea* corresponds pretty closely to the German *Vorstellung*. *Idea* in its Platonic, archetypal meaning — equivalent to the German *Idee* — can then be distinguished by means of a capital.

Later translators have rendered *Vorstellung* 'representation' or 'mental presentation'. In the 1939 American edition of *Occult Science* it is translated 'visualization'. But a mental image in the sense of *Vorstellung* need not be visual; it may equally well be auditory or related to any of the other senses (taste, smell, touch, etc.), as for example when in the silence of thought we experience a melody, whether remembered or improvised. In the present edition *Vorstellung* has variously — according to the context — been translated 'mental image', 'mental picture', 'thought-picture', or 'idea', and *das Vorstellen* 'the forming of mental images', or 'ideation'.

Among the problems inherent in the translation of Rudolf Steiner's spiritual-scientific works is the fact that words of Latin or Greek origin, at first sight the most easily translated, have quite another *timbre*, another shade of meaning in German and in English. English, like German, Dutch and Scandinavian, is in its roots a Germanic language, but unlike German it is enriched with countless words of Latin origin, whether derived from Latin directly or via Norman-French. In German, words of Latin origin are comparatively rare and practically every Latin form has its Germanic equivalent, which is the word in common use,* The outcome is that when a Latin word is used, it conveys a subtle shade of meaning, apt to be lost when rendered by the most obvious English translation, often identical with the German or nearly so. To take one example, for the English word 'spiritual' the ordinary German equivalent is *geistig*, but side by side with this there is the word *spirituell*, and when this is used it suggests a spiritual quality in a peculiarly delicate and appreciative sense.

There are many such duplicates, more or less synonymous and yet conveying different shades of meaning, as for example, *Sinnbild* and *Symbol*, *Einweihung* and *Initiation*, *Einbildungskraft* and *Phantasie*, *Schauung* and *Vision*. Both in his written works and in his lectures, Rudolf Steiner makes full use of the subtle shades of meaning made possible in German by the alternative use of less familiar words of Latin or Greek derivation. For the translator, this presents a problem all too easily overlooked.

Among other things, the words of Greek or Latin origin in German, being in less common use, can often be adopted as technical terms pure and simple.. This applies (though in varying degree) to the names Rudolf Steiner gave to the three higher stages of cognition: *Imagination*, *Inspiration* and *Intuition*. The words are identical in the two languages, but whereas 'imagination' for example is a word in common use and as such indispensable in English, the same does not apply to

* Synonyms of Germanic (Anglo-Saxon) and Latin origin are of course frequent in English too; here however, both are in common use, indeed, the Latin form is often the more common. In German this is not so.

Imagination in German. In such instances we distinguish the word by a capital when used in the technical meaning of spiritual science.

This new edition of *Occult Science* is a free translation. While trying to be true to the essential meaning, we have translated into the English idiom, which for the most part involves a considerable departure from the original. Notably in dialectic — in the way a logical sequence of thought or reasoned argument is presented — the style and construction natural to English are as different as can be from the German. Directly rendered and especially when the argument is prolonged, what appears crystal-clear and straightforward in German is apt to become ponderous and wordy, over-insisting on the obvious in English, until at last the reader is befogged. Since it is Rudolf Steiner's method of spiritual-scientific teaching to evoke wakefulness and clarity of thought, it surely is important that the thought be conveyed in the way that comes natural to one who thinks — and is at pains to think clearly — in his own language, whichever it may be.

In this and other ways, we think a free translation can often be a faithful rendering rather than one which adheres more closely to the style and structure of the original. To translate freely is however an added responsibility, obviously exposed to dangers. For one is then *interpreting* the author's meaning and the interpretation may not always be the right or the only one. We do not pretend that our translation will be free of mistakes. In view of future editions we shall be grateful to have our attention drawn to any seeming discrepancies or errors.

We are indebted to a number of friends for valuable help and suggestions. Mr. A. C. Harwood kindly read through the finished manuscript. Above all we have to thank Miss D. S. Osmond, to whose encouragement and practical help at every stage the present edition is very largely due.

* * * * *

An introductory word should also be said concerning the Synopsis. Rudolf Steiner's basic works need to be read and studied continuously. He never included an index; rarely, if ever, a detailed list of contents. Even the longest chapters of the present work he left undivided by sub-headings.

The Synopsis is intended above all for those who already know the book. Those who are reading it for the first time, or even re-reading it as a whole, will do well to disregard the Synopsis entirely. It is intended for students who may recall a particular theme and want to find it again without too great loss of time. Leaders of study-groups will find it helpful in this way. The Synopsis does not pretend to be exhaustive; we trust, however, that a sufficient number of references have been given. Nor is it meant as an analysis. Careful analyses — revealing, for example, the inner structure and the many correspondences implicit in the long Evolution chapter — have often been made by students. They can be most helpful — helpful perhaps even more in the making than in the finished outcome. No such intention underlies the following synopsis. It has the purely practical purpose of enabling the reader quickly to find the passage he is looking for.

G.A., M.A.

SYNOPSIS

Chapter I. The Character of Occult Science

Concerning the term 'Occult Science'. The 'manifest secret' (25–6).

What is the essence of a 'science'? Science and supersensible perception (26–9). Sundry aberrations (29). The character of 'proofs' in natural and spiritual science (30–1). Riddles arising from contemplation of the outer world, to which the outer world gives no answer (31–2). Concerning 'frontiers of knowledge' (32–3). Contrary viewpoints mentioned and answered (30–2).

Universal, impersonal validity of spiritual-scientific insight (34–5).

Spiritual knowledge a source of renewed life and strength (35–36). Spiritual-scientific study and the development of one's own higher faculties (36–8). The student becomes an active participator in supersensible knowledge (38). In supersensible cognition, man himself is the instrument of knowledge (37–8).

Chapter II. The Nature of Humanity

Physical body; relation to mineral kingdom (39–40). Etheric or Life-body (40–3; *see also page* 314).

Misunderstandings to be guarded against: the hypothetical ether of physics; discarded notions of a 'life-force' (41–2). Wider use of the term 'body' (41). Etheric organs — heart, brain, etc. (41).

Astral body (43–4).

Waking and sleeping (43). Relation to animal kingdom. Fallacious reasoning concerning 'sensitive' plants (44).

The I or Ego, the fourth member of man's being (45–53).

Life, consciousness and memory in relation to etheric body, astral body and Ego (46). Memory characteristic of man; mistakes concerning 'memory' in animals (45–8; *see also page* 326). Learning, remembering and forgetting (48). Distinction of body and soul. Astral body as soul-body (48–9).

338

The Archai or Spirits of Personality attain their human stage (121–2).

Germinal beginnings of human sense-organs (122).

Entry of the Fire-Spirits (Archangels) and the Sons of Life or of Twilight (Angels). Participation of the Seraphim and Cherubim (122–4).

Renewed activity of the Thrones. The germ of Spirit-Man (124).

Transition from soul-warmth to outwardly perceptible warmth; earlier, purely spiritual stages.

Beginning of Time. Time and Duration (126).

Meaninglessness of questions endlessly pursued; example of cart-tracks (126).

Summary and recapitulation. Progressive advancement of the Hierarchical Beings (127).

Interval of spiritual rest between Saturn and Sun evolutions (128).

Sun Evolution (129–37)

Recapitulation of Old Saturn. Outpouring of the human life-body by the Spirits of Wisdom (129–30).

Beginnings of Life. Interval of cosmic rest. The human being becomes twofold (129–30).

Entry of the Spirits of Movement (130–1).

Movement within the human body, comparable to that of sap in plants (130). Differentiation of warmth into air, warmth and light (130–1). Interval of rest (131).

Entry of the Spirits of Form (131).

Interval of rest (131).

Middle period of Sun Evolution (131–4).

Advancement of the Archai beyond the human stage. Imaginative or wide-awake picture-consciousness (132). Co-operation of the Seraphim. Beginnings of reproductive process (132). Some of the Archai stay behind in evolution. Resulting differentiation of two Nature-kingdoms. Separation of Sun and Saturn (133–4). The Archangels attain their human stage (133). Beginnings of human glandular system (135). Interval of rest (135).

United activity of the Cherubim and the Angels (135–6).

The Angels attain dreamlike picture-consciousness (135–6). Interval of rest (136).

The human being and the Thrones. Man receives the germ of Life-Spirit or Budhi (136).

Interval of rest (136).

341

343

Evolution of heredity, memory, breathing, the nervous system (172-3). Three distinct human types (176-7).

Before the separation of the Moon, human souls — all but the strongest — had to leave the Earth for a time (177-9).

The several groups of human souls and the planets: Mars, Jupiter and Saturn. Evolution of animal, plant and mineral kingdoms on Earth (178-81).

Influence of the rebellious (Luciferic) Spirits (182-5).

Sickness and death (185).

Protection of human life-body from Luciferic influence by the Sun-Beings (185-7).

Rhythms of day and night. Movements of Earth, Sun, Moon and the other heavenly bodies (186).

Return of human souls from Jupiter, Mars and the other planets (187).

Beginning of Reincarnation and Karma (188). Reproduction and the spiritual protection of man's life-body (188). Highly developed memory. Power over the life-forces of Nature (188).

Loss of the faculty to divine the future. Fear, error and the possibility of freedom. First explicit mention of the Ahrimanic Beings (190).

Exalted spiritual Beings of the planetary and solar realms who protected the human life-bodies. Higher Egos of the Jupiter, Mars, Sun, and Saturn humanity (190-1). The Sun-Being and the Christ (191).

Names of the evolutionary epochs: Atlantean, Lemurian, Hyperborean (and Polarian) (191-2).

Biblical tradition of Paradise and the Fall (192). The Lemurian Fire-catastrophe (191-2).

Atlantis (192-201).

Saturn, Sun, Jupiter and Mars races (192). Relation of Man to the Hierarchies in waking and sleeping (192). The Atlantean Oracles or Initiation-centres, turning the Luciferic influence into an instrument of progress (193). Christ and the Sun Oracle (194). Saturn, Jupiter and Mars Oracles (194).

Origin of the Planets Venus and Mercury (195).

Venus and Mercury Oracles (195). The Vulcan Oracle; development of science and the arts (195). Diverse methods of the Oracles, in relation to Thought. Special position of the Christ-Initiates (195). Higher human faculties — notably that of speech — gained through the transmutation of the Luciferic influence (196-7). Memory of ancestors. Erroneous concepts of reincarnation (196).

Organs of cognition in the etheric or life-body, developed through the exercises for Inspiration and Intuition (276).

Relation to the 'lotus-flowers' of the astral body. Etheric centres in regions of head, larynx and heart (276–7). In Inspirational cognition, the concepts and ideas are given in and with the percepts (277).

*

Exercises for Intuition affect the physical body too (275–8) Influence on breathing (278).

*

Separation of Thinking, Feeling and Willing (278–80).

Dangers which this involves (279–80). Consequent sevenfold development (279–80). Imaginative pictures permeated by one's own subjective being. Deeper self-knowledge needed for discrimination (280–1).

The Ego and its yet unfulfilled Karma. The 'Double' — a necessary first experience on entering the spiritual world (281–82).

Hidden feeling of shame, veiling the spiritual world from ordinary consciousness (283–4). Study of cosmic and human evolution prepares man for the meeting with the Double. The Double as *Guardian of the Threshold* (285). The Guardian at the moment of death (286).

Illusions inevitable if the Guardian is not properly encountered (286–8).

Two main sources of illusion: (i) Man's own soul-condition colours all that he sees in the spiritual world. This source is overcome by the self-knowledge which the meeting with the Guardian involves (286–7). (ii) Mistaken interpretation of what is seen. In the spiritual world the mistaken judgment becomes part and parcel of the perception (287–8). Criteria of spiritual reality. Spiritual training and study enhance the powers of thought and judgment (288). Imagination, Inspiration and Intuition in this regard; pure spiritual reality in Intuition (289–90).

*

The Double as 'Guardian of the Threshold' and the new-born Self (291).

Temptation to abandon the burden of the ordinary self. Premature illusion of having reached the goal (291–2). Successive influences of Lucifer and Ahriman in human evolution. Lucifer and the ordinary self (292). Ahriman prevents man's recognition of the spiritual Beings underlying the outer world (292).

The meeting with the 'Greater Guardian of the Threshold' (292).

Untold fear the alternative, if unprepared for this experience. The Lesser and the Greater Guardian and the two sources of illusion above-mentioned (293). Many individual forms of the experience with the Guardian of the Threshold (293).

*

Relation between the Microcosm and the Macrocosm (294-5).

Seven stages of the Way of Initiation described in this book: 1. Study of Spiritual Science; 2. Imagination; 3. Inspiration; 4. Intuition; 5. Knowledge of the relation of Microcosm and Macrocosm; 6. Becoming one with the Macrocosm; 7. The synthesis of all these becomes the prevailing mood of soul (295-6).

*

Through Intuition man learns to know his higher Ego as a spiritual being in the spiritual world (296).

The Greater Guardian and the Christ (296). With the Intuitive perception of Christ in the spiritual world man learns to understand the history of the Earth and the entry of Christ as the Sun-Being into earthly evolution (296).

The Way of Initiation, always adapted to the evolutionary epoch.

Changes since the 12th and 13th centuries A.D. The Way as here described is suited to the conditions of modern time. (296-7; *see also page* 225).

Chapter VI.
Present and Future Evolution of the World and of Mankind

Spiritual perception of cosmic past and future (298-9).

Old Moon and future Jupiter (298-9). Old Sun and future Venus; Old Saturn and future Vulcan (300). Inadequacy of intellectual constructions (300).

The seven post-Atlantean epochs of civilization (301-7).

Changes in human consciousness during the fourth epoch, and the Christ-event (302-5). Beginning of the new Initiation (304). Some Initiates still enjoyed the old clairvoyance and helped in the transition (303). Powers of supersensible cognition necessarily in abeyance during the early stages of Christianity (304). The interval in the 13th century (304).

Related works by Rudolf Steiner

Knowledge of the Higher Worlds
The Philosophy of Freedom
Christianity as Mystical Fact
Theosophy
At the Gates of Spiritual Science
Man's Being, His Destiny and World Evolution
Stages of Higher Knowledge
Ancient Myths — Their Meaning and Connection with Evolution
Between Death and Rebirth
The Christ Impulse and the Development of Ego-Consciousness
The Driving Force of Spiritual Powers
The Effects of Spiritual Development
Life between Death and Rebirth
Man as Symphony of the Creative Word
Man: Hieroglyph of the Universe
Manifestations of Karma
The Road to Self-Knowledge *and* The Threshold of the Spiritual World
Spiritual Guidance of Man and Humanity
Supersensible Man
True and False Paths of Spiritual Investigation
The Wisdom of Man, of the Soul and of the Spirit

Works by other Authors

K. König: The Human Soul
S. C. Easton: Man and World in the Light of Anthroposophy
F. E. Winkler: Man the Bridge between Two Worlds
C. Unger: Principles of Spiritual Science
T. S. Hughes: Reincarnation
G. Wachsmuth: Reincarnation as a Phenomenon of Metamorphoses
O. Palmer: Rudolf Steiner on his Book 'The Philosophy of Freedom'